A Whimsical View of Life

By Hobo Jack Sophir

Copyright©2023 Laughin' Jack's Good Humor Publications

Litchfield, IL U.S.A.

Print Version: ISBN 978-0-9625074-1-0

Cover Design & Re-format by
Robert Whiteside

This work is available
as an eBook from
Amazon.com

Attribution: Grunge Frame By PKParketer

Dedcation

This book is dedicated to the memory of my many little canine friends, all of whom have contributed to some degree to my mental well-being over the years.

In particular, I want to dedicate this book to the memory of "good Guy", a miniature Afghan hound. His love and devotion helped make three of the most difficult years of my life more bearable, thus allowing me to complete the first of several stories.

The rest of the stories were either written or completed almost twenty years later. I wish to dedicate this book also to two other little dogs; "Pippin", a minipin and "Foxy Boy", a mostly Chihuahua. Their continued love and devotion has helped my strength and concentration on the completion of the rest of the stories.

Hobo Jack 11/2011
a.k.a. Joaquin, "Backwoods Jack" and
"Laughing Jack"

Table of Contents

Preface to "A WHIMSICAL VIEW OF LIFE"

(opportunities gained, opportunities lost)

Life…is not always what it seems to be -- and often it is not what we would like for it to be. That, at least, is the way my own life has been. But my life, like most others is almost never spectacular -- so no one ever hears about it.

Each day, the news media reports a plethora of stories about war, violence, robbery, acts of hatred, acts of stupidity. Occasionally there are even stories of acts of kindness and of various achievements. There are almost all "big" stories. "Little" stories hardly ever make the news.

I thought I would like to write about some of the "little" stories of the "little" people who never seem to make it into the papers or on T.V., but whose whimsical, quirky lives should have been part of that news.

Some of these brief life experiences are sad, some happy, some amusing -- some just whimsical. All are part of an absorbing essence of the human existence.

Joaquin,   December 1993

Addendum

Although most of the stories and sketches in this book are based on either my own personal experience or the experiences of people I have known personally, there are some which are completely fictional. Some of the other pieces have been partially fictionalized so as to give continuity to the storyline or because in certain instances either my knowledge or memory of the facts was incomplete.   In many cases I have changed, at least somewhat, the real names of the characters.

Since these liberties are usual "writer's license" taken by most other writers, I feel no qualms of conscience in having used them myself. There are those (particularly in news reporting, I understand) who seem to think that life itself is something of a fiction – so perhaps from that perspective the edges are rather blurred anyway, between what is fact and what is not.

The Author

Preface for "Just Ask For Marty"   11/20/01

The following events took place in 1951 when I was nineteen years old, while visiting in New York City. I was in the process of returning from the first half of a hitchhiking trip of over a thousand miles each way (my first such trip). Starting from my home in Saint Louis, Missouri, I had ended the first half of the trip at Marlboro, Vermont, where I had chased after my girlfriend, Judy Wasserman. Judy won a high school senior English class contest to participate in a writer's conference at Marlboro College and I thought it would be quite a surprise for her to see me there. (It was – but that… is another story in itself.)

I had stayed a few days with the family of my mother's cousin in Brooklyn when I returned from Marlboro. My relatives very generously took me to see the usual sights in New York City, but drew the line at taking me to see the Bowery. That excursion, I was forced to make on my own.

The next day after my experience in the Bowery, I wrote down as accurately as I could remember, the events of that extraordinary few hours. The handwritten manuscript remained untyped for eight years. In 1959, I finally typed it, making only a few minor changes and additions. That typed copy of the story was entombed inside a briefcase for another thirty years. In 1989, I came across it again while sorting papers and thought I'd let my wife read it. I removed the story (12 pages stapled together) and placed it on top of a camel-back trunk in the loft of my barn where I had kept the briefcase. Absentmindedly, I forgot to bring the story down with me that day. Several days later, when I looked for the copy again, I had forgotten where I had placed it, and by then, it had slipped off the curved top of the trunk, falling behind and underneath.

For almost 13 years, I looked from time to time for that only existing copy, never being able to locate it in the massive disarray inside the barn. Finally, in November of 2001 when sweeping the loft, I noticed a corner of one sheet protruding from under the trunk and retrieved the very badly silverfish eaten pages. They were fragile and fragmented, but almost completely legible.

Since deciding in 2000 that I had enough hobo poems and short stories to do a book of them, I had agonized over the loss of "Just Ask For Marty", since it definitely fit the category. I knew that I could never rewrite it to be more than a mere shadow of the original.

In the preparation for inclusion in a book, I have again made some extremely minor changes, most of which are corrections of typographical or punctuation errors. Also, the very dated word "negro" (Spanish for black) was changed to the English "black", to make this story conform to our current standards of political correctness (about which nearly everyone now seems to be almost psychotically over-sensitive).

As I think back on this story, the first I ever wrote, it seems rather fitting that I should have written it about bums because in an ironic way, I started out life with a lot of talent, yet I ended up spending such a large part of my life living like a bum – a hobo. Even though I never became an alcoholic like all the bums in this story… perhaps in some inscrutable esoteric manner, there is at work here a perverse form of poetic justice…

Jack Sophir 1951 and 2001
AKA "Backwoods Jack"

(I signed the piece at that time using my given name, since neither my nom de plume nor my hobo moniker existed yet.)

Just Ask For Marty

It was one of those damnable hot days in New York; the kind when the sun is so bright that it makes you blink your eyes to look at the sidewalk. And humid – so that if you scrape your nails on the back of your neck, they rake off little globs of black, oily sweat. I'd walked too far already. Maybe I should get on a train and go uptown – Central Park, that'd be better – anything would be better.

I crossed under the third street el from Division, and was walking up Bowery toward the bridge. Stopped for a second. The time – just after four. That gave me another three hours to kill before I could head back to Brooklyn. I looked around hopefully, wondering.

"Hey deh, muh fren'!"

My eyes focused on the strange human contrivance before me. It was a black man, short, very hefty, in his later thirties, as nearly as I could ever gather – and shiny black, extremely so. He was dressed in style – Bowery style – a slightly ragged suit coat with unmatched pants, and a dirty red striped tee-shirt. His thick lips smiled and his drunken eyes were laughing; and I smiled.

"Say, you won'ta he'p out a fella? Ah needs ten cents fo' a glass a ale; jus' a thin, lil' ol' dime."

I shook my head, still smiling.

"Aw come on – it ain't gon' break you."

"Look", I said, "if I give you my last dime, then how will I get back to Brooklyn? I hafta have a dime to ride the subway."

"Well, you a nice, fine lookin' young man, you don' hafta worry."

I shook my head, "Why don't you try working?"

"Hey, ah bin wukin', man – ovah on Broadway a'haulin' rags outta cellah fo'' a Chine'man. Ah wuk 'bout fo' days haulin' a couple ton dem rags out dat cella an' all's he gave me wuz one lousy dollah! Ah nevah ast him how much he's gon' give me when ah stawt, an' ah figge'd on makin' 'bout three a' fo'."

"Well, you *should* have asked him before you started."

"Ah know, but Ah wuk roun' yeah a long time, an some time dey tells you two a' three dollahs, an den dey gives you five a' six when you's finish."

At this point I was about to step away from my portly solicitor, I noticed one of the several occupants of a nearby cluttered doorway, ambling in our direction.

"Can't you see that this young man does not wish to impart to you the price of a beer?" came a deep voice.

"Ah know, but it ain't go' break him" the black man replied, "an Ah drinks ale, notno beer. Ah don' fool roun' drinkin' beer, man, ale's srongah!"

The owner of the deep voice approached closer, gazing at me with great curiosity. Now the eyes of the others of the profligate populace turned upon me – I felt something like a new animal in the zoo – or the latest side-show freak.

"You go to school?" asked the deep voice.

"Yea, I'm an art student." I replied.

"You looked like an artist or writer or something like that." Deep voice talked as though he might have had a cultural background, but in all other respects, he appeared to be just an ordinary Bowery bum. Dressed in typically shabby clothes, he stood about five feet eight inches – average weight. His full head of hair was neatly trimmed and combed back straight and the grayness of it seemed to reflect from cold blue-grey eyes; he looked fiftyish.

"Yo mama 'n daddy livin'?" asked the dark one suddenly.

They were feeling me out, I thought; probably some sort of game with them – getting people to buy them drinks.

"Yes, they're alive," I answered.

"An you got bruthas an sistas?"

"One sister, four years younger."

"Now tha's a nice fambly, an y'all do' hafta worry none 'bout nobody takes caeh you."

Momentary silence.

"How 'bout you buyin' us a cold drink?" the dark one asked me "You know you kin affo'd it, man. An sides, Ah's been a good man all my life. Ah do' drink no hard lika – maybe jus a lil' wine sometime. Ah do' smoke – Ah haven' tetched a cig'rit in a yeah – yeah an nine munts; an Ah ain' neveh bin a sweahin' man, evah since Ah wuz jus' knee-high." And he gestured appropriately.

Again, silence.

This time it was the newcomer who approached me.

"Let me see your hand." He said politely.

He took my left hand and scrutinized the palm.

"You are indeed fortunate. You see this line?"

I nodded.

"This is your life line; you have a long life ahead of you; and you will have much money." (Indicating another line). "You will be famous; your fame line is long. And you'll have only one love."

"Now look at my palm." (He held it up). "Fairly long life line, long fame line, very short wealth line."

"Now," he said, "surely you can spare some of your fortune with us, we who are so neglected by Lady Luck."

I made an obvious indication of my indifference to his plea.

Then his next offering burst forth upon me.

"I regret that I have but one life to give for my country! Who said that? You should know, you're a student! Do you know? You don't! It was Nathan Hale, a mere boy of twenty-one. Let the world take note! He said gravely, amid pompous gesticulation.

Several avenues of possible polite escape were busying my mind when another of the dramatic outpourings started.

"Give me liberty or gimme a beer!" he shouted, with heraldic gestures. "Who said that/" – and he laughed.

I looked at the black man, who looked at him – then we both laughed.

"Come on." I motioned, and the three of us walked over to a nearby saloon.

My new-found acquaintances sat down on either side of me as the barkeep approached. "Beer," I said, pointing my finger to my left and right, "and a lemon soda here."

After paying the modest bill, I turned to the left and addressed the intellectual. "Have you ever written anything?"

"Yes, much" was the dramatic answer.

"About what?"

"Of cabbages and kings – and many things."

He was talking to impress, I thought or else he'd been half-drunk when I met him, or both.

"What's your name, kid?" he asked between gulps.

"Jack."

"Ok, Jackie, call me Marty. Tell me kiddo, whater yuh down here on the Bowery for?" He answered for himself, "Yer no artist, yer a writer, aren't yuh?"

"Possibly," I said.

11

"An' yer down on the' Bowery t' see life in th' raw an' get material for a high school essay or somethin'."

"Nooo, I…"

"Well yer a writer, I'm right about that aren't I?"

"I guess so", I answered.

Marty looked down pensively into his fast-receding beer. "How old are yuh, Jackie?"

"Nineteen, and you?"

"I'm forty-five years old," he lamented, "old enough ta be yer father."

Our black companion had been engaging me in conversation off and on as Marty drank and talked, and my head was flying back and forth as I attempted to keep up with the separate conversations.

Finally, I turned to the ebony face who had just about finished his beer: I was going to let him finish his talking as well.

"An Ah say, Ah don' min' a lil' wine or a few glassa ale, but Ah ain' nevago be a habichul drunk; Ah see what's happen ta dem."

He had a very sing-song manner of speaking, and his body seemed to sway with the rhythm of the voice.

"A man come outta tavehn with a bottle in his han' an' his bowels wuz jus runnin' down his pants leg – you know, right on de street. An he wuz jus' drinkin' all de time…"

His words drifted away as he walked out.

Marty was just coming back from the men's room (we were siting near the front), when he called to me.

"Hay, kiddo, commere! I wanna show yuh somethun'."

We walked back to the middle of the bar – I think it must have been a restaurant also, because – there was a little old man with a beard eating his dinner in a booth.

"Hi yuh pop; how yuh doin'?"

Marty's face beamed as he extended his hand. The old man grasped it and grunted cheerfully. He smiled.

"Meet the kid from Brooklyn" was Marty's introduction.

I extended my hand – the old fellow shook it and again grunted – cheerfully.

"You see this guy," Marty continued, "If I can be just half the man he is when I'm his age, I'll be doin' *dam'* good."

A Whimsical View of Life   Hobo Jack Sophir

We walked back to the bar, and I began to take a closer look now at Marty. He had been a handsome man when he was younger. His face was pasty now, but he still had clean, clear skin; his smile lines were about average depth and except for the eyes, he looked very, very average for his age. Those eyes, though, were peculiar. They hadn't any of the discolored, puffy, sagging skin beneath them, as typifies men his age, but the upper lid was completely overlapped by the skin above it – only more than just that – it formed almost an outer "lid over lid" effect, slightly closed; and it gave him a strange, sleepy appearance.

We sat down again, and Marty called for another beer.
"What d'yuh want, kid?"
"Wh, I – I guess I'll have another lemon soda" I said without even thinking. I was still contemplating, wondering.
"Don't drink do yuh kid? Don't ever start."
He reached into his pocket to pay for the beer and soda.
"Hey! That's ok, Marty – I'll pay for 'em" I said.
"Naah…" he pulled out a handful of change and put a quarter on the counter.
Marty drank in silence; then he looked over at me, scrutinizing – holding onto his empty beer glass.
"You know, Johnnie, yer a good kid; I like yuh!"
"Thanks, Marty, " I said, "And you're okay by me."
My new friend seemed at once inspired.
"Say, you wanna see the *real* Bowery, kid?...Chinatown?...Not what the tourists see, but the *real* stuff?"
"Sure," I said.
"Then you stick with me. I'll show you the places where th' big shots hang out. Th' big boys – gamblers, gorillas, th' whole works; but you gotta keep yer trap shut – an' don't laugh, cause they'd just as soon kill yuh as look at yuh. I'll show yuh th' Bowery in action – tonight! Okay? You *with* me, Johnnie?"
"Sure, I'm with you Marty," I assured him.
"An' don't you worry about anything, cause if anybody stawts givin' yuh trouble jus' tell 'em yer with *Mawty*, cause if anybody tries anything with me, well, huhh…just let em try! Com on let's get outta heah."
It was peculiar, and a little ludicrous, the way he sometimes spoke with a pronounced Brooklyn accent (he claimed to have been born and

13

raised in Brooklyn) but I think he must have felt more ferocious when he talked that way. At any rate, it was an interesting diversion from his usual Bowery jargon.

"The only good thing about that place is that they give yuh a big beer" was the verbal conspectus he offered as we walked along. "No sense sittin'; in that place – besides, I want yuh ta meet th' boys. Andy, an' Joey, an' Ernie, an' Tommy 'n Viola, an' – oh yeah, I wancha ta meet Chinatown Mary. Half Chinese – she shacks-up with Chinamen, but she's *okay*. Great kid – I   bin studyin' her for over a year now. I want to see what you think."

We had reached the corner of the block by now – and there was another tavern.

"Yuh see this bar?" Marty thumbed it. "This is where the guy that wrote 'Guys and Dolls' usta drink. There's a picture of him in there. Whatsamatter, doncha believe me?"

"Sure, I believe you, Marty" I returned, not intending to appear incredulous.

"Yuh don't believe me – come on we'll go ask th' bartender."

He grabbed me by the arm and led me in. We stood there.

"Hey, Eddie, commere. Tell him, does Damon Runyon come in here or don't he?"

"Yeah, he usta come in here" was the reply.

"Uh, Eddie – how 'bout a whiskey 'n beer?" Marty asked timidly.

"I'll make it good Monday – been workin' every day this week – except today. How 'bout it, okay?"

Eddie sighed – "Okay". He turned toward me with a defeated smile and set up the drink.

Marty gulped the whiskey and washed it down quickly with the beer, and we left.

We were beginning to walk through Chinatown now, and Marty in turn began talking in subdued tones.

"Yuh see all these shops? Well, every one of 'em's just a front. All them Chinks belongs to a Tong. An' they got hatchet men that'd chop yer head off as soon as look at yuh. Believe me, when one of them Tong wars gets goin', there's nuthin' like it. Even the big-time gorillas an' gangsters don't compare."

"What's a Tong?" I asked, in ignorance.

"A Tong's a secret society, like the K of C or the Klue Klux Klan – you know. Yuh see, every Chink that comes into this country hasta

14

belong to a Tong; an' they pay the Tong so much when they're workin', an' if they lose their job, the Tong keeps 'em going'. There's two main Tongs, an' every so often, they get to fightin'; but there hasn't been a war in – oh, ten years.

A group of tourists were going into a Chinese souvenir shop as we passed.

"Lookit 'em, walkin' around lookin' in those god-dam' shops. Hungry! That's all – just plain hungry fools. They'll go back home tonight an' think they've seen Chinatown – th' Bowery. But if they only knew what goes hon behind those innocent looking fronts."

"Look in that shop over there Johnnie." He motioned left with his head. "See those Chinks in there?" They were for the most part elderly men, well dressed, conversing. "Well, they're all gorillas – every one of 'em!"

With that, a young Chinese boy crossing the street in front of us glanced our way.

"Yeah, yuh see – even him; old ones, young ones – all gorillas." About this, I confess I really *was* rather incredulous, but – ah well, who was *I* to question Marty?

And so we finally came to 'his' bar; I never did find out the name. But it was across from the 'Tombs', the criminal courts building.

"Well, here we are, Johnnie – yuh still with me?"

"Sure", I said.

My name somehow became changed to 'Johnnie' some time back, but it made no real difference, and it suited the occasion better anyway. So I was 'Johnnie'.

I waited now for Marty to open the door, and take the lead.

"Whatsamatter, Johnnie, yuh scared?"

"No", I insisted.

"Yuh worryin' about money? Yuh don't need it."

"I know," I said, "everything's okay."

Marty just couldn't seem to get used to a person being unafraid. Later I found out why. The whole degenerate populace there was like a bunch of rabbits – frightened rabbits – scared of the cops, scared of the 'gorillas', and even of each other.

We walked in. Marty looked around until he'd spotted his objective.

"Come on, kid, I want yuh ta meet two of the finest people in the whole world, muh two bes' fren's, Tommy 'n Viola."

Marty guided us toward the bar.

"Hi, Tommy."

"Hi there, Marty. Where th' hell ha' ye been th' last week?"

"Workin'. Worked every day this week, 'cept today."

Viola looked at him.

"Yer not workin' – look at y er shirt!"

"I swear I bin – got money commin' Monday."

"Tommy," and he turned to me suddenly, "I wancha ta meet Johnnie. He's from Brooklyn – Irishtown."

Well, that sold Tommy Lochran. The little old Irishman extended his hand, smiling warmly.

"So, you're from Brooklyn are ye? Now that's fine."

Tommy looked every bit the Irishman he was – a wiry five foot five, wavey, gray hair; must have been around sixty. His suit was clean, but shabby, and his dark green sport shirt was ironed to a gloss.

"An' this is Viola, Johnnie." Marty was saying as I popped from my reverie.

"What d'yuh think a th' kid?' he directed at her. "He's okay, huh?"

I looked up into her smiling, homely face; she was quite a contrast to her husband. I judged her to be about forty-five. With her stylish clothes, excessive makeup, and great overabundance of height, (she appeared to be about five-eleven or six feet), she looked like an exaggerated caricature of some third-rate clothing store's window dummy. She regarded me dryly.

"Yeah, he's okay," she laughed.

Marty was thirsty.

"Say, Tommy – how 'bout a drink for us; me an' th' kid from Brooklyn?"

Tommy looked across the bar.

"Give 'em a drink, Gene" and he threw a bill on the counter.

Marty waited anxiously for the whiskey and beer.

"Tommy 'n Viola 'er th' bes' frien's I got in th' whole world," he muttered.

Feeling a hand on my shoulder, I turned to find Tommy motioning to me to follow.

"Commere, me boy, I'm goin' ta make a call I want ye ta hear." We walked over to the phone booth, where Marty could no longer see us.

"Listen now," he said softly, "Yer a good kid. I don't know what yer doin' with that bum, but ye'll do best ta stay away from 'im.

"Aw, he's alright," I scoffed.

Tommy shrugged his shoulder and looked at me as if to say: "Hey, y' can't say I didn't warn ya'."

"Well, I've got ta call a friend of mine now – over in the Tombs." And he motioned with his head.

"Ye see this?" He reached in his wallet and took out a piece of ragged yellow paper, unfolding it; there was a name and an address in the Criminal Courts building.

"I've fixed things for more than one poor guy this way."

"Just exactly what *is* the 'Tombs'?" I asked.

"Hah! Ye don't know what the Tombs is? Well, I'll tell ye. It's the place ye never want ta get inta, 'cause once ye do, ye won't get out!"

"Oh," I said.

He picked up the receiver and dropped in a dime, dialing operator.

"I'll get the dime back," he assured me.

"Hello, operator, I want ta call Rector 2-6200." He waited a few moments in silence.

"Warren Murphy, please – yeh. Tommy G. Lochran – that's right." He waited again. "Hello, War..." The juke box blared out 'Old Soldiers Never Die'; Tommy closed the booth door, and I walked away.

Marty had just finished his drink, and he began introducing me around.

"Hi, Andy."

"H'llo Marty."

"Andy, I wancha ta meet th' kid from Brooklyn, Red Hook. He's okay!"

We shook hands.

Next we proceeded to a row of booths along the wall; we neared one at which were seated two men about Marty's age. They had a bottle of wine set before them, and both grunted a sort of unwelcome hello as we slid onto the bench opposite. Marty introduced me with the usual Bowery formalities, and began again his endless quest for whiskey and beer.

"What's in the bottle?" He asked its red-faced owner as a start. Joe, red-face's name, was a Swede. Heavy-set, ruddy skinned and

17

thinning, red-blond hair would be almost sufficient description – a laborer – and a bum and a rather shabby one at that.

His friend was a Frenchman, by the name of Earnest, who's appearance was pretty much the same as for being laborer, bum and shabby, but he had the added garnish of an old felt hat pulled down shapelessly over his matted white mop of hair. They both looked out at us through bulging, blood-shot marbles. They weren't really drunk yet, though.

"Dis es California muscatel – good vine; you want some – go over'n get a glass," offered Red.

"Ah, hell, you know I don't drink that shit! I want a whiskey 'n beer. Which one of yuh is gonna buy me a drink?"

"Marty, ya know ve can't afford whiskey, or ve'd be drinkin' it ourselves."

"Hay, Frenchy, how 'bout you buyin' a drink for me 'n Johnnie here?"

"Why don' zhu buy your own dringh?"

"Cause I won't get paid till Monday. Look I bought you plenty a drinks when I had the dough. Now, how 'bout it?"

Frenchy emitted a reluctant "Awrighd".

Marty had finished that drink in short order, and was getting nowhere in his efforts to obtain another.

"I just wanna see how good you guys are," he was saying. "Frenchy, you wouldn' buy yer gran'mother a drink on her death-bed."

The Frenchman sat there with utter disconcern.

"Lissen ta me Earnie ya cheap sonuvabitch, yer sittin' there not even spendin' a dime a yer own money – drinkin' Red's wine. Come on, buy me an' th' kid a drink!"

"Awrighd – I buy you a beer," was the exasperated answer. Knowing Marty's solicitations to be an interminable affair, Red and the Frenchman left our booth. I turned to Marty, who was sulking over his beer.

"Well kid," he said, "yuh wanted ta see th' Bowery in action, an' yer seein' it. But wait a little while, 'til th' big-shots get here an' let their hair down."

I looked over at the clock; it was quarter to six.

"Yuh know, Johnnie, I jus' can't figure you out. Why 'er yuh down here sittin' in a Bowery bar? Yuh don't drink – what-er yuh down here for?"

"You know why," I said.

"Yeh, yer a writer – or are yuh an artist? I dunno." I was sure the drinks were catching up with him now.

"Tell me, Johnnie, what's a nineteen year old kid doin' down here? Why, you're youth! You should be watchin' a ball game, or out dancin' with girls, or seein' a play on Broadway! But yer down here with a drunken bum in a Bowery bar." He shook his head.

We sat for a while in silence, watching the coming and going of after-diner-hour patrons. Chinatown Mary was among the shifting group. She settled herself at a nearby table, where she displayed a disappointing homely Chinese-American face atop an averageish body of a woman in her late thirties. Yet, something bout her made her stand out in the crowded room. She sat alone with a drink, as though waiting for someone; saying nothing and giving the impression of a suspiciously paranoid personality as she glanced around at her surroundings.

Marty finally realized that she was sitting there and pulled me over to meet her. She gave a silent nod of recognition at Marty as we approached. Marty began with his usual introduction for me.

"Hey, Mary – this here's Johnnie, the kid from Brooklyn. He's okay!"

"Yeah? Hi kid..." Then she turned her attention away from us. Marty hesitated a few seconds not knowing what else to say and we walked back to the booths, where we slid into one.

I continued to look at Chinatown Mary and diverted my eyes away from her from time to time so as not to be too obviously watching her. In one of those moments, she seemed to evaporate – as suddenly as she had appeared.

Whatever had been the strange attraction Marty had found in her, it would, at least for me, be forever lost in that morass of Chinatown humanity.

Red and Ernie were in the booth next to us, and the latter being now dead drunk, caused the former to seek new company. He carried over his wine bottle and glass and sat down across from us – a very calm sort of man.

Marty was saying "Yuh know, I like yuh, Johnnie, yer a good kid."

I smiled, showing my teeth.

"Ay yust ta have teeth like that," said the red one. He smiled slightly "Yost like that – with two buck front ones."

"Will yuh buy a drink fer Johnnie 'n me?" Marty asked him.

"Ay tol' you, you want wine, okay – otervise, *no*!"

This was more than Marty could take.

"Red yer a dirty, lousy stinkin' bastard – yer *no good*!"

"Ah, Ay'm no good," he sighed with agreement. "Bot Ay *was* fair four years, before th' first World War. Ay didn't smoke air drink; Ay was a runner. Ay ran an' yomped an' swam. Th' Germans only shot me in the knee, bot it killed me here." And he pointed to his head. "They thought Ay'd never walk again."

The mood of drunken sulking prevailed on Marty.

"Red, yuh stink!" he yelled. "Yer just like all th' others, yuh stink – yuh stink, yuh *stink, YUH STINK*!"

He raised his voice a step with each repetition, until the crescendo reached a scream.

"Take it easy, Marty," I said. "You're getting; all riled up over nothing."

"Whadd'ya mean nothin'?" he sneered, "It's what's wrong with all of 'em; every god-dam one of 'em – th' whole world's stinkin' lousy rotten. Yuh know what I think of it? This – haach pooh! POOH! I spit on it; I spit on everybody – pooh – no good!"

Red left again.

"Marty," I said, "You denounce the world, but are *you* any good – any better?"

"Naw, Johnnie – I'm just a drunken bum."

Marty tried to lean his head against the padded booth back. He grimaced. Then he looked at me with a booze-glazed-almost agonized expression that could have been a protest – a demonstrance. The smoky air and dimness of the lights gave a dream-like quality to the indistinctiveness of the room. I found it hard to keep my mind from wandering off into that dream.

"Who are you, really?" I asked him.

"Y' see, Johnnie," he went on, "I was a good average kid. I went t' high school, I saw ball games, an' took girls out dancin'; I got someplace – had money an' plenty a' friends. I married a beautiful girl… and things were going alright."

His eyes began to fill with tears, and he put his hands up against them to try to press the drops back.

"Then one day I came home from the shop – it was just like any other day. I kissed my wife; I looked at her an' I asked her if she loved me. She laughed! I called my oldest daughter over. 'Bobby' I said, 'come here to daddy'… He exploded into a cloud-burst of tears.

"They tried to poison me – they put arsenic in my food! They took everything I had; my insurance policies, my home, my job, my friends – my family."

I watched him as he sat there sobbing.

"Johnnie, if yuh ever love a girl, an' make the decision to marry her – make *sure*; oh so *dam'* sure!"

"Don't worry, Marty, I will."

I meant it; and I looked at him again – and meant it more. It didn't matter how distorted his story was, there must have been an element of truth in it, I thought.

As we sat there, each of us with his own thoughts, the rest of the world seemed to shut itself away in the gloom of the twilight that filtered through the misty windows. Marty startled me when he spoke.

"Well, yer really seein' things tonight, Johnnie, seein' life. You've seen Bowery bums drinking, and you just saw one cry. Naw, I'm not cryin' on anyone's shoulder, kid, I – I'm just tellin' yuh what it's been. Your doin' it right though, Johnnie. You come down here ta see how the other half lives, and why; and I admire yuh for it, kiddo. Yuh got a good brain in yer head, 'cause if yer gonna write or paint or draw or sing – no matter what yer gonna do, *live* first, then go ahead an' do it; then you'll succeed.

"Yeh, Johnnie, th' whole dam' world stinks – meanin' th' guys like me stink; th' guys that made me what I am stink.

"But what keeps me goin' is that I still got faith," he said.

"Faith in what?" I asked cynically.

"Faith in God."

"Oh, come now! What *do* you believe in, Marty?"

"Lis'en, I wonce worked for a Greek fella; worked as a chauffeur. He paid me good; I slept in his house, had clean clothes – plenty of food. One day he ast me – said 'Marty, what th' hell's th' matter with you? Here I'm givin' yuh all yuh want, an' yer still not satisfied'. So I said, 'Look,' I said, 'I'm 'n American, you're a Greek. I been livin' here all my life an' you come here from Greece an' I hafta work fer *you*!' 'That's the way it is, Marty' he sez. So I sez, 'Well then, if that's th' way yuh feel about it, yuh c'n take yer god-dam job back; I don't want it.' An I even gave him back the uniform."

'Just a minute,' he sez, 'There's one thing I want ta tell yuh – I want yuh always t' remember – then yer through. I'm Greek an' you're American'. 'Okay, Greek', I sez, 'shoot!'

'It don't make any difference *who* yuh are,' he sez, 'There's only two things in this world that any man needs to succeed – one's God, n' th' other's a dollar bill.'

An' that's what I believe in, Johnnie. That guy today is one of the most successful men in New York, an' he's one of th' best friends I have. Why, he'd do anything for me if I asked, but I'm just too proud."

"What do you believe in, kid" he asked me.

"I don't know," I told him. "Nothing like that, probably just don't know *what* to believe in yet."

I hesitated to tell him what I really thought, afraid he wouldn't understand.

"What religion are yuh, Johnnie?"

"None" I said.

A smile of approbation appeared.

"I'm with yuh kid. I was brought up as a strict Catholic; but no more!"

He sneered and cut the air with his hand.

"No good."

"Why?" I asked.

"Yuh couldn't believe it if I told yuh why."

"Certainly I could."

Lissen, kid, they put guys that talk about things like this in th' nuthouse. You wouldn't believe it anyway."

"Well, try me and see if I do; nothing's really *too* incredible." I offered.

"I was sick", he started. "I was on my death bed. They took me to a hospital; an' I thought sure I was dyin', so I said Sister, go get a priest, I'm dyin' an' I want to make a confession; I want somebody to say th' last rites over me'. When I looked up an' saw him I said, 'Father, I want to confess; I'm goin' to die'. He looked at me an' he laughed! Can you imagine a Catholic priest laughing in th' face of a dying man? I said to him 'You're no Father'. He sez 'Yes I am; you're not going to die Marty'. An' he laughed in my face!"

"I'll tell yuh something else, kid. Yer not gonna believe this, but I'm of the immortals 'My house hath many mansions'," he quoted, "'but no man has ever seen them an' lived to tell about it'. They tried to kill me, Johnnie, but they couldn't do it."

I was about to ask…

"Drink, Johnnie, for he who drinks with me becomes immortal also." Our glasses clinked.

"Yuh don't believe it!"

"Maybe."

"No," he said softly, "you can't."

In the silence that followed, he folded his arms on the table and laid his head across them. A few moments passed, and he popped up like a lazy jack-in-the-box.

"There, but by the grace of God go I," Irishly, he said. I thought the same.

With his money and credit for drinks gone, I suggested that we leave, the hour being late. No one seemed to take notice as we walked toward the door and into the street. A light rain was falling, and we moved in silence.

We crossed Division, and when we reached the foot of the steps leading up to the third street el, I stopped.

Marty grasped my hand firmly.

"So long, Johnnie."

"So long Marty," I said.

But somehow I felt that I couldn't leave – not just yet – it wasn't exactly an unsatisfied curiosity, or the desire to hear another yarn, or even the thought that I might never see the man again (though I was sure this would be the case). I suppose what made me continue to stand there looking at him was simply that there was so much left to learn – the why and wherefore about him and the others like him. I still didn't know, in truth, why he was what he was, or did what he did, or said what he said – or why he was standing here on this street corner shaking hands with me. Why was anybody down here? Or why was anybody anywhere, for that matter?

We were standing in the rain, just a drizzle, and its coolness felt good because the air was still warm and humid.

"Marty…"

"Kid, my name's not really Marty." "Well,"
I said in amazement, "What *is* it?" "Doesn't
matter, kid."

"Maybe it does," I said. "Suppose – suppose I want to look you up again/"

"Just ask for Marty. Ask anybody here; they all know me."
"But…"
I began to see the fruitlessness of pursuing it further.
"Sure," I said, "just ask for Marty."
I was about to walk up the steps when he tugged at my arm.
"Look there, Johnnie – you see that?"
He pointed to an American flag painted on a store window.
"There's a wonderful tradition in that flag Johnnie. An' it's up to the youths like you to carry on those ideals – 'cause it's the guys like me – an' a lot of 'em *not* like me either, who've got the world all screwed up the way it is."

Turning to me, he pantomimed dramatically.
"Oh youth, I give you this flag to carry forth."
He held out his arms with the imaginary banner, and I grasped it and turned, walked up to the platform. The reaction was automatic – we were both playing parts in a fantastic one-act play.
When I reached the top of the stairs and looked back, he was gone.

J.S. 1951

Addendum for Just Ask For Marty

A few days later I went back to the Bowery. I got off the 3rd street EL at the same station – I thought it was the same station, but it wasn't. Nothing looked the same. I could not find any of the bars or restaurants that Marty had taken me to. All of the Bowery bums I asked about Marty told me - they'd never heard of him. After wandering around for over an hour, I gave it up and got back on the EL to Brooklyn.

Three years later, I hitchhiked again to New York to join several of my Art School friends who had taken a rented room at the edge of the Bowery. They had intended to stay for the summer and possible sit in on classes at the Art Students League... or just walk around the city and be "inspired" to do drawings or paintings. I stayed only a few days, not feeling really welcome, but again tried to locate the area where Marty had taken me and if possible to find him. I tried to find the 3rd street EL station where I had gotten off. The 3rd street EL no longer exited! Once again I asked every Bowery bum I encountered if they knew of Marty. They all told me the same thing! They had no idea who I meant.

That was now... nearly 70 years ago. Almost all of us die rather inconspicuous deaths... as I am certain Marty finally did. So, what does it all mean – life and death? And if we touch each other's lives just momentarily, will that help to change the direction of any cosmogenic impulse? I would like to think so. But that is the most I can do: just to think so.

"Hobo Jack" April 22, 2023

Preface for A Royal Flush

Many decades ago, my cousin Peggy told me this basic story about our grandparents. Knowing my grandfather and grandmother as well as I did, I was able to elaborate – fill in the gaps in the story to give a continuity to it to make it more understandable.

A Royal Flush

Recopied from version dated 1/27/97 on 12/19/11
(with minor revision)

Stubborn shadows clung with a resolute tenacity, to the grimy, dingy rows of time-aged apartments that evening. Those shadows, like stealthy villains, crept even into the inner edges of unlit cobblestone alleys.

There were fanciful shadows, as well – dancing under the street lights when the breeze shifted the branches of overhanging trees into phantasmagoric patterns.

As though he were monitoring some cautious culprit, Oscar watched from the window of his first floor apartment. Moving his massive, almost shapeless body slowly, like an old turtle unsure of which direction to take, he shifted his weight from one foot to the other, then back again with impatience, yet without letting any sign of anxiety show on his face.

His expression seldom ever changed; even smiles and frowns were subdued. Usually imperturbable, he found his patience was finally being tried to the limit by the extraordinary circumstances over which he had never attempted to achieve control previously.

A staccato tapping of high-heeled shoes, then – her door opened. Dressed simply, but elegantly, she had neither tried to hide, nor flatter her late middle-aged figure. She wore it well.

"I'm ready… but I don't think you'll have to take me this time. Eli said he might be able to pick me up at eight. It's just about that now – and I can ride back with him. So don't wait up. You know my brother – he'll probably want to stay up late again."

"Alright, Dearie."

The basso profundo reply rumbled out of Oscar's throat - a tone that belied his short stature. At a glance, and without perspective, one would think that he was six feet tall and weighed three hundred pounds. In reality, he was a six inch shorter, miniature version of that. But it was perhaps his blocky jaw and stern mouth, overset by what could best be described as a 'prize fighter's nose' that contributed to the illusion.

Dearie stepped briskly to the coat closet and selected a light weight jacket, stopped momentarily at the hall mirror to view herself and dabbed another puff of powder on her nose. She reached the door just as the bell rang.

"Bye, hon – if anyone calls, tell them to call me back in the morning."

Oscar nodded a silent goodbye, then ambled with seemingly slothing feet back to his room. He removed the beige, light wool jacket of his suit, but left on the vest. As he pulled his reading glasses from the leather case in the vest pocket, he reached with his other hand into the opposite side of the vest for a fountain pen.

A plain iron bed and an equally plain and even more dismal-looking dresser adorned the tiny back room, with its only window facing toward the alley. Crowded each against the other was a battered metal wardrobe and a small desk. The green, glass-shaded early-deco desk lamp and the desk upon which it sat were the only remnants of Oscar's business office.

He sat down and leaned back in the badly scuffed desk chair, then twisted the switch on the base of the brass desk lamp. His gray eyes focused as though he were looking through the wall – in a meditative trance.

Delicate whisps of fine hair atop the dome of his mostly balded scalp seemed to attract his hand almost magnetically during extended musings like this. Then he would draw his hand down smoothing the cropped tufts of white hair around each ear.

There were some bills that he needed to pay. He reached into a desk drawer and removed a check pad, thought for a moment, then laid down the pen.

It was the sixth night in a row that Dearie had left him alone in order to play cards with her friends. All of this had started innocently enough months ago with a group getting together for an evening of poker at one of their homes. Every other week or so, someone would host a game. Then it became every week – then twice a week, and as the participants became increasingly obsessed by their card games, it had progressed into an every night event. Now, only one of the group was able to host it.

Even the stakes had escalated. Starting out with pennies, it had slowly risen to nickels and dimes – then quarters and finally dollars. Now, it was possible for someone to loose – or gain in one night, a rather handsome sum – even in the value of a nineteen-forty dollar.

The apartment felt more empty than usual tonight. Throughout his adult life, Oscar had never made what you would call close friends and his former business associates never called or dropped by. Even his daughters brought the grandchildren over only on occasional Sundays or holidays. There was an almost suffocating silence in the apartment that night. He reasoned, without even perusing the thought, that he was, indeed a 'poker widower'.

It was not that he had anything against the game itself. He'd play a few hands when the family gathered on holidays. Actually, he found it rather enjoyable sitting there with some of the adult family members at a card game around the dining room table after the dishes had been cleared. And maybe it wasn't as much the game that he liked as it was the conversational interchange – business trends – the war in Europe – whose child was doing what... Then he would light up one of those plump after-dinner cigars, the smoke so rank that it soon drove away all but the most hardy souls. But thinking about that made him feel all the more isolated.

Oscar switched off the desk lamp and went over to sit on the bed, his back propped by a pillow against the headboard. With the light from a small reading lamp, he picked up the top book on a pile of paperback mystery novels stacked on a nightstand, and opened to the first page. The words simply wouldn't register.

He tried to concentrate, remembering how he often used plots and scenarios from some of these mysteries in his own chimerical and somewhat quixotic stories that he told his grandchildren. Even though he could almost see, in his mind's eye, those diminutive figures crouched there by his bedside – with their delicate features totally enthralled, listening to him as they had, so many times, there was just an impasse, a road-block tonight.

It was obvious that no amount of self-prodding was going to induce his fertile imagination to create another adventure for his 'Captain Jimmy and the Hole in the Wall' series. If Captain Jimmy succeeded in crawling though the hole in the wall tonight, all that would be awaiting him was a game of poker!

In a fit of impetuously whimsical exasperation, Oscar went to the telephone table in the hall. Flipping through the phonebook, he located the listing for the nearest police precinct station and dialed the number.

The somewhat somnambulant-sounding voice that answered verified that Oscar had, indeed, reached the correct number.

"I want to report a gambling operation in the fifty hundred block of Pershing."

There was a protracted silence, followed by a low-keyed muttering. Oscar repeated his assertion. Now, we have to consider that a night desk sergeant *could* rightfully have been a little irritated by this kind of complaint – which might take the attention and time of many of the men at the station. And this evening had thus far been pleasantly uneventful. The 'big crime' of neighborhood gambling was hard to prosecute anyway. It was much easier to handle one of the usual auto accidents – or even an early evening domestic flight. All of these thoughts were spinning around in the desk sergeant's mind when he answered the telephone.

"So exactly where is this? Ya got any address number?"

"No, but I've been by the place many times; they've got something going on there every night. It's on the north side of the street… and it's the only apartment house in the middle of the fifty hundred block with front porches on each apartment. It's on the second floor, east side. There'll be plenty of lights on."

With his deep, commandingly authoritative voice, Oscar was very convincing.

"Fifty hundred block of Pershing, eh? Okay, we'll check it out – so, who is this anyway/"

"I'm just a concerned citizen – don't like to see illegal gambling going on in a residential neighborhood like this."

He placed the receiver back on its hook and lit up one of his fat Havanas. An incontrollable chuckle rumbled out between drags on the cigar. Had there been anyone there to ask him, he would have argued that having been in the dry goods business for many years does not necessarily insure that one will have a dry sense of humor.

It was forty-five minutes before Oscar's cigar had burned down to a stub in the yellow plastic holder clinched between his teeth. Those minutes seemed to tick away more slowly than usual on the ornate mantel chime clock, as he sat in the living room… in his usual well-padded and well-worn overstuffed chair – feet propped up on a footstool as he tried to look through the newspaper. Anticipating the phone's ring, he hurried into the hall to answer it.

"Hullo?"

"Oh… I'm so glad you're still up… you've got to come down to the police station right away!"

"What?"

Dearie's voice began breaking up between tears. "It's awful – simply *dreadful*! The police came up there and arrested all of us – took us to the station in a *paddy wagon*!" She was now sobbing between breaths. "And they charged us all with… *gambling*!" Dearie ended with a wailing gush of tears.

"Don't cry now, Dearie, I'll be right there as soon as I can."

Oscar carefully hung the receiver back on the hook, went over to the bed to get his jacket and laboriously squeezed into it. Then, like a lumbering automaton, he proceeded to the closet and selected a topcoat. Several more minutes had elapsed by the time he had walked to the garage behind the apartment, blocked open the heavy wood-slat door and carefully backed out his little Chevy business coupe.

During the brief trip to the precinct station, Oscar refused to even think about what he would say to anyone, He would let everything flow naturally – dictated by the events.

Inside the station there was general pandemonium. The bustling of people coming and going – seeking fathers or mothers – husbands or wives. With a brisk, but emotionless movement of his wrist and hand, the desk sergeant motioned Oscar to enter a room where several family members stood talking to the police chief, who himself had been summoned away from his leisurely evening.

By the time everyone had emerged from this unprecedented consultation, the 'gamblers' were already out of the lockup and were seated on the waiting room benches. Dearie was still mopping her eyes with a delicate lace-edged handkerchief when Oscar sat down with her.

"Oh… I've *never* been so humiliated!"

"There, there – everything's going to be alright, Dearie." Oscar put his arm around her. "We talked to the police chief and he says that he's willing to drop the charges against all of you if you'll just agree to limit those games of yours to maybe once every week or two – so that it's not like somebody's running a gambling den up there…"

Dearie hung on to Oscar's arm as they walked out – and she continued to hang onto it even after they arrived home. Lonesome shadows still danced under the midnight street lights. Oscar watched them again for a few seconds before he walked back toward his room. He stood momentarily in the doorway between the dining room and the hall that connected it to his room and the bathroom. Dearie was bustling nervously around the dining room table – straitening table scarves that didn't need straightening.

"You know… it must have been that woman in the apartment down below. She must have been the one who called the police. Every time one of us gets up and scrapes a chair along the floor a little – or when anyone laughs or talks a bit loud, she gets out a broom and keeps bumping the handle on the ceiling."

Oscar stood attentively, still in the doorway, saying nothing, but nodding as if in agreement.

"I…," Dearie began dabbing at her eyes again, "I just can't get over it! It was so humiliating – I've never been so completely *mortified*! Thank goodness no one else I know saw me in the police wagon or at the station. I would have been so ashamed and embarrassed."

Waiting for her to finish her catharsis, Oscar kept standing in the doorway.

"But listen, Papa – that's not even the worst of it; listen to *this*! All evening long I'd been losing and finally – finally just when the police knocked on the door, I was about ready to lay down a *royal flush*! Then the police came in and gathered up all the money."

Oscar did a quick pivot, took three steps into the bathroom and turned on the water in the sink so as to drown out the sound of his basso guffaws.

Mud Baby

Midday heat sizzled from the glaring Mississippi Valley summer sun. A drenching storm the night before had left a stiflingly heavy humidity that hung like the weight of one of Annie's wet blankets. She reached into the wicker clothes basket, grabbed out a couple of pieces of wet wash and deftly hung them on the clothes line, pinning as she proceeded. During each cycle to the clothes basket she would give a protective glance over her shoulder toward the vacant lot next door where Jackie had wandered.

"Y'all stay wheh ah kin watch y'now, y'heah?"

Annie's black brow glistened with beads of perspiration; her small, rotund figure bounded rhythmically as she moved from basket to line and back again. Her motion was accentuated by the two bars of a nameless melody that she constantly whistled and hummed alternately.

As Annie worked, Jackie aimlessly walked around the lot, eyeing the depression in the center where he and his playmates had dug a series of "roads" and tunnels in the dirt. As the toddler approached his play-spot, he remembered having left his favorite red cast iron toy car there the day before. Only the roof of the toy now protruded from the sticky yellow mud. Accumulated rain had collapsed the roads and tunnels into the center of the hole and only slick sides remained along the edges.

With both feet planted firmly at the edge, Jackie reached out to rescue his car. He bent over further, until he had lost his balance, then quickly moved his feet into the hole to avoid falling over. He tried to lift his feet back out, but the mud oozed further around his shoes as he struggled to free himself.

With a cry that became a long moaning wail, the trapped youngster bellowed his agony. In an instant his "mammy" put down the wash and hurried over to rescue her charge. She reached out to grab his flailing little hands, placing herself far enough away from the mud so as not to be pulled into it herself.

"Com'mon now, Annie go' get you out." She tugged, then tugged again harder. With an explosive release, the boy flew up into her arms, his socks pulled nearly all the way off, dangling like a couple of muddy white flags in the breeze. He continued crying even harder.

Annie carried Jackie back to the yard; she sat down on the porch steps with the ferociously crying child still snuggled in her arms.

"You safe in Annie's arms now – why you still cryin' like dat, chile? W'ut be d'matta' wif you?"

Jackie clung closer – put one arm around her neck and pointed to where Annie had pulled him from the mud hole. "My feet – my feet came off!"

Best of Friends

11/24/93

Lucian Hunter moved into our area when we were in second grade. He was actually a rather nice looking boy – but there was just something about him I didn't like. More than didn't like – there was something I *hated* about him! I *hated* him and, not surprisingly, he *hated* me. From the first brief moments of our encounter far across the classroom, we were mortal enemies.

The day after we had been placed into our school class, we somehow found ourselves alone together after school in the basement athletic room. How that chance meeting ever happened, I will never know, but we both realized from the instant we spied each other that – this was IT!

We sped suddenly at each other like two frenzied lions fighting over a lioness. But there was no motivation like that. We weren't fighting over a girl, because we didn't know any of the same girls. We weren't fighting over territory – obviously neither of us owned the school, nor were either of us even "dominant" males. We weren't fighting over food or books or clothes or – anything – but *hatred.*

Fortunately we collided near a thick athletic mat. As we fell onto it pummeling and pounding away at each other, I screamed "I hate you!"

He returned my compliment. "I hate you, too!"

We rolled around, on and off the mat, hitting, screaming, pulling, kicking… POW! Wham! SLAM! THUD! WHUMP! The fight seemed like it lasted for 3 hours – but it was probably more like 3 minutes.

I felt blood trickle down over my chin. My nose hurt with a fierce aching. Lucien backed away at the sight of blood. He felt his own face. Blood also dripped from his nose. We sat on the mat staring at each other for several minutes.

"Where do you live?" I asked.

"Just right across the street." And he pointed out the window. "You want to come over to my house? My mother always has milk and cookies for me after school."

"Yeah – sure."

From that day on, Lucian and I were inseparable pals – until his family moved again when we were in 6th grade. I've often wondered what ever happened to him – more than that, I've wondered why 6th graders weren't given the option of maintaining their relationships…after all – that *was* a very hard-won friendship!

Cigarettes, First and Last

11/29/93

The bell rings out in the hall; end of the day and beginning of usual commotion. Richard sidles up to me. "Come out in back and wait with me – and I'll show you something!" he speaks in hushed tones without even looking at me. I'm as curious as any other 9 year old boy would be. "Ok!" I tell him.

We wait for about 20 minutes. Everyone is gone from the halls and the janitor is busy pushing his huge dust mop on the floor below. The janitor's closet is next to our classroom on the upper floor; its doorknob is unlocked as my friend turns it and opens the door. The light is still on inside. The "closet" is more like a small room, cluttered with buckets, string mops, brooms and a variety of soaps, sponges and rags.

On the side of one wall, a vertical steel ladder is anchored a few inches away from the surface. In the ceiling 10 feet above the floor, directly over the ladder, there is a small trap-door. Richard quietly closes the door to the hall and begins climbing the ladder. When he reaches the top, he pushes the trap-door open, climbs through and silently but vigorously motions for me to quickly follow. I sprint up the ladder and suddenly find myself in a belltower on the roof of the school. I am too amazed to even notice Richard close the trap-door, pull out a pack of cigarettes and light one.

"Here," he says, handing me a cigarette. "Ever smoke before?"

"No." I'm still a little dumbfounded by the whole situation.

The belltower has no bell and probably never was intended to have one. What it does have, though, is an impressive supply of pigeons. Nests and droppings are everywhere. There is no place even to sit.

The smoldering cigarette in Richard's mouth glows brightly as he sucks in on it. He holds it out and I push mine against it. "Okay, now draw in and it'll light."

I follow his instructions; then I just stand there.

"What's the matter? Your parents smoke, don't they? You see them smoking all the time, right?" I nod affirmatively. "Well – just do it like they do. You have to draw in on it like this." He demonstrates. "Then you just breathe out. See – it's real easy."

I draw in as for a deep breath. Smoke pervades my mouth and nose, searing my eyes. Immediately there is a sharp, intense pain in my lungs. My head begins spinning – and I clutch at the walls of the tower.

"See, you did it!"

Richard's voice is full of gleeful admiration. I say nothing – keep hanging onto the wall. Slowly, with glazed eyes I reach up and remove the cigarette

34

from my mouth.   I look out over the streets
and houses, then turn and look
back at the field behind the school. My companion is busily puffing his
smoke – jabbering aimlessly and paying very little attention to me.   I
continue to stand, preoccupied with nothing.

Finally, Richard finishes his cigarette.

"Want another one?"   Then he laughingly corrects himself. "There isn't
time; we better go. The janitor will be coming back."

We open the trap-door, slither down the ladder and carefully swing the
broom closet door open slightly. We peek out. The janitor is still nowhere in
sight.

Several more times during that year, my friend and I had our secret
smoking sessions in the school belltower – but I never made the mistake of
inhaling again. The next year and for many years following, we graduated to
occasional casual smoking rendezvous with other boys – in the woods or in
someone's garage – or in a vacant lot; wherever it seemed convenient. And
we all felt very adult. We were entering a forbidden part of the world of the
"big people", albeit from the back door.

By the time I was 16, most of the boys smoked. It was just part of growing
up in that era. Another important part of growing up was owning a motor
vehicle. Cars for 16 year olds were too expensive, so we bought motor
scooters. I had my first scooter – and my first experience with engine
trouble.

It seemed that many of us with scooters and even the older boys with
motorcycles and cars often congregated at the home of the best mechanic of
the bunch. Because his parents seldom put their car in the garage, we were
able to utilize the space for working on our vehicles.

My little Powell scooter had finally burned the exhaust valve so badly that
it would no longer start. I took the head off, borrowed a buddy's "expensive"
$2.50 valve grinding kit and went to work on it. The evening was unbearably
hot, even with the garage doors open and the job was tediously slow working
with such crude equipment.

Mosquitoes were swarming into the garage like a fleet of enemy fighter
planes. I bummed a cigarette from one of the guys, lit it and set it on a box
near the scooter, hoping the smoke would effectively keep away most of the
little probocid devils.

After what seemed like an eternity grinding the pits out of the valve seat,
there was still the touchy job of installing the split keepers. I hated that
"balancing act" on the bottom ridge of the valve stem – especially with the
distraction of a mosquito chewing on your ear lobe. The first cigarette had
long since burned out. I approached the same friend for another.

"Hey – don't you *ever* buy cigarettes of your own? You been bummin' cigarettes from me or somebody, ever since I've known you." He fumbled in his pocket. "Here!" – handed me a cigarette.

"You know, I'll bet you never bought a pack of cigarettes in your life!" he chuckled as he put away the pack. "Bet you don't really even know how to smoke!" he was laughing hard. Everyone smiled, watching us. "Tell you what – that's the last one you'll ever get from me!"

He was just having his little joke at my expense – not even half seriously, and I knew it...but it affected me profoundly: because he was right.

I put the lit cigarette down on the box next to the scooter – finished reassembling the engine...After that, I worked many times on scooters and motorcycles and later on cars – often out in the summer night...but I never did ever light up another cigarette.

Why Did You Do It?

9/10/11

I can't even remember her name. After all, it was seventy-two years ago. That's *really* a long time – almost a lifetime...but I can remember the incident – just as if it were yesterday.

I was standing there in Miss Palmer's fifth grade classroom at Jackson Park Elementary School, not thinking about much of anything. Of course, that wasn't unusual – I seldom thought about much other than the final bell for the day releasing me from my pedagogical prison. But when I was suddenly confronted with the wide dimension of her extraordinarily fat abdominal expanse, well, it was just more than I could take.

Something snapped inside my head: I must have been thinking about doing it subconsciously for a long time. You see, her extended stomach protrusion looked just like a punching bag to me – and so, I punched it! Hard!

Ah yes...you already know the rest of the story: the girl crying ferociously; the teacher dragging me by the arm to the principal's office; their heatedly animated voices in the inner office while I waited in the outer office for them to have a short conference on my punishment.

But they decided to question me first. Perhaps, I might have had some understandable reason for having done something so cruel. They ushered me in:

"Why did you hit that girl in the stomach?" my teacher asked very pointedly. I just stood there in stony silence.

"Jackie, *why* did you hit that girl?" The teacher was really bearing down on me now, and I knew I was going to have to say *something*.

"Uh...uh...uh. Well, I ...uh"

"You *what?*" growled the principal, "come on...out with it!" Mister Drury stood over me like a bespeckled vulture. His six foot stature dwarfed my ten year old frame and I was virtually shaking in the thunder of his wrath.

"*Why* did you do it?" he asked again.

"Yes, why did you do it?" Miss Palmer followed. Did she ever hit *you?*"

"No."

"Did she say mean things to you?"

"No."

"Did she laugh at you or make fun of you?"

"No..."

"Then why on *earth* did you hit her?"

I stood there looking down at the floor and shrugged.

"I...I...I. I dunno..."

"Yes, you *do* know! Now *why?* WHY did you do it?"

"I guess," I said tearfully, "I guess...'cause she was *FAT!*"

Gullies and Ravines

11/25/93

Third grade boys really do like to play softball. At least they did when I went to grade school. But I wasn't the average third grade boy. Oh, I did enjoy playing softball once in a while, even though I was a scrawny little kid who couldn't hit well and didn't throw or catch any better.

Most of the time, my playing softball at recess depended on whether there were enough kids to make up a team without choosing me. On those days when I didn't play, I would wander to the back edge of Jackson Park School's athletic field which adjoined a badly eroded former corn field. There was a fascinating strip of sassafras saplings along one side and paralleling that, little gullies that grew wider and deeper as they proceeded downhill.

Time after time I would walk those little gullies top to bottom, where they ended at the cross street. Never did I find anything; never did I see anything unusual. Always, there was just dry mud – yellow clay subsoil; but it was as though I *expected* to find something or see something unusual.

My aunt and uncle had a "weekend farm" which we visited regularly. There also, I had little to do other than walk the gullies in the fields. But there, the gullies were different. The hills were steeper and the gullies became rapidly deep – so deep that they were over my head. At the end of the field where they joined the creek, they were truly ravines – like great canyons to a small child. Still, I never saw nor found anything in them that could help to account for my fascination with walking them.

In later years, I wondered if other people are as mesmerized by their own "gullies" and "ravines" that have become the daily routine of their lives. Maybe they're looking to see something or find something that they never see or find…

At the very bottom of the hill on which our "subdivision" was built, there was a storm water drain that everyone called "the ravine". It was man made and drained storm water from many streets into the River Des Peres. That ravine was about thirty feet wide and twelve feet deep. It ran along the old streetcar line nearly a quarter mile.

Many afternoons after school, I spent walking along and sometimes down into "the ravine", where brush hadn't grown. As an open storm sewer, it had been there for more than fifty years, because there were huge poplar trees growing by it and even in it. Those poplars were full of blue jays and cardinals – flickers – all sorts of birds. Maybe they weren't really unusual, still they were an attraction for an inquisitive boy.

There was also the remains of a tool shed built into the side of the ravine – just the concrete walls were left. Once a couple of young hoboes built a sheet metal roof on it and tried to live in it for a few days. At last I had found something unusual in a ravine. They were indeed unusual - unusually dirty, unusually ragged and unusually and desperately poor in both an era and an area of affluence. I'm not sure what else I expected to find in a ravine, though…

One day when I was walking by the "ravine", I took my favorite marble out of my pocket just to admire it. The color of that marble was a deep translucent red with swirls of milky orange and yellow and white – the most beautiful marble I ever owned. And it was a wonderful shooter too – big, and easy to "thumb". I put it in the shooting position in my hand – and then, unintentionally, shot it into the air as my thumb slipped.

For months I searched for that marble by the big poplar tree. Finally I gave up and never went back to the "ravine" again. I wondered if somebody else might have found it. I wondered if there were anyone else who walked that ravine – or any ravine. It never occurred to me then that other people might be walking all their lives in ravines of their own making. At least I could *see* my ravine – step out of it if I wanted to.

I've never decided that ravine walking is something that has to be bad. Maybe there's someone out there walking a ravine, who someday will look down and find a wonderful, beautiful, huge red marble at his feet and look up and see a lovely red cardinal – and proudly walk home with his marble in his pocket…and a cardinal in his mind.

Jackson Park School is Falling Down

2/10/2007

Sixty degrees at the end of October is not exactly chilly weather. That was what nearly everyone thought at recess. When the bell rang, all of the children and the teachers fled out into the playground of Jackson Park Elementary School…all, that is, except Del, who first got up and went to the front of the classroom, then hesitated a few seconds waiting for everyone else to leave.

Del immediately returned to a seat – not his own. It was the desk next to mine in the very back row of the room. With my seat in the rear of the room, this meant that I was often one of the last (or last) to leave.

Noting Del seated in the desk next to mine, I went back to my desk and sat there next to him. He then quickly pulled a small adjustable wrench from his pants pocket and with a swift twisting motion unscrewed a nut from a seat back bolt of the deck in front of him. Then he gently topped the quarter inch carriage bolt out and dropped the hardware into his pocket along with the wrench.

He looked over at me with a foxy smile.

"Don't say anything, okay?"

I looked back at Del inquisitively, as if waiting for a further explanation, but he said nothing.

Del and I had been friends for a long time – but only briefly what you'd call close friends. He lived just a block away from school, but I had never been to his house.

"Come home with me after school." He nodded with another foxy grin.

Then he slipped a screwdriver out of a different pocket and reached under the desk top of the one in which he was sitting. He found the screw slots in two of the six screws that held the desk top on, removing the screws with a dexterity that truly amazed me. He dropped the screws into one pocket and returned the screwdriver to another.

Del got up and pulled the lower edge of his sweater over the protruding screwdriver handle. I had wondered why he always wore the same long, pinkish beige sweater with plaid geometric designs.

I sat there, a bit in wonderment... and a bit in fear; but Del beckoned me to follow him. We left Miss Farmer's room and went on down the hall to the schoolyard door, then outside on the playground. Before we had reached the group of children playing ball, Del pointed down to the bulge in the lower part of his pants' front pocket.

"It's not what you think it is," he chuckled. "It's full of nuts and bolts and screws – all of 'em I got today at the other recess... and in the boy's room every time I had to use it. You ought to see what I've got at home!"

Like me, Del was a little guy - though we were almost all still small at the age of ten. But his small size didn't seem to hold back Del's peculiar but ambitious extracurricular activity. That became readily evident when we rode our bikes to his house an hour and a half later at the end of the school day.

"My mom's not home yet; let's go out in the garage."

Along the back wall was a typical jumble of yard tools, old tires, lawn chairs and other middle-class American miscellany. Behind a folding chair reposed a small, gray wooden cabinet. Del pulled the chair away from in front of it so that he could swing open the roughly hung doors of the equally roughly constructed cabinet. On the bottom shelf were three nearly full gallon glass jars of nuts, bolts, screws and washers, as well as two number ten tin cans, also nearly full. Reaching down into his bulging pocket, Del removed the current day's hardware and deposited it into one of the open cans.

"I got all of this since school started in September," he said with a degree of pride that I could understand, considering the quantity of what he had amassed.

"Gee... but... but... Del, what are you going to *do* with all of it?"

Delmar stood there with an almost dumb expression. He shrugged his shoulders smiled slightly.

"I don't know. It's just a lot of fun getting it. Someday I could have a hardware store, maybe..."

"Wul...wul – what's gonna happen? I mean, if everything at school falls apart. I mean..."

"Oh don't worry about that." Del smiled slyly. "It's *not* gonna happen. Every day, when they find something loose, the teacher tells the janitor and he puts a new screw or bolt in and tightens it up again. Then I can go back later and take the new ones out."

"What!"

"Yeah, that's how it works."

Del laughed, showing his small, even teeth, which made him look less foxy, but still very crafty, indeed.

"You want to help me? I've got another screwdriver and here's another wrench."

He picked up the wrench from the top of a workbench and pulled a screwdriver from its slot in a wall rack.

"Yeah... I guess so. I don't know what I'll do with all the bolts. Maybe I can make something out of them."

"Sure," Del agreed, "you need some for your bike. Maybe we'll have motorcycles when we get old enough. Bet they lose a lot of bolts."

I dropped the two tools in my pocket just as Del's mother walked in the front door. Del closed the cabinet and pushed the chair back, covering and hiding the door.

The next day, Delmar was already seated at his desk in the front row when I arrived. He smiled and winked at me, and as I passed by going toward the center isle he whispered in a low tone: "Get a book out and act like you're studying."

I nodded. "Okay."

Throughout the day, there were several opportunities to remove bolts and screws, and I took advantage of every one of them. At the end of the day, my own pocket bulged with an assortment of hardware.

But the screwdriver handle protruded out of my pocket and I had to place it with the blade facing up so as to be less noticeable. I had a sweater myself, but had forgotten to wear it.

Del looked at my bulging pocket and smiled approvingly.

"Here," I said, "you want them?" And I reached into the pocket and took out a handful of bolts. He looked at them for a moment, then shook his head.

"Nah... my pockets are so full I don't think I can get any more in 'em. Just take 'em home."

When I got home, I immediately went up to the kitchen pantry and dug through the shelf of folded paper bags that my mother had saved. She saved every bag – every piece of string – every rubber band, with her 'waste-not-want-not' mentality. I chose a small brown bag, just large enough to accommodate the bolts, nuts and screws and carried them down to the garage, placing the bag inconspicuously in a corner on the floor.

The next day, I remembered to wear my sweater. And the day after... and the day after that.

"Well," my mother observed one morning as I pulled on the sweater, "I didn't think you liked that sweater your Aunt Alice sent you."

"I don't... but it's warm."

What I had failed to say was that not only was it too large, but it was too long as well – which was exactly what I needed to cover the tools and bulges of hardware.

After a couple of weeks had gone by, I was beginning to amass a fairly large quantity of bags of bolts, nuts and washers of my own – but nothing that would even vaguely compare to Del's truly massive collection.

It was a bright Monday morning – everything looked fresh and new. Del had an idea. When we were in the downstairs hall at recess, Del whispered to me: "you know those big, shiny brass bolts that hold the door handles – the push bars on? They're kinda neat. I never have got one yet. They always turn on the outside of the door when I try to get one. Someone needs to hold the screw slot on the outside of the door while I turn the head on the inside."

"I'll do it." I told him.

"Now listen, " he said, "you stand with your back to the door and hold the screwdriver in the screw slot and kind of lean against it to put some pressure on it. That way you'll just look like you're standing there waiting for someone and you can see everyone on the playground that might be coming in… and you can warn me."

"Okay," I agreed.

We went to the back lower door leading to the playground and Del quickly began twisting the head on the brass bolt after I had taken my place in front of the door.

"Oooh, this one's really tight. Try the one next to it." I heard Del say in a muffled voice through the door.

"Okay, I've got it – go ahead," I replied.

Del gave the bolt head a mighty twist and I felt the resistance against my screwdriver. Then it suddenly released and Del turned the screw slowly out of the female threads on the end I was holding.

Del was so intent on removing that large brass bolt that he did not hear the dainty footsteps of petite Miss Farmer as she approached him down the hall from behind.

"Delmar! What *are* you doing…?"

Miss Farmer had reached a point almost directly behind him when she spoke. The horrified tone of her voice shook Del back into the unwanted reality of what both he and I knew would soon be a series of embarrassing and ego-shattering reactions to our crime. I watched through the door glass shaking so hard I hadn't the presence of mind to put my screwdriver back in my pocket. With a frown, Miss Farmer pointed at me through the glass of the door, then beckoned for me to come in.

The small, delicate stature of our teacher was disproportionately large when she was angry; we two little ten year old boys seemed dwarfed by her. I liked Miss Farmer; she was plain-featured, but pleasant and rather easy going. And I felt very bad about having contributed to her anger.

"Oooo – so it was *you* two! I should have known! Yes, I should have known…" (she did *not* tell us *why* she should have known and we were too fearful to ask.) She grabbed each of us by our arms and guided us down the hall. We knew where we were headed long before we got there.

As we walked into the principal's office near the main entrance, a number of students and teachers stood around the counter tending to business. The heavy, glass-paned oak door closed by itself behind us with a thud of finality. Miss Famer led us into a small room off to the side, where the privacy was even more stiflingly intrusive than our public display in the outer office might have been.

Almost immediately, Mister Drury came into the room frowning and looking imperious. He was a large man with a booming voice. He peered down his long, aquiline nose through gold-rimmed spectacles at us. And he reminded me of a vulture in a grey- pin-striped suit.

"So... what have we here?"

The words rumbled in a nasal echo from the mouth of the large man.

"These boys... these boys... " Miss Farmer hesitated in her own embarrassment at the fact that we were in *her* class. "Oh, *these* are the boys who have been stealing bolts all over the school!"

"Hmm... I see... hmm! Alright – *you!*" Mister Drury pointed his finger at Del. "What is your name?"

"That's Delmar," offered Miss Farmer, not waiting for the boy to answer.

Mister Drury turned his head slightly to the side and squinted.

"*Why* did you take all those nuts and bolts?"

Delmar stood with just a hint of an embarrassed smile, dwarfed by, but not trembling in the shadow of his interrogator. He shrugged his shoulders and said nothing, gazing vacantly.

"And the other boy – what have *you* to say about this?"

I was too frightened to be able to let out whatever meaningless words that I might have mouthed. I looked away in embarrassment.

"Boys!" said Miss Famer in desperation, almost crying, "why – why did you *do* such a thing? Don't you realize how much trouble and expense you've *caused* the school?"

Obviously, we ten year old boys did not. Finally Del looked up with a blank expression of innocence:

"I guess... I just like to take stuff apart..."

"Oh Delmar..." Miss Famer began again in a pleading tone, "You simply *must* begin to understand that this is not acceptable behavior!"

"Yes, ma'am..." he nodded and looked down.

Mister Drury again stepped toward us, towering, but bending over to face us squarely. He narrowed his left eye and stared with the other, a bulging buzzard-like intensity to it.

"How would you boys feel if the school fell down on all of us – including the two of you? And because *you* two caused it!"

I knew that Del was too smart to believe something that silly; even I didn't believe it. I kept wishing that this ordeal would soon end –

because I knew we had even more to endure once we got home. And... it could be even worse!

Finally, Mister Drury called over his secretary:

"I want you to prepare notes to the parents of these two boys. Say in the notes the nature of what they have done and that I wish to speak with one or both of the parents – oh, and that they must bring with them those bolts that the boys took home."

Again, Mister Drury turned his attention to us: "Now tell me boys, what on earth were you going to do with all those bolts and screws?"

"I guess we were gonna make things?   Huh?" Del looked questionably at me.

"Yeah – I could make a car!" I said, evidencing my love for automobiles.

Mister Drury grimaced, "Look," he said, "the time will come when both of you are older to 'make' things. But it will *not* be from bolts and nuts taken from this school! Now... is that clear?"

Both Del and I looked down and nodded.

"If I made a car," I offered with a sudden inspiration, I'd give it to the school!"

Taking a deep breath, Mister Drury rapidly exhaled it in exasperation:

"Alright boys... since you seem so intent on making things, you can both go around and *make* repairs on the desks and other items that you took the hardware from. When you put the bolts and screws back into the holes you took them out of, you'll save the janitor the trouble of doing it – and... you'll be 'making' something – repairs!"

Delmar and I did manage to matriculate from Miss Farmer's fourth grade class that year – of course, minus all the nuts and bolts and screws. I figured that we had done the school no favor by our presence there. Still, we managed also to graduate from fifth and sixth grades as well and left the school really not much the worse for our having been there.

Years later, after I had been through the entire University City school system, I even felt some tinges of nostalgic affection for that old elementary school building. Every time I would pass by it, I would remember the massiveness of that steel and concrete structure. How silly for anyone to have ever suggested that we might make it fall down. That building, with its attractive architecture and its solid construction, should stand there forever as a monument to those who learned and those who taught there – even if the school were to become no longer practical from changing demographics.

You know something... now that I think about it – in all those following years that I attended University City Junior High and then the high school - never once did I go back to Jackson Park Elementary School to look up any of my former teachers. And I did like some of them. I will always regret – and never understand why, I never gave a thought to returning to that school – though I passed by it nearly every day for years. Perhaps there is just something about the passage of time that creates a finality to the termination of a difficult achievement.

But beyond that – today, although all those teachers have passed into the oblivion of obscure deaths, I do wonder what they might have thought of me now. That new penny-bright little boy, now living like an old bum in a ramshackle hovel – still disassembling nuts and bolts – now from discarded 'things' left in the trash at the edge of the street. So, is that poetic justice – or just perverse bad fortune? Where is that fine line drawn between 'acceptability' and disreputability? And what *is* success – and what is failure? That is, if we look at the meanings of those words in terms of the global impact of each of our lives.

I will never know what the teachers at Jackson Park School might have thought today of the little boy who passed through their classroom over seventy years ago. Would they understand who he was – or who he became? Or would they even, at this point much care? In the greater scheme of things... does it really matter?

Nathan Liner, The "Dumb Guy" and a Bad Accident

Walking home from the third grade at Jackson Park Elementary School, there were usually about four of us: myself, Ronald Chaderosky, Norton Fendelman and Billie Hamilton- sometimes also Ronald Henges. We all lived in the same area of University City and often would pass Cranson's Drug Store.

Many times, near the drug store we would encounter Nathan Liner, the "dumb guy". Nathan was severely retarded with the intelligence of about a three year old. Why his family allowed him to roam the streets I could never understand. Perhaps for exercise and fresh air (such as it was on the city streets), but there he would be when we walked home from school.

Nathan was a very short – possibly only about five foot tall adult, maybe in his late twenties or early thirties. (My memory of him from my own age of eight or nine is not especially good after over eighty years.) I *can* recall, though that Nathan would usually be dressed in a man's suit, not shabby but quite ill-fitting. No doubt, for someone of his short stature it had been necessary to have the suit custom tailored. And because of his rather odd proportions, it must have been very difficult for the tailor to accurately fit every dimension.

In addition to his clothes giving Nathan a somewhat odd appearance, I seem to recall that the diminutive guy had a habit of drooling just slightly out of one side of his mouth! And that *definitely* did not enhance his attractiveness when he approached someone!

But Nathan was a good natured little fellow and very open to our suggestions. If there were some girls from our class walking nearby, we would say to Nathan: "Hey Nathan, go tell those girls over there that you want to marry one of them!"

Poor, portly little Nathan – he would amble over to the girls and with a big vacant-looking smile on his homely face say to them: "I wa' get ma'wied! I wa' get ma'wied!" The girls would be extremely agitated and disturbed by this unwanted encounter with a strange-looking and disturbing sounding – freaky little "adult".

We boys would just "break-up" laughing until Nathan ambled away down the block. I and my classmates, as very young little children, did not seem to have any understanding as to how truly sad life would be for a severely retarded person like Nathan. Perhaps, if we had known, we might have reacted differently to him… (but, knowing myself and my friends… I have my doubts!)

Cranson's Drug Store was where the kids would stop in after school to buy penny candies. Mister Rich Cranson was not a particularly friendly guy – oh yes, he would always sell us those penny candies that we wanted, but with somewhat of a scowl on his face. Obviously, there was no profit in selling penny candies; he did it only as an accommodation to our parents, who might be his customers for his drug and miscellaneous items.

It was one of those days when I had just left Cranson's Drug Store with Norton Fendelman. Nordie lived just east of Chanson's across the large vacant lot. After Nordie went in his apartment, I looked in the vacant lot at Cranson's large trash burner. It was filled to the top!

47

Intrigued, I cut across the weed-filled lot to look in the burner, not following Cranson's path to it. Right near the burner, I tripped on something and fell near the edge of the pile of ashes and broken bottles. Putting my hand out to break my fall, the base of my thumb slashed open on the edge of a piece of glass. The cut was fairly deep and blood poured down my arm. I ran to the drug store and went in, dripping blood all over Cranson's antiseptically clean floor. My loud crying brought Rich Cranson out from behind his counter immediately. He was *horrified*! Not because a little child was badly cut, but because his super-clean store was being contaminated!

Cranson immediately grabbed a package of bandaids and tore open the wrapper on the smallest bandage that would *barely* cover the cut. He then placed the tiny bandaid with considerable pressure over the cut so as to stop the bleeding. He then gave me a paper napkin to put around my hand so that no more blood would drop on his floor.

"Now go home – and don't come in here again with cuts!" Cranson's comment chased me quickly out of the store.

In spite of its small size, the bandaid soon stopped the bleeding. When I got home I showed my mother the injury. She washed off the blood and put a much larger bandaid over the cut.

"Ooo... that cheap Cranson!" she muttered, "How could he do something like that to a little child! It would have cost him a couple pennies more to put a decent size bandaid on the cut! I'll never buy anything again from that Cranson's Drug Store!

I could not remember that she had *ever* bought anything from Cranson's in the past so it was a kind of empty threat – but I personally never went into Cranson's Drug Store again. I began walking home down Balson Ave. and stopping in at "Doc" Winningham's Drug Store at Midland. It was only a half block further and "Doc" was an extremely friendly older man who not only gladly sold us penny candies, but often gave us an extra piece or two that we hadn't paid for.

Well... that's all in the past now – long, long past...

Cranson's Drug Store is gone; "Doc" Winningham's Drug Store is gone. Most of the stores are gone – *all* the businesses are gone. Everyone's dead and gone except me, I guess. And it's an uncomfortable feeling... sort of like being left behind. It's almost a little bit funny, though I don't seem to find any humor in it today. But maybe I will tomorrow... that is, if there *is* a tomorrow...

Hooky Tadpoles

7/17/23

Ann McKinney was the school "Tomboy" at Jackson Park Elementary School. Her father was the science teacher at the Hanley Junior High. We never saw him but we knew about him, so Ann was something of a celebrity. And Ann was fun to be around because she was more like one of the boys than a girl.

Ann's family's house was a full half mile or more west on Olive Street Road – out near Beckman's Feed Store. She didn't like having to walk it alone every day so one day she said to Delmar Brimble and me: "Hey, my mother fixes something really good to eat when I get home. Bet she'd give you guys some too!"

So Del and I followed Ann all the way out to her house that afternoon. We went up on the back porch and waited while Ann went in. She came back out looking glum. "My mom's not here this afternoon. She didn't even leave anything for me to eat!" Ann shrugged as if to say "sorry".

We quickly trundled down the steps and began walking back east. "Hey Del, did you se that little swampy pond we passed a couple blocks back?"

"Yeah, let's go look at it!"

We stop at the pond. It covers just about the area of a vacant lot. It is quite shallow, just a "springtime waterhole" with rusty tin cans around the edge and brush and small trees growing in and around it.

"Look, Del! Look at those tadpoles! They're *huge*! And they're even starting to get legs!"

"Yeah… let's try to get some to take home!"

We look around the edge of the pond but can find nothing suitable to use for a container.

"I've still got those gallon glass jars I had the bolts and screws in last year," Del says.

"Well, then let's come back tomorrow and bring jars to put 'em in. IT's too hot to come all the way out here again today," I comment.

It was another warm mid-May day. Delmar sidled up tome at the first recess.

"Let's go get those tadpoles now – before it gets any hotter," Del says.

"But Miss Palmer's gonna know we're gone!"

49

"Aw… I'll leave my books on my desk so she'll know I'll be back… or maybe she'll just think I'm still around here someplace. She might not even miss you with your desk all the way in the back."

"Well… okay."

We walk off the playground to Del's house to get the gallon glass jars, then proceed out Olive Street Road. We play for a while around the edge of the swamp-pond, then fill our jars about half full of water and tadpoles. We leisurely carry the jars back to Delmar's house and leave them, then go back to school, waiting until afternoon recess before going in class again.

Miss Palmer immediately confronts Delmar who is sitting at his front row desk.

She stands in front of him frowning, her solid five foot five inch stature firmly planted in front of his desk. With her hands on her hips she vocalizes emphatically: "Delmar! *Where* did you go?"

"Uh… uh… wha… uh… see, we found some huge tadpoles in a pond, an' uh, what we…" Delmar gets one of his foxy grins.

"Now you *listen* to me, Delmar!" Then Miss Palmar beckons to me to come forward, so that I'm standing next to Del's desk.

"Boys, you simply *cannot* do something like that *ever* again! Do you understand? That is unacceptable behavior. I was ready to call the police to have them search for you!"

"Well, Miss Palmer, we were afraid the pond might dry up and we wanted to get some of those big tadpoles – they're so neat!"

"Alright, Delmar," Miss Palmer said calmly, "I understand your motivation, but you simply cannot do things that way.   You cannot come to school and leave unannounced. Going to the pond is an after-school project! And I will not report thi8s to Mr. Drury's office if you promise to bring some of those tadpoles to class so that we can watch them develop. That would be a good class project."

That afternoon, I went to Del's and took home my jar of tadpoles. In the morning, Del brought his jar of tadpoles to Miss Palmers class and ;left them there to develop. Miss Palmer was quite pleased with the great amount of interest that the rest of her class took in watching the tadpoles develop into frogs. But I suspect that our teacher was a little less than happy that she had unintentionally tuned Delmar Brimble into something of a celebrity. Well… things done' always work out exactly the way we planned. What more can you say?

"Jew – you killed Jesus!"

7/17/2023

When I was only six years old and had to walk to our new home at 7045 Cornell Avenue in University City, I was instructed to wait and walk home with my cousin Charles Sophir who also attended Jackson Park Elementary School. My Uncle Leo lived only about a half block away, so it was no trouble for my cousin Charles to see me safely home. Charles was two years older than me and a couple of inches taller – much stronger and heavier.

Whether we walked home on Balson or Dartmouth, we had to pass by the schoolyard and playground of the Christ the King Catholic school. On Dartmouth, the Catholic school playground was four feet above the sidewalk bordered with a rock wall. On the Balson side, the playground was level with the sidewalk. Usually, we walked Balson because it was close to our school's front door.

One spring day, Charles was delayed for some reason after school and I decided to begin walking home by myself. I knew Charlie would quickly catch up with me, being taller and a faster walker.

But when I passed the Christ the King playground, one of the older, larger Catholic boys ran out and yelled at me "Dirty Jew… you killed Jesus!" The boy then grabbed my sack of school books and threw them up into the branches of a small tree in the area between the sidewalk and the street. The bag caught in a lower branch, too high for me to reach. The harassing Catholic boy stood there laughing as I attempted to reach the strap on my book bag and pull it down.

Charles soon caught up with me; he reached up and got my book bag down. The Catholic boy ran off back into his schoolyard.

But for a long time after that, I wondered why that Catholic boy had attacked me. Although I had no religious instruction of any kind at that time in my life, I was aware of what "looking Jewish" meant. And I did not think I looked like the Jewish boys in my class. Their hair was dark and curly and some of them had pronounced "bumps" on their nose bridges. My hair was blond and straight, my nose had no bump on it… though maybe my features were somewhat semitic… But I didn't even know who this "Jesus" was. I knew I certainly hadn't killed him – or anyone else at the age of six!

About a year later, they put a five foot chain link fence around the Catholic school playground. And it was never clear to me whether the fence was to keep out anyone from going into the Christ the King schoolyard... or to keep the Catholic boys from going out and attacking children walking along the sidewalk. And I still don't know the answer to that and I guess I never will. The Christ the King school is gone as well as anyone who might have known the answer to the question.

Ah well... things change! Times have changed... and I wonder if it still really matters.

The Ferns in My Grandmother's Wicker Planter

1993

Trailing expanse of green profused down the wicker sides; the burgeoning planter, painted white, stood resolutely defiant with living growth in the otherwise moribund dismay of the depression era second-floor flat.

My grandparents were Old-World Jews, driven from the 19th century's age of European intolerance and memories of militant bigotry with outright pogroms, into the blissfully skewed vision of an ethos of American justice and economic abundance.

I had watched my grandfather wood-grain his stairwell mouldings by hand, just as he had done in the railway cars before he left Europe. His skill fascinated me... and the great effulgent planter of ferns fascinated me, but did little to overcome the dismal lifeless aura of the late-depression times into which their flat – and their lives were relentlessly entwined.

As I remember them, my grandparents were poorly assimilated into the matrix of much of the American society and economy. Between themselves, they spoke mostly Yiddish, of which I understood none – and so felt largely shut out from the best of whatever they might have imparted to me. Both of them were, however, very loving and helpful in the few ways they could be, but communication with me came only within the many limitations of their adopted language, English.

Coming from Poland and Hungary respectively, my grandmother and grandfather never showed the slightest inclination to share with me anything about their early years in the old country. And I, for some odd reason I shall never fully understand, didn't feel the least necessity of *asking* them about it.   At some point, those things, of course, become too late to pursue…

Grandma did, on many occasions say to me "Jackeleh – should marry a *nice*, Jewish goil!" And then she would elaborate in a stream of mixed English, Polish and Yiddish, much or most of which escaped my comprehension.   Whatever Grandpa said to me – and there was little of it – I have no recollection of even one word.   Mostly, what remains now is the mental image of Grandma's round, smiling face with her antiquated wire-rimmed spectacles and Grandpa's placid, rather emotionless expression – like an indelible imprint on my mind.

Behind the apartment where they lived, there was a trolly line, which at that point had the tracks laid at the bottom of what seemed to me to be like a steep-sided ravine.   Trees and shrubs grew in a vast proliferation of unidentifiable verdure – but I recall enjoying most, the sweet-scented flowers of the little strap-leaved lily of the valley – and occasionally finding a box tortoise digging for grubs in and around them.   Whenever we visited during the summers, I would spend my time crouched in the woodsy dell behind the flat, waiting to see birds, tortoises and ferociously loud street-cars; in the cold months, I would be seated in their porch room, viewing that enormous planter with it's happy bit of winter greenery.

When I was a young child, I could never determine exactly what all of that meant – how and where it fit into the scheme of my life… as if there *were* some kind of discernable scheme or pattern.   And now, as a very, *very* much older child, I still am uncertain as to how or whether there is, or ever should be, some inflexible paradigm with which one is behooved to identify.

Although the language barrier made for somewhat limited access to my grandparents, I could always enjoy my grandmother's ferns and her lillys of the valley and I could enjoy having watched my grandfather graining the stair well – and I think there are some secrets locked with in all of that… Perhaps – just perhaps… as unintelligible to me now, as Yiddish was to me then.

Richard Antwell, The Obedient Boy

4th revision 4/24/23

On those hot summer mornings back in the late 1930s, all of us kids on the eighty hundred block of Cornell Avenue would pedal our trikes down to the bottom of the hill where Cornell started at Jackson to wait for the milkman.

I seem to remember that there were at least four of us about the same age as myself, Bobbie Momme whose house was above the vacant lot next door to my house, Dickie Laskey from right across the street, and Ed Sievers from across the street and further down. Then there were occasionally a couple of older boys on their small two-wheelers, who came from another street. I don't think I ever knew their names – or the names of two very young girls at the bottom of the the hill who followed on their tiny trikes only a few houses up.

We would all wait for and then follow the milkman as he made his deliveries on his route up Cornell until he reached Hanley Road at the top of the hill.

"The Milkman" was the only way all the kids referred to him. He never told us his name – at least if he did, I can't remember it. But I can recall his face well. He could have been of Italian decent. The hard lines in his face were accentuated by his dark eyebrows and wavy black hair with a tinge of gray in it. I remember him being rather small in stature, but muscular... really a very nice man – because he always had a big smile for each of us kids. And he was so friendly – the way he would take his ice pick every so often and chip off slivers from the 10lb ice blocks – give them to us kids to lick – refreshing on a hot summer day!

"The Milkman" drove that old Divco stepvan milk truck carefully, but confidently. He even let me ride in it a few feet with him once. The milkman was almost like a "Pied Piper", the way we kids followed him.

You could always tell when the milk truck started up at the beginning of our block. The hill was so steep that it taxed the full power of the Divco truck to pull its heavy load of milk packed in blocks of ice, on the constant starts up the incline. All the kids loved

54

to follow that truck up the hill on our tricycles – though it taxed our leg power to the limit.

I had heard stories some of the older boys had told about a kid who lived on the street just behind Cornell. Anyone who had been unlucky enough to have walked home from kindergarten on Stanford, had been chased by, and if caught, attacked by Richard Antwell, the neighborhood bully. My shortest route home was directly to Cornell, so I had never encountered him.

One morning, we had all congregated at the bottom of the hill awaiting the milkman; we were waiting in front of Bobby Breslow's house, Bobby Breslow was a larger, older boy I'd never met. One of the kids said: "don't mess with Bobby Breslow – he'll beat you up!" I had no intention of "messing" with Bobby – or anyone else. I was small and the shyest kid on the block. I nodded to Bobby Breslow and got back on my trike as the milkman approached. We all followed the milkman back up the hill. This was the pattern for weeks.

One morning, though, someone saw a kid peering through the wire fence behind Bobby Breslow's house.

"Hey look! There's Richard Antwell!" the boy shouted.

I couldn't see Antwell's features clearly, but I could tell that he had black hair and a deep scowl… and it made him appear owl-like. Very quickly, he was gone.

"Did you see Richard Antwell?" the older boy asked me. "He lives in the middle of the block behind us; don't ever go in front of his house; hell pull you off your trike and beat you up!"

I had never been on Stanford and I really had no reason to want to go there – so I gave it no thought.

It was obvious; I was beginning to outgrow my little tricycle. The older boy on the block now had a two-wheeler; and I wanted one. I had pleaded with my dad unsuccessfully many times to have him buy me a two-wheeler.

"Son, you're only five years old," he would say, "I don't think you'd be able to balance yourself well enough on a two-wheeler to be able to ride it."

"Aw', Dad, Bobby Momme has one – an' he's only a year older'n me…!"

My father flatly refused. But on my 6th birthday in May, he made a compromise – he bought me the largest, most elaborately made tricycle I'd ever seen. It was huge! And it had pneumatic tires front and rear. The frame was made of cast aluminum and the front wheel stood 2 feet in height. It's gleaming white paint had narrow pinstripes down the sides and as I climbed up on the seat, we could tell that my feet barely touched the pedals. My dad lowered the seat slightly so that I could pedal the trike without having to stand on the pedals to do it.

Proudly, I rode my new tricycle down our drive and out onto the sidewalk.

"How do you like my new tricycle?" I asked a couple of the kids.

They were *not* impressed.

"We thought you were going to get a two-wheeler."

Well, I had to make do with what I had. And at least going *down* the hill, I could almost keep up with the boys on their two-wheelers. But coming back up... that was a different story. That huge, heavy tricycle had to be pushed back up the steepest section.

For weeks, I rode my new tricycle following the milkman to the top of the hill on Cornell. Then, one day, I became curious to learn where he went when he left our street. I knew that he turned right onto Hanley Road, so I followed behind on the sidewalk until it became Stanford, the next street north.

The milkman made each of his deliveries with me pedaling just behind as usual. Without even thinking about it, I suddenly found myself at the middle of the block. And... there he was! Standing in front of his front porch: RICHARD ANTWELL!! In an instant he saw me. And in another instant he came tearing out, arms outstretched, with a frightening scowl and a grumbling roar!

I turned the heavy trike around and began pedaling furiously up the slight grade back toward Hanley Road. Antwell came racing after me. Even as I picked up speed, he seemed to be getting closer by the second! I could hear his heavy breath and almost feel his hands closing around my neck!

Finally, I reached the corner and swung the trike to the left just as Antwell's hands were about to close and yank me off. Still racing along the sidewalk, I took a chance, turned my head and looked back. And there... there was Richard Antwell, standing at the corner, his hands outstretched, his face frozen in a paroxysm of intense hatred!

I pedaled on back home and *never* ventured onto Stanford again. It took me many years to finally understand what had happened. But it was simple. You see, Richard Antwell's parents had obviously told him never to go past the end of his own block... and he was, of course, a very obedient boy!

56

Aunt Mae's Summer Camp

4/30/23

I'm not sure of when it was that my parents first heard about Aunt Mae's summer camp – or how they heard about it. My parents usually never revealed any of the details about much of anything.

All I knew was that rather unexpectedly one summer when I was about eight, it had been arranged for me to spend two weeks at Aunt Mae's summer camp on Long Lake near Granite City, Illinois.

Along with a grip full of clothes, shoes, towels and swimsuit, we drove over to Long Lake in our '38 Chevy four door. How long it took for us to find the unmarked, unadvertised location of the camp, I simply have no memory. But we did eventually find it, and "Aunt Mae" turned out to be a very warm-hearted, though not very attractive-looking woman in her late 50's.

Mae Delaney had married "Uncle Harry" only a few years before. She had been previously married to a wealthy Jewish business man who had died suddenly. Mae had inherited some money, but not enough to last her lifetime. When a fishing camp on Long Lake came up for sale, Mae got the idea to buy it to start a summer camp for young kids.

The main house had a tiny kitchen and attached bedroom and a very long porch-like addition which became the "dormitory" for the campers', there were at least 8 or 10 campers at any one time, all of us sleeping in the porch-like addition.

After we had been at the camp for about a week, our parents brought our bicycles over so that we could ride out on the county road. We could than "explore" nearby places and it gave us kids something else to do other than just swim and fish in the lake,

A Tar Baby

We had all been riding our bicycles regularly on the road in front of Aunt Mae's when the county decided to re-tar the road surface.

"Uncle Harry" gave all of us kids a stern warning, "They're gonna put road oil- tar on the road today. I want all of you to stay *off* of there until it has a chance to harden up! That'll take several hours. You understand?"

We all nodded.

It was about noon when the road crew poured the road oil on the road surface. By three o'clock, the intense summer sun had still prevented the tar from hardening. One of the campers, Marty Wallace, figured he had given the oil plenty of time to coagulate. He got on his little 24" bike and went riding merrily out to the middle of the oiled road.

Instantly, the bike began skidding and sliding around on the slick tar. Down went the bike and the boy – flailing, stumbling – slipping and sliding back down into the tar again, Marty screamed in agonized fright, finally managing to drag his bike and himself out of the road.

"Uncle Harry" and "Aunt Mae" came hurriedly out of the house expecting to see the worst; and their expectation was completely justified.

We kids stood next to the garbage pit for the entire hour that it took "Uncle Henry" and "Aunt Mae" to first wash Marty and his bike down with kerosene; then with alcohol and then with strong soap and water.

"Uncle Harry" went out to the end of the driveway and took a stout rope, tying it across the end of the drive. We all stood there and watched.

"You kids listen to me!" he said. "All of you – *stay off* of that road! Cleaning up one nitwit is enough for one day!"

We heeded his warning. We had heard enough of Marty's screaming and crying as he was being cleaned up and we certainly didn't care to go through it ourselves.

My First Freight Train Ride

After I had been at "Aunt Mae's" summer camp for about a month, we learned that there was a confectionary about a mile away on the lake, but on the other side. The only easy way to reach the confectionary was to cross the lake on the railroad track which was nearby and which actually divided the lake.

One day, after having gone to the confectionary to buy a bottle of soda with our one dollar a week 'allowance', I and another boy were returning across the railroad track. When we reached the other side, there was a freight train just starting to move away from us. I set my bike on it's stand and ran over the end flatcar.

"Watch my bike for me, will yuh?" I called out to the other boy. I really expected to ride only a few feet and then jump off and walk back.

The train picked up speed very quickly. I was afraid to get off! For about a half mile; it moved on away from the lake with me standing on the step of the last car. Finally, it pulled into a siding and stopped. I jumped off and ran back to my bike.

I will never know if the engineer spotted the little kid standing on the step of the last car and purposely pulled into the siding – or if he had intended to do that anyway. But I was at least saved from having to get someone to pick me up possibly in a rail yard somewhere in East St. Louis! Obviously, I had not considered where I might end up. When you're only eight years old, such possibilities are not usually worth considering!

The Great Gang War of 1944

1/2/11

To say that Wolfgang Kirch was a great gang leader would be stretching the truth…more than a little. In fact – it was difficult to say how 'Wolf's Gang' ever received its tenuous title; our minute clubhouse wasn't even on Wolf's parents property; it was behind my house – underneath the clingstone volunteer peach tree alongside the fence.

But Wolf was older and taller than any of the other kids on the block; and he had a more mature, commanding aura about him. I remember him as being a nice-looking, pleasant boy with dark hair and dark eyebrows. He had, actually, quite a charming personality. Even my parents had nothing particularly bad to say about him – which was unusual enough in itself.

Wolf and his younger brother, Martin, lived only three doors up the block, but on the street below. Their house was right on 'Varsity Walk', which cut our long blocks of 7000 and 7100 Cornell and Stanford in half. So Wolf and Martin and I were at each other's houses nearly every day after school.

Although Wolf was a couple years older than I was, (Martin, two years younger), it was I who was the builder and who began construction of the tiny 'clubhouse' in the back yard. With scrap lumber that had been thrown out along the street in weekly trash pickups and with discarded apple boxes from groceries, we put together what was probably no more than a six by six foot shack, with minimal siding and roofing.

It was only a few months after we had constructed our clubhouse, that we began to hear stories of a ferocious new group called "Lloyds Gang". The leader was a boy who had been in my own class at Jackson Park Elementary School since at least first grade. While I would never have considered Jerry Lloyd one of my close friends, I would certainly not have called him an 'enemy' in any sense. Since the Lloyd family lived in the west edge of the school district and my own family in the east edge of it, distance alone tended to prevent much contact – or confrontation.

But there it was: Jerry Lloyd's gang was becoming known as the gang to be most feared of any gang or individual. There was, in fact, no other gang that we knew of, and we of Wolf's Gang feared the inevitability of some kind of confrontation.

It was through one of our schoolmates that I first received the information: Lloyd's Gang was soon to attack and destroy our clubhouse! We did not wait idly, but in anticipation, began to reinforce our fragile little edifice into a veritable fortress of Bastille-like proportions, we nailed more boards on the outside, the fence side by the vacant lot. We placed more boards on the roof and then began stockpiling bricks, stones, short pieces of lumber – anything that could be heaved and hurled at the attackers.

We had been warned in advance of the day for the confrontation – after school on Thursday. All of us of Wolf's Gang were there that afternoon. Hidden inside our fortress, Wolf, Martin, I, my little nine year old sister, and two other younger boys from down the block waiting in nervous anticipation.

Suddenly it began – the ghastly horde of Lloyd's Gang savages came pouring into the lot, yelling – roaring with barbaric screams! Onward they pushed, hurling rocks, bottles, bricks, boards – every missile that they had brought with them, as well as anything hard and heavy that they could find in the vacant lot.

Wham! Crash! Thump! The missiles pounded against our fragile fortress. Bricks, rocks and bottles showered down on us like a torrent of miniature meteorites. Wolf grabbed the nearest missile and heaved it back indiscriminately.

"Come on, guys," he shouted, "Let 'em have it! Give it back to 'em!"

We rushed outside and began hurling back the pieces of bricks and rocks that had been thrown by Lloyd's Gang as well as our own stockpile of similar missiles.

Back and forth the projectiles flew, most of them ending up hitting the clubhouse after having been thrown by the members of Lloyd's Gang. But we were badly outnumbered; and boards began to fall off the clubhouse – the roof started to cave in from the weight of all the stones and bricks that had accumulated on it.

As the explosive commotion continued, my mother happened to come out to the narrow walk alongside of the house on that east edge of the building. She stood in incredulous amazement, watching the bombardment – feeling powerless to do more than stand there as a horrified, yet fascinated bystander.

With their fury now seemingly satisfied, and with the additional discouragement of being watched by an adult, Lloyd's Gang quickly heaved their final bottles and bricks, gathered themselves together and evaporated in the same suddenness with which they had appeared.

The two young boys from down the block as well as my little sister still were trembling and barely able to speak a word. Even Wolf, Martin, and I were visibly shaken by the intensity of the rock, brick, and bottle barrage.

"Well" said Wolf rather dubiously, "I think we beat 'em…"

"Uh huh," I agreed with equal dubiousness.

Then we looked at our clubhouse. Actually…it seemed only a little worse than before the attack. The fence had protected the east side and the projectiles had not reached very well onto any other side. But the roof…well, that might have to be replaced. The windows and door were unhurt; there had been no glass in the windows anyway and the door was merely an opening as well.

None of us of Wolf's Gang had been hurt by a missile. How that miracle had taken place, no one knew. Although we weren't sure that the members of Lloyd's Gang could say the same, we were, understandably unconcerned about our 'enemies'.

Later, when my father arrived home and surveyed the damage, he confronted me about it at the dinner table.

"Well…what happened out there at your clubhouse?"

"Uh…it was Lloyd's Gang."

"What do you mean? Who's *Lloyd's* Gang?"

"They…they tried to tear it down."

"Looks like they did a pretty good job of it! But they probably didn't have to work very hard to do it."

"Aw dad -- what do you mean? And we tried to stop them."

My father was already pretty well fed up with my 'apple box shanty' as he termed it.

"You better get out there tomorrow and clean up that mess! Get rid of those rocks and bottles…*and,* take the rest of that pile of junk boards you call a clubhouse out to the curb for the trash pickup Saturday! Okay?"

"Yes, Dad…but…"

"No 'buts' about it, I'm tired of seeing that relic from Hooverville being in the back yard!"

"But, Dad…"

"No!" "But…"
"No!"
"Oh, alright."

Lloyd's Gang hadn't succeeded in demoralizing us – we who were the members of Wolf's Gang…still, it was only shortly after the Great Gang War of 1944 when Wolf Kirch's family moved away and I never saw them again. Gangs do not continue to exist without a leader, but it was not the end of just Wolf's Gang. Lloyd's Gang seemed to fade into oblivion as well. Why, I could never say; pressure from parents or authorities – an attrition from the process of simply 'growing up'… who knows?

And so…Lloyd's Gang had *not* succeeded in tearing down our clubhouse…hmmm…or *had* they?

The Funniest Ride Ever

Just exactly what gave the idea to try it, I really can't remember. But it was on our way to a cub scout outing at Rockwoods Reservation, about thirty miles from Saint Louis. This was actually a family event, with my mother (the den mother) my father and my little sister. In another car just behind us, was my classmate Ronald and his family. We were driving along smoothly at sixty.

My sister and I were riding in the back seat and as I looked down on the floor…there I saw Patti's favorite stuffed animal – Bosco, the monkey! Why she had brought along Bosco and one of her dolls… is hard to say. Poor Bosco, he had been around for so long and was *so* badly worn, that there was hardly anything left of his original long, plush fabric covering.

Old Bosco had been used as a "catch ball" in water games at Aunt Mae's summer camp for several seasons. He always ended up thoroughly soaked and it took weeks to dry out his stuffing. The drying process did *not* enhance either his appearance… or his odor!

On the seat next to me was a rather long length of very heavy string – almost a light rope – that we were to use for practicing cub scout knots. I tied the cord around Bosco's neck and under his arms, using my best cub scout knot.

"What are you *doing* to Bosco?" my sister asked.

"Oh... I'm just going to give him flying lessons." I answered nonchalantly.

My sister looked *very* apprehensively at me.

"That won't hurt him?"

"Well... it'll be *really* funny. Watch!"

I quickly rolled down the back window and eased old Bosco out into the air rushing past the car. He was so light that he literally floated in the breeze, swaying, bouncing, gyrating, as the air currents lifted him and spun him head over heels. He was indeed, *very* funny to watch.

"What are you two kids doing back there?" my father asked in his usual somewhat irritated manner.

"Uh... nothing."

"What do you mean 'nothing' – what *is* that you've got dragging behind the car?" He was able to see something in the rear view mirror, but not clearly.

"It's just Bosco," I answered. "We're giving him flying lessons." My dad laughed in spite of himself. "Well, you better pull him back in here. What if that flies into someone's windshield?"

"It won't; I used a real strong cub scout knot!"

My mother turned around and addressed me:

"You better do what your father says. Just stop that nonsense!"

"Aw, Mom..."

I let more of the line out until Bosco dropped to the pavement. He hit hard, spun back into the air and did a couple dozen summersaults as his arms and legs began to lose their stuffing. We could see that in the car behind us, Ronald and his younger brother were in the front seat pointing at Bosco – the two boys were laughing so hard they were almost in hysterics.

Bosco took one great soar toward the sky and nose-dived into the pavement, scraping along until he had lost nearly all of his stuffing.

"Better bring that thing back in now." My father commanded.

"Okay. I guess he had a pretty good flying lesson," I laughed.

I untied the string from around what was left of Bosco. My sister looked rather sadly at his remains:

"Poor Bosco... We can't fix him, can we?"

"No, " I said, "but we could give that doll of yours on the floor – which one is that Gwendolyn? We could give her flying lessons too!"

Pattie nodded gleefully, now in anticipation of another hilarious comedy.

My mother and father were conversing and paid no attention to what I had told my sister.   I quickly attached the cord around Gwendolyn's neck and under her arms with the same cub scout knot. Then I lowered her out the window.   The dolls head, arms and legs were made of some type of composition material which weighed a great deal more than the lightweight cotton stuffing of Bosco.

Gwendolyn went crashing into the pavement. Part of an arm and leg went spinning off down the road. Ronald's father had wisely dropped further behind us when he saw the doll first make its appearance behind our car. Suddenly a large truck passed us causing a great air turbulence. It picked the doll up causing it to gyrate and jump high above the car. Then as the truck sped past us, the vacuum it left hurled the doll against the road so hard that its head exploded. The top half of it went bursting off to the side along with whatever sawdust or paper it had been stuffed with as well as any brains it might ever have had. Next went another am and another leg; very quickly there were just a few fragments left.

"Alright... now *stop* that nonsense!" my mother even laughed a little as she scolded us.

I pulled what there was left of Gwendolyn back into the car, untied the knot and handed the remains to my sister.

"I don't want that; that's no good!" And then she laughed again. At first she smiled, then her face took on a slight frown.

"First it was Bosco – and now I don't have Gwendolyn either" she said wistfully.

"Aw, you have plenty of other dolls," I said.

"Yeah, but they're not Gwendolyn."

"Well, just think of how much fun we had watching her take her flying lessons!"

"Oh...I guess...", she said with finality.

Almost seventy years later, I mentioned the incident to my friend Ron. "Yes, I remember it! It *was* funny! Maybe we could do it again sometime!" he said with great enthusiasm.

I thought about that. I wondered if we ever actually *had* done it again. Certainly I had *wanted* to. And I had *thought* about doing it again over the years. But maybe it's like so many other things we do. The first time is spectacular. But after that it loses its impact. The comedy no longer seems as humorous. And another thing: although we wouldn't have had any trouble finding another doll… where would we have ever been able to find another worn out monkey like Bosco?

The Hobby Shop

12/13/11

It was only about two weeks before Christmas; the weather was cold and blustery. There was a wind blowing so strong that it made the temperature feel as though it were already into January.

Larkin McKibbin, my best high school chum and I had been walking along Delmar Boulevard from my house on the seventy hundred block of Cornell Avenue. The tall houses and commercial buildings along Delmar blocked a lot of wind…and we walked fast both to keep up our energy levels and thus warm ourselves – and to get to our destination as quickly as possible. We were only fifteen – too young to be driving.

At the Delmar loop, I asked Larkin: "Where'd you say that hobby shop was?"

"It's on the north side of Delmar – 'bout half a block from Hamilton. Haven't you ever been there before?"

"No…I think I know where it is, though. I've ridden by there lots of times; but I never stopped in."

"That's where I got that neat Dusenberg model kit." Larkin said.

"Yeah?"

"An' they've got a really neat Packard Phaeton Model too!"

"Oh yeah – I wanna see *that!*"

When we reached Skinker, the wind began to blast ferociously down the long, wide, open lanes of that large boulevard. Larkin pulled on the World War II gas mask which had been hanging on his chest by its neck strap. People on the street began to gape and gawk at him, many smiling, some even pointing and laughing.

"Let 'em laugh." He said in a muffled comment though the mask, "They'll be the ones with cold faces!"

"I know – but you really look like some kind of giant bug!"

"So what happened to the mask's filter can?" I asked, seeing the hose just dangling down.

"Aw, I didn't need that heavy canister hanging in front of me. I took it off, I'm not tryin' to filter poisons gas – just stop the cold air."

"Well, the hose looks like a long wrinkled nose!"

I laughed and pulled the center of my scarf up over my face, leaving only an eye slit between the scarf and my knit cap. We walked rapidly in silence past the Wabash Train Station and across Des Peres, then down the block to the hobby shop.

Just as we reached the door, a mother with her young son was attempting to enter. Inside, the young boy, still clinging to his mother's hand, looked up at Larkin with his gas mask on and his long, black hair down to his shoulders. Larkin's height, even at fifteen was nearly six feet, the tiny boy gazed up at this giant monster and screaming in terror. The mother pulled her son along to the back of the store, picked him up and tried to console him.

After engaging the shop owner in a conversation, the woman placed her now only whimpering son back on the floor and continued her inquiry. The little boy walked several feet toward us, fearful curiosity overcoming his previous rampant terror. Larkin waited until the boy was just a few feet away then raised his arms menacingly and growled in a deep, raspy voice;

"Oooo…boogie, boogie, boogie!"

The boy went shrieking again back to his mother, who immediately dragged the child out of the shop, giving Larkin an angry stare on the way.

Moments later, the shop owner came over to us;

"Boys!" he said aggressively. Then realizing that we, too, were potential customers, he moderated his tone. "You nearly frightened that little boy to death! That gas mask…"

"Yeah, I know," I said "He's wearing it cause it's so cold and windy out there today."

"Well, it's not cold in *here!*"

"I know."

Larkin slipped the gas mask off, letting it hang by its neck strap.

"That kid must have not ever seen any World War II movies where the soldiers have on gas masks."

"Well, I wouldn't think he'd seen any. After all, he's only about five or six years old!" Remarked the shop owner.

"Lark, he must have thought you were some kind of giant grasshopper." I offered. "It's those oval eye lenses; that's what it makes you look like!"

We both laughed.

Later, after Larkin had bought some small model accessory, we left the shop and he immediately pulled on the gas mask again.

"Boy," I said, "the people out here are really laughing at you!"

"So, let 'em laugh – my face is warm…and theirs isn't.

But I still can't figure out why that little boy was so scared of me. Maybe he got frightened by some great, big grasshopper. Ya think?" Then Larkin laughed.

"I don't know, I said, "Maybe he just got frightened by some great, big boggie man!"

We both laughed half-way back up to the Wabash Station.

The "Cave Men"

7/16/2023

We had just completed our junior year in high school. Early in June, I was only 17 and my friend Dan Leavitt was already 18. Often, Dan and I would discuss Thoreau's Walden Pond – how it might relate to our lives in the 20th century. Dan thought it might be interesting to try to live briefly like "cavemen". Maybe for a few days at the "Rockwoods Reservation". We were both very familiar with the place, having hiked around in it many times.

There were huge "caves" quarried out of the rock, but as to the wild food, neither of us had even the slightest bit of knowledge.

But we were young and enthusiastic; we decided to try to live like "cavemen" for three days at Rockwoods. We'd bring blanket rolls and each of us would bring a bag of food for the three days.

I cannot remember who it was we got to drive us the 25 miles to Rockwoods, but we made no provision for them to bring us back.

We arrived in the morning on a beautiful early June Friday and spent the day hiking around the entire park trying to find a spot where we could establish our "caveman" location.

The huge quarried "caves" were off limits – loose rock was constantly falling from the ceilings. The entrances were barricaded. Late in the afternoon, we found a partially quarried south hillside with an overhanging area of rock. It was densely overgrown with brush and groves of sassafras saplings.

We each had brought large machetes and began cutting away a space to create a sleeping ledge and site for a campfire. As we began to cut saplings, we also attempted to weave them into a rough framework that could be covered with tree branches still containing their leaves.

This crude "shelter", as I recall, was only partially successful, as the wind would blow the branches off of it. Our leaf branch "beds" turned out to be far less comfortable then we had expected them to be. We were so hungry by dinner time that we ate over half of our 3 day food supply. Water, of course, was available from the park's well water fountain.

In the morning, after a fitful nights sleep, we two "cavemen" began a futile search for "wild food". Since we had no knowledge of what to look for, we would easily have passed it by, had we been lucky enough to have encountered any.

By the end of the second day, we had both consumed all of what was left of the food we had brought. In the morning of our third day, we were ravenously hungry with no food left! But Sunday was the day for picnickers to visit the park. At noon there were several cars with hikers parked along the park's picnic area road.

We watched from the hillside by our camp and observed one of the picnic tables with food left by picnickers who had gone to the nearby washroom. We swooped down and grabbed anything we could lay our hands on to eat, gobbling it down the instant we put our hands on it.

After that raid, we moved on to the next picnic area, but found it occupied. As we were walking by one of the picnic tables, a girl about our age beckoned to us to come over. She could tell that we were not the ordinary picnickers and she was curious to know why we were there.

After explaining to her what we were trying to do and talking a bit about Thoreau, we left.

"Dan, we didn't even get her name" I commented. "And she was kind of attractive and seemed like an interesting person."

"Oh... tomorrow she won't even remember who we were" he replied.

"Yeah... well you never know..."

"Agh... just forget it!"

We then walked to the park curator's building to say hello to Geroge Moore, the park naturalist. We knew him well from our many

69

previous visits to the park often several times each year, usually with our parents on family outings.

Moore had been there since the park's founding and had watched us grow into true "nature boys". He was always very friendly to us and quite knowledgeable about Missouri animals, birds and plants. Moore was already in his 70's and retired not long after we saw him that time.

Although I did make one last trip to Rockwoods Reservation the following year, Mr. Moore had retired and was no longer there. Neither Dan nor I ever heard from or about him again.

Some things are simply beyond explanation. I had continued to live in Missouri for several decades after that, yet I never went back to Rockwoods... and I had been going there since I was about 2 or 3, before it became a park... when it was still Glencoe Quarry. I remember sitting in one of the little rock cars with my grandmother watching the tiny steam locomotive pull a string of loaded cars out of the quarry to Glencoe where the rocks were crushed into gravel. All now memories – but vivid memories.

When we left Mr. Moore's office, Dan and I went back to our campsite, packed our blanket rolls, walked out to the highway and tried to hitch a ride to St. Louis. After several unsuccessful attempts to "hitch", a delivery truck stopped for us. I immediately recognized the driver. "Dan look, that's our classmate, Louis Linhardt!"

We squeezed into the front seat.

"I'm going to St. Louis, guys, but not to University City. I can let you off at some place where you can get a bus there though. I took this delivery job for the summer."

"Yeah, great, Louis."

Thus ended our experiment to become "cavemen". And that was the only time we ever tried it. But I've often thought about the girl at the park... wondered about her. It's a big world out there... I never saw her again...

That Old Dirt Road Out Behind Beckman's

Rewritten 4/24/2023

There were no cars in the driveway when I pulled in at Lark's house on Shaftsbury that summer evening.   I drove all the way up to the house. Larkin came right out:

"Better move your car over there under the apple trees. My mother'll be back in a few minutes and she'll want to park her Hudson as close to the house as she can get it; you know she can't walk far on those crutches."

"Yeah – alright, Lark."

I drive over to the trees and shut the engine off. Before I can even step off the running board, Bill Stehle pulls his raggedy '30 Model A coupe in at the end of the driveway. He sees my car, gets out and calls to me:

"Hey, Jake – yuh wanna race me?"

"Yeah! But where?"

"Agh… how 'bout on that old dirt road out behind Beckman's?"

"Okay!"

"Wild Bill" jumps in his coupe and starts the engine.

I have been on that old dirt road out behind Beckman's Feed store only once before. Someone had told me about the elderly couple who lived in the end house – how they still wore clothes from the 1890s. I had driven out and seen them working in their garden, he in his ancient four button suitcoat and string tie, and she in her long skirt and antiquated pink and blue granny bonnet. Willie had no interest in seeing them, it was just to be a race. And I knew I could never beat Willie's coupe – it had a higher rear end ratio than my tudor and much lighter body – but it was always fun to try.

By the time I could get turned around and go back out to Shaftsbury, Willie was already making a right turn onto Brentwood. The traffic and two stop signs at Brentwood and Olive Street Road slowed Willie's coupe and I caught up with him. By the time we got to Beckman's, Willie was already several car lengths ahead of me. He raced into the side drive leading to the old dirt road. By the time he had to turn left, he was already doing 30 mph and he could not make the sharp right angle turn.

Up and onto the lawn of the first house, Willie went screeching in second, leaving deep ruts in the soft ground and knocking over the mailbox on its post.

Now, driving like a wild man, Willie dropped the coupe into low and intentionally drove up onto the lawn of the second house, knocking over *its* mailbox and leaving even deeper ruts.

I had tried to follow in the tracks of the coupe, but stayed on the road after going across the lawn of the first house.

Willie went flying down the road to the third house. The old couple was still out taking an evening "stroll"; they stepped aside when they saw Willie roaring toward them. When the coupe reached the end of the road, it was still doing 35mph; Willie threw the steering hard to the left; the light little coupe skidded into almost a half-circle, ending up facing in nearly the opposite direction. Willie immediately jammed the shift lever down into low and went screeching away!

By the time I could get backed up and turned around and then drove out to Olive, Willie was already a quarter mile west. I followed him until I saw him turn left into the entrance to a new subdivision just before Lindbergh. When I reached the subdivision entrance my engine began to sputter; the rough dirt road behind Beckman's had shaken more dirt loose in the gas tank and the gas line was beginning to clog. I pulled the car to the curb facing east.

Willie had driven down the new subdivision drive, a long steep hill ending in a wide circle. No houses had been completed yet, but concrete curbing had been poured and the circle paved with loose gravel. Around and around Willie drove the little coupe screeching and throwing gravel in every direction the noise was absolutely ferocious as it resounded in the empty hollow.

After a few minutes, Willie drove back up, wondering why I hadn't followed him. When he saw me sitting against the fender disassembling the gas line, he knew what had happened; the gas line had clogged so many times before.

Laughing, he stopped just long enough to call out: "See yuh later, Jake!"

As I was picking up my tools and was ready to close down the hood, a cop car pulled in behind me. The cop got out and came over.

"Havin' trouble?"

"Yeah – just dirt in the gasoline. But I got it cleaned out now."

"You been here long?"

"Just a few minutes, why?"

"Well, the neighbors around here been complaining about a little coupe raisin' hell driving around the circle down there in the new subdivision drive. I know it wasn't you, but did you see anybody drivin' a little coupe around down there?"

"No," I said with complete honesty, "you can't see anything from up here."

The cop must have figured I was with the coupe. "Now listen," he said, "if you do happen to see someone in a little coupe, better tell him that if we catch him raisin' hell down there in the new subdivision again – or tearin' up lawns on that road behind Beckman's Feed Store, we're gonna give him a ticket for peace disturbance and destruction of private property, and it's gonna cost him a *big* fine!"

I drove back on Olive Street Road and turned right on Brentwood. Willie was still out in front of his house by the coupe. I stopped for a minute and relayed the cop's message. And I don't remember either of us ever going again out to the subdivision – or on that old dirt road behind Beckman's.

That was now... over 70 years ago! Our Model A's are long gone; Willie is long gone. And on the few times I've driven out to Olive Street Road... I can't recognize *anything* anymore. All of the familiar places from my youth are no longer there; the world changes so rapidly now...

Beckman's huge frame feed store – a fixture on Olive Street Road for 75 years... is gone! As is the old dirt road behind it. And all three houses that were on it. And even the farmer's *fields* that adjoined it!

Now when you look out there – it's nothing but acre after acre after acre of concrete and new subdivisions. Subdivision of little, architecturally uninteresting cracker-box houses that all look alike – occupied by intellectually uninteresting people who all look alike... and dress alike... and think alike. And I guess that's what they call "progress". But I'm not so sure I'd want to agree with that definition.

A *limited* technology – which we had earlier in the last century seemed to be good. But now, replacing it with a technological madness – a money and morality and power madness and an animal-agriculture madness… where will it all end? And *how* will it all end? And *will* it all end?

I have never been good at making predictions. And with the 21st century's vast human overpopulation to consider, I would be even more hesitant to try to do so. But there are immutable, natural laws that will eventually predominate on our planet – of that I am confident… thought I'm sure I will not be here to observe it!!

Graveyard Blues

1/9/95

The necktie is too constricting. I tug at it loosening the knot then pull it off. I had taken my date directly home; she turned out to be no more remarkable than her school play that we attended…and now, I am bored.

Tossing the keys to my dad's car on the front hall table, I go in the garage and get on my motor scooter without even changing out of my dress clothes. The autumn evening is still fairly early and the temperature is warm and inviting.

My dad's new 1950 Mercury is still parked at the curb in front of the house. I decide not to move it into the driveway so as to make it easier to get the motor scooter out. Once on the scooter, I head directly to my friend Lee's house.

Lee is tightening down the last two nuts that hold on the front spring of his army Jeep, shop light dangling from the inside fender brace.

"What happened?" I asked him.

"Frame horn finally broke off. We welded it, but we had to pull the spring loose so the rubber grommet in the spring eye wouldn't get too hot and burn up. And see…see how we reinforced both sides.."

"Yeah…but gee, I wouldn't of thought sumpthun' they built for the army would be *that* flimsy."

"Listen, remember when we took the Jeep across those gullies in the field at Piotraschti's Farm?"

"Remember? How could I forget, 'bout shook my teeth out." "Well, that's what started it. It just got worse every time you'd hit a bump er sumpthin'."

The shop light slips off the fender brace, I pick it up and hold it close so that Lee can get the best use of it.

"Hey, yuh wanna test out the Jeep...now?" I ask.

"Yeah!"

Lee puts the wheel on and tightens the nuts. Mac, Dave and Willie have been standing around – kibbitzing more than helping, Willie taps Lee's arm.

"Where yuh goin'? Let's go over ta my girlfriend's house."

"Willie...Janis is *not* your girlfriend. I told you- she's goin' out with a lot of other guys."

"Uh...she's my girlfriend..."

"No, she's..." Dave shakes his head and laughs in a tone of final frustration.

I have a bright idea:

"I know where we ought to try it out...Let's go over to the Chinese graveyard they're tearin' up."

"Yeah!"

"Yeah!"

"Come on, guys – let's go!"

We climb in the Jeep, Lee starts the engine as we tear out of the drive, screeching into the street almost on two wheels. After we reach the intersection where Shaftbary meets Hanley, we make a left and drive a couple blocks north where the cemeteries reach to the street.

"Hey...man – look at that – they got the Jewish cemetery all torn up too."

"So what – who cares? Chinks – Waps – Kikes – Spics, they're all dead, aren't they?"

Lee laughs, puts the Jeep in four-wheel low and drives up over the sidewalk into the mounds of earth, stone, and crushed trees. Fires still glow with traces of smoke rising from some of the brush piles. Although the atmosphere is not as eerie as we had expected, the terrain is not as easy to negotiate, either.

We raise great clouds of dust as we maneuver through this macabre landscape of what seems reminiscent of how Gahenna might be. As we bounce and jostle the growling little machine, dust clouds float out over Hanley Road.

After a few minutes, a pair of headlights appears at the edge of the construction site. A spotlight casts into the smoky, dusty night.

"Cops! It's the cops, Lee! Look!"

Lee shuts off the lights and engine and waits. The spotlight arcs across the dismal landscape for several minutes. Because we are far enough in from the street and because the Jeep's khaki paint is excellent camouflage, the police car moves on.

We watch its lights slowly travel north toward the corner and turn right on Olive Street Road. Again, the spotlight pierces the darkness around us. After a few more fruitless probes of the light, the police cruiser drives into the old cemetery road, going as far back as possible. This puts them much closer to us.

Lee starts the Jeep and pulls it into gear with the lights still off. Carefully creeping around stumps and earth mounds, we see the spotlight again almost touching our location.

"Alright, you guys, c'mon outta there!"

The two men from the patrol car are standing outside of it, trying to peer into the dusty smoke. Suddenly the second patrolman screams at us:

"Hey, don't you guys know what your doin's against the law? Get the hell outta there!! Right NOW!!"

Our intrepid driver has by now worked his way close to the back edge of the cemetery grounds where it adjoins a small patch of woods running alongside The River Des Pere.

"Listen, Lee, there's an old dirt road that goes all the way back here through the woods – get on it and it'll take us out to Midland." I tell him.

With the lights still off, we proceed through the woods and out onto the city street.

"Lost 'em – we lost 'em!!

Everyone is jubilant.

We then drive east on Midland, away from the graveyard. At Vernon, we turn left and continue east past Pennsylvania stopping the Jeep to check on the welded area of the frame. Lee looks back before getting in. He jumps into his seat, jerks the Jeep into gear and leaps it up over the curb toward River Des Peres.

"What's 'a matter?"

"Where the hell yuh goin'?"

"Down there!"

"U. City cop car coming this way, back there on Pennsylvania." He drives over the steep flagstone banked side of the river (which is really only a large storm sewer). Straight down we go, effortlessly across the bottom and up the steep, stone covered opposite side, then out onto another street.

The police, having watched our lights, drive over and again try unsuccessfully to catch us in their spotlight. We are in a subdivision with only one exit – and that exit is perilously close to the University City Police Station.

"Just drive far enough up to make 'em think we're coming out on Delmar." Mac suggests. "That way they'll go up there and you can go back down and out the way we came in."

We wait for about three minutes before going back to the bottom of the hill and into the River Des Peres again. As the Jeep is about to climb over the top edge onto Vernon, the police car appears at the barricade inside the subdivision with lights cutting the darkness, spotlight swinging madly, red lights flashing and siren screaming.

In an instant, we have moved out of the range of lights which are being blocked by the barricade boards anyway. Lee drives in a large semi-circle, ending in an easterly direction on Olive Street. All of us are laughing so hard we don't even hear the siren at first – but the flashing red lights behind us are unavoidable.

A young burly-looking, rookie cop walks up to the side of the Jeep: "Okay, lemme see your license!"

"Uh – uh, what's the matter officer? Did I …uh…miss a stop sign or sumpthin'?"

"Get off my back smart-ass. Two officers been chasin' you guys for the last half hour. Don't give me a lot of grief. Just drive that thing down to the station."

We proceed him to the U. City Station and park the Jeep, waiting for the cop to walk over.

"All right – go on in there – all a 'yuh!"

We stand inside looking rather sheepishly at the desk sergeant.

"Wanna book 'em?"

"Yeah."

"For what – peace disturbance? Destruction of private property…?"

"Dunno – hafta figure out sumpthin'. First, I'm gonna question these two." He points to Lee and me.

Before taking us into a room for interrogation, he brushes his hand toward the other three.

"The rest of you guys get lost!...or I'll figure out sumpthun' t' charge you with too!!"

I attempt to follow Lee. He attempts to follow me, neither of us wanting to be the first one to be interrogated. We pass through a long hall into a well-lighted room at the back of the station. Inside, Lee is confronted:

"So where were you before I stopped you?"

"Well…just drivin' around…y'know…lookin' fer sumpthun' t' do…"

"Sumpthun' t' do like raisin' hell in that torn up graveyard? Sumpthun' t' do like drivin' up an' down the wall of the River Des Peres? Two of our men chased a Jeep in those places earlier this evening – in fact, it was just before I stopped *you*!"

"Well…how could they be sure it was a Jeep? Did they *see* it? An' if they did see it, how d' yuh know it was *my* Jeep? Did they get a license number?"

"Okay, smart-ass…d' you really think we don't know what you 'n' yer buddies are up to?"

"Hey – that Jeep of mine isn't the *only* Jeep in St. Louis – there are other army Jeeps even in U. City. I know 'cause I've *seen* 'em!"

"So what're yuh tryin' t' tell me – that wasn't you…? PUNK!" Lee stands up to his full, though lean six foot one inch height, towering over his accuser. He returns an equally sneering look. I'm trying to hold back a laugh which has proceeded only into a very faint smile, when the man in blue wheels on me.

"And you! We been watchin' *you* for quite a while! We know you been operatin' a 'midnight auto parts' out of your garage."

"A WHAT a 'midnight auto parts' – whater' you talkin' about? What the hell is *that*?"

"Don't act so stupid, you little scum. You think we don't know that a young kid like you with shelves full of parts from floor to ceiling around his old man's entire garage hasn't been out stealin' that stuff? We see it every time we drive by there when the door's open. An' you got guys comin' an' goin' at all hours! You can't tell me you're not the one who's been stealin' hub caps an' spotlights off cars in this area!"

"Hey…wait a minute! Listen, man – there's no modern hubcaps or spotlights in there. It's *all* antique car parts. And every bit of that stuff I *bought* – at junk yards!"

"Okay punk – you got receipts for it?"

"No – I don't keep the receipts from that stuff – why should I? Do you keep receipts on all the food you buy – or on your clothes? How 'bout your furniture?   D' yuh get a receipt whenever you get a haircut?"

"Why you *lousy, lyin' punk*…!!!"

The rookie cop stands three inches taller than me and outweighs me by sixty pounds. He grabs my shirt collar and gives me a ferocious shake. My new white shirt rips the full length down the front…all the way to the belt line. Then he shoves me away.

Moments later, the desk sergeant opens the door:

"Uh – office Patterbain, are you through yet? It's just about time for the shift change. You'll be off duty in five minutes. Do you want me to write them up on some charge?"

"Nah." He shakes his head in exasperation. "Just get 'em out of here! Get 'em out…"

"Uh…pardon me…before I leave," I tell him, "I really need to get your badge number so that I can have my father's cousin who's a lawyer over in Clayton bring suit against you in court for tearing my new shirt. Also, I need your name…what is it…Puttybrain?"

He points to the door, gnashing his teeth: "OUT!   Get out! NOOOOW!!"

I can almost feel his seething rage searing the back of my neck like a blowtorch. As we walk through the door, we hear one final comment from the sergeant.

"You know if you guys got any sense at all, you'll take that Jeep of yours straight home and stay there with it."

Lee turns back to him "Guess neither of you'll believe this either, but that really is exactly what I was plannin' to do".

Mac, Dave and Willie have been waiting in the open Jeep, smashing mosquitoes.

"What'd they say?" Mac looks at my shirt. "What the hell happened to you, Jake?"

"They're crazy! They think all those model A and American Austin parts – and all the other stuff like it in my dad's garage, are the parts somebody's been stealin' off *new* cars! He tried to rough me up when I denied it!"

Smiling, Lee turns back to us: "They even tried to accuse me of being the one who was driving a Jeep tonight through the graveyard and up and own the walls of the River Des Peres – can you believe *That*?!"

All of us roar with laughter.

The little Jeep is cramped in back; Dave and Mac are seated on fender wells and I'm scrunched down squatting in between them. We're all hanging onto the hand holds. Willie sits in front jabbering away aimlessly. A few blocks from our homes, we pass by the high school. Hanging onto the windshield, Willie leaps up and points to one of the school rooms.

"There's Turbyville's room, see?"

"So what – who cares?"

"He's my shop teacher."

"Oh yeah…I didn't know that?"

"Huh, huh, huh…Turbyville went up the hill to fetch a pack of rubbers, he screwed his wife with a paring knife and out came little flub-de-dubbers. Huh, huh."

"Hey, that's brilliant, Willie!"

"You're a great poet, Willie. Y' ought t' get that published."

"Think so?"

"Sure, Willie! Write it out and take it up to the gal who's editor of the school paper. Bet she'll like to see it!"

"Yeah, she might publish it!"

"Yeah."

"Uh…I dunno…"

"Sure Willie – *do* it"

All of us laugh uncontrollably.

We pass the high school and start down the hill to the River Des Peres bridge.

"Who wants to go home first?" Lee calls to us.

"Me!" says Willie.

"No, Me!" Mac shouts.

"Me!" counters Dave.

We reach the bottom of the hill and cross the bridge heading for the 'y' in the street where Shaftsbury comes in on the left.

"Turn left."

"No, right."

"Left."

"Right."

Even with our speed reduced, we are rapidly approaching the middle of the 'y' intersection. With only thirty feet left before we drive up onto somebody's lawn, Mac yells "Go left!"

Lee whips the steering wheel left. Wham! Crunch!! K'whuump. The Jeep does a three-quarter rollover ending on its left side. All of us are thrown out clear of the wreckage.

I pick myself up off the street, shake around a bit and decide I'm okay. Lee walks up to me, somewhat dazed.

"Didn't expect *that*!" *God Damn*! You okay, Jake?" "Yeah – yeah I guess...where's Mac and Dave?"

Willie is bouncing up and down from one foot to another.

"What's the matter, Willie?"

"Aw, stubbed m' toe on the curb"

Mac and Dave are sitting nearby on the curb, both of them have visible bruises on their faces. Dave walks over to us limping a bit. Porch lights have come on by now and soon neighbors begin milling around in pajamas and bathrobes.

"Anybody hurt?" someone asks.

"Better call the police" another says.

"No, call an ambulance. Did anyone call an ambulance yet?"

The Jeep's engine has stopped but its lights are still on. Lee shuts them off as a police cruiser pulls up and a captain going in for the shift change gets out.

"Anyone here hurt?" he asks us.

"Nah – not really, just some bruises." I tell him.

He examines the Jeep, questions Lee and begins making out a report. In a few more minutes an ambulance arrives. The driver goes over to the police car. By now both Mac and Dave have begun to ooze blood from their bruises and scrapes, but are refusing medical attention as the ambulance driver and the police captain talk with them.

"Boys," the captain admonishes them "I'm not trying to tell you that you have to get those injuries looked at, but you do know that head injuries can be pretty dangerous and sometimes it *is* possible to have a concussion without knowing it. Look, the ambulance is already here, so you may as well go back with him to County Hospital and let them check you out. I know both of your parents would feel a lot more at ease about it if you do."

The two boys agree to go along.

"If they try to charge you for the ambulance," says the police captain, "you just tell them that you didn't call it, okay?"

As the ambulance leaves, another car pulls up. Officer Patterbain is on his way home and has stopped because of the accident. Lee is still standing by the police car as the off-duty officer approaches:

"You! YOU!! I should have known…"

"Yea…it's me…huh." Lee's eyes scan the ground in embarrassment.

The two officers confer inside the police car.

"What'er you gonna write 'em up on, captain? Speeding and careless and reckless?"

"Doubt it – no one saw it. Besides they all claim they were going fairly slow – just cut the wheel too quick. You know how those stubby little Jeeps are with that quick steering."

"Destruction of public property?"

"Nope, only damage was to the vehicle itself. And even that just smashed the windshield flat."

"Peace disturbance?"

"No, not really."

"Creating a public nuisance?"

"Doubtful – very doubtful you could make it stick."

The captain gets out and comes over to the three of us attempting to push the Jeep back onto its wheels. All the neighbors have long since retired back into the sanctity and security of their houses.

"Patterbain, get over there and help 'em stand that thing back up – we can't leave this wreck here in the middle of the street for someone else to hit tonight!"

With a great heave the Jeep thuds back upright.

"Boys," the captain advises us. "I don't think any of you have the least idea just how lucky you are that one of you wasn't killed in this." He shakes his head in disgust.

Lee looks directly into the man's eyes, "Yeah," he says with a genuine contrition "you're probably right…"

With more confidence than reasoned thought, Lee climbs in behind the Jeep steering wheel and attempts to start the engine. It grinds over for more than two minutes. Patterbain is standing next to him glowering with a contemptuous half-smile.

"Quit runnin' your battery down, stupid – just push this junk pile over to the curb and come collect it tomorrow!"

Lee continues to turn the engine over.

"Hold the gas to the floor!" I shout at him.

The starter spins the engine a few more seconds, until it finally catches, sputtering and coughing; then it levels out.

We jump in. Lee smiles derisively.

"Hey Puttybrain....thanks!"

As we speed off, Willie leans out and waves to the cop, screaming: "Puttybrain went off to Spain to fetch a pack..."

Street Car

12/25/22

Re-written from memory. Elaboration of true experience from about 1953. Somewhat fictionalized.

We had all collected at the garage behind Lark's "Gasoline Alley" home on Shaftsbury that summer evening, when someone said: "Hey - let's play *streetcar.*"

Lark countered: "Aw, you know those Creve Coeur line tracks were torn out a couple of years ago."

"Yeah - but there's the rail line to the big lumber yard out there near Beckman's feed store."

"Yeah!"

"Yeah!"

"An' you can get to the track real easy at Delmar an' McKnight!"

"Hey Lee – what about usin' your Plymouth? You still have those two empty wheels don'tcha?"

"Yea, but the Plymouth's track is way too wide."

"Well, then, let's use your Jeep! That's narrow. You got a couple empty wheels for it, right?"

"I guess...but I think one of 'ems warped."

"Won't matter. It'll still hold on the track an' we'll only be goin' ten miles an hour anyhow. Can't go faster 'cause the other side with the tires'll be bouncin' on the ties."

"Okay...let's go!"

We all pile in Lee's Jeep and drive down the street to his house to get the empty wheels.

When we get to Delmar and McKnight where the railroad tracks cut across both streets, there is a large flat graveled area next to the track where we pull the Jeep in so that we can change two of the wheels. After slipping off the two left side wheels with tires, and putting on the empty wheels, I tell Lee "Just use two wheel nuts. That'll be enough to hold 'em, slow as we're gonna be goin'…just put the others in your pocket."

We drive onto the track and begin heading north toward Olive Street Road, a half mile away.

As we go bouncing along, Willie whoops it up again as usual: "Hey… Turbyville went up the hill to fetch a pack of rubbers, he screwed his wife with a paring knife an' out came little flub de dubbers!"

"Aw, shut up, Willie!"

"Why? Thought you liked that."

"Yeah – once or twice."

We pass along an extension of Brittany Woods.

"Hey, Look! There's a deer!"

"Where?"

"Don't ya see it over there?"

"Oh, oh yeah. Now I see it. I don't think I ever saw one come in this close to town."

"An' there some kind of animal up ahead on the track. See it?"

"Yeah, what is it?"

"I dunno – now it's gone."

We drive on to Olive, bumping along at a creeping speed. When we reach Olive Street Road, the track becomes an overpass. Lee drives right out to the center of the span and stops. We all stand up and wave to the cars driving below. Many see us and slow, creating something of a traffic jam. A few minutes later, a cop pulls over to the side and gets out, walking close to the overpass.

"Hey, you guys…what th' hell are ya doin' up there?"

"Nothin!"

"Well, get th' hell offa there!"

"Why?"

"What d'yuh mean why?"

"It's against the law. That's why!"

"What law?"

"Uh…uh….I dunno…It's just against the law! And you're causin' a traffic jam. There might be an accident!"

"Yeah…well, you're makin' it worse!"

"Now listen you…you come down from there!"

"I can't…you come up *here*!"

We all laugh.

By now, it is starting to get dark, the cop shines his flashlight at the steep side of the overpass, littered with rocks and a tangle of brush, vines and tall weeds.

"What's your name?" The cop asks Lee. "I think I know who you are!"

"Uh… Bobo uh… stickin stew"

"That's no name!"

"Sure it is! What's *your* name? Jo Jo Emptyhead?"

We boys all roar with laughter.

"Now listen you! God damn it! Just get th' hell offa there! Where'd you get on that track anyhow?"

"Delmar and McKnight." "Well, go back there and get off."

"I gotta go across an' find some place to turn around."

"So *do* it!"

"Why'd you tell him where we got on? Now he'll go there and wait for us." I tell Lee.

"We don't have to go back there," Lee says, "We'll go to the rail siding for the lumber yard on the other side. It'll be low enough to drive off after we put the tires back on."

We cross the overpass and go a quarter mile to the lumber yard's siding, jack the Jeep up and reinstall the wheels with tires.

Lee puts the Jeep into four wheel drive and we go down and across a field over to Olive Street Road, then head home.

Willie is jubilant. "We fooled 'em – We fooled 'em! Ha! Ha! Turbyville went up the hill…"

"Ahh shut up, Willie!"

"Why…I thought you guys liked that!"

"Yea – the first few times…think up a *new* one!" "I can't! Thurbyville's my shop teacher."

"We *know* that! So use a different shop teacher!"

"Turbyville's the only one that teaches shop."

"Then change his *name*!"

THE END

4th of July Fireworks

Rewritten 3/12/23

Old Mister Mac was somewhere in his mid 70s when the McKibbins decided to sell their home on Shaftsbury and move into the city.

They had lived on Shaftsbury – probably about 15 years. The house was a tiny vine covered frame with no basement but on a quarter acre tract with several large apple trees.

I never asked why they had decided to move – maybe Mr. Mac got tired of cutting all that grass. Larkin never helped with it; his father probably felt lucky that his son was at least keeping the mower running.

The McKibbins owned a small, two-story brick residence in mid-city and no doubt had wanted to move there for some time, however, their son Larkin was still attending U. City High. But in 1950, Larkin did not graduate with his class – he instead went to work for Walter Ashe Radio in downtown St. Louis. With Larkin's knowledge of radio parts and electronics in general and with his charismatic personality, the radio company was glad to have him as a counter-man for retail sales.

The McKibbin's house on 1113 Kentucky Avenue had originally been a single family residence, but someone had converted it into three separate rentals: first floor, second floor and basement. The McKibbins used the rent from the house to supplement their rather low income from other sources. When the renter in the first floor apartment moved out, the McKibbin family moved in.

I remember the first floor apartment having a front "sitting" room, then a small dining room, a kitchen and two bedrooms. Larkin's bedroom was in the very back.

If Old Mister Mac thought that by moving he would rid himself of his son's 'gasoline-alley' group of hang-arounds, he was wrong. It was only 3 miles down to the house on Kentucky Avenue and although Larkin was working 5 days a week, we would still drive down and kibitz – just hang around on weekends.

Lee stopped by my house one Saturday. He was driving his rather raggedy '38 Plymouth four-door.

"I'm goin' down t' Larkin's – wanna come?"

"Yeah – I wanna see how he's doin' with the '27 Chevy I sold him." I had bought the '27 out of its original garage in University City. The car had very low mileage – a beautiful original body – even original interior. But the engine was locked up! I tried everything I could think of to free it up, but without success. I sold the car to

Larkin for what I had paid for it! Sixty-five dollars!

That Saturday, when Lee and I went down to visit our buddy Larkin, we expected to see him out and about. He was not. Mrs. Mac answered the door, "Larkin's still sleepin'" she said in her southern accent. "Go back there an' see if y'll kin wake him up."

Larkin was dead to the world.

"Hey Lark – c'mon – wake up! It's late!"

Larkin grumbled and turned toward us.

"Awright – awright! I'm gettin' up. I'll be out in a few minutes."

We go back outside and sit on the running board of the '27 Chevrolet. 20 minutes go by. We have to repeat the waking process. But this time Larkin actually gets up.

"Worked late on the Chevy" he tells us. "I couldn't free up the engine either. I still had that good engine from my '28 Chevy I kept when we junked it. It took three of us last night to get the old engine out and put the '28 engine in." Mr. Sutton and his friend helped (they were reformed alcoholics from the Salvation Army and Mrs. Mac let them occupy the basement apartment in exchange for helping around the building). "Everything fits up perfectly. Just a minor difference in the cover over the valve pushrods. I still have to hook up all the lines and controls."

A few hours later, the engine is running and Larkin and Lee go to Lark's tire pile in the side yard to see if they can find tires to replace two flats. When they return, Lee says "It's gettin' late – I gotta go back home. Common, Jake, See yuh, Lark!"

We get into the Plymouth and head for home. Lee drives out Manchester to Kingshighway and turns right going toward the highway 40 entrance. The entrance ramp is a long curved downhill sweep, ending in a sharp curve where it enters highway 40.

Lee guns the engine as we enter the ramp. "Ha, ha…watch this!" We race down the curved ramp to the bottom curve. Lee cuts the steering sharply throwing all the cars weight on the right rear tire.

"KABAM!!" the right rear tire explodes!

Lee stops the car and looks over at me:

"Oh shit!"

"What's the matter?"

"I just remembered – no spare! I had to use the spare on the right front a couple days ago when I had a flat."

"Well, now what?" I ask him.

"Oh…I dunno…"

"Maybe Lark's got a tire we could put on it," I suggest.

"Naw. We just looked through his tire pile for the Chevy- all he has is 19" and 21".

"What about that kid that lives over the tavern on the corner. He has a car that uses 16 inch."

"Lark said that kid's back in reform school for havin' sex with a minor girl."

"I could walk back to Lark's in about fifteen minutes – but his mother took the Chrysler somewhere. No tellin' when she'll be back. She could have driven us out to your place to get a tire."

"Yeah an' we can't leave this car here on the highway much over an hour. They'll tow it!"

"So what'll we do?"

"Gonna just drive on the shoulder real slow. It's a half mile to the park entrance, another half mile to Skinker."

We proceed at about five miles per hour with the flat tire thump–thumping along.

Just after the park exit the tire disintegrates and comes off the wheel.

"Well, at least we can go a little faster now." Lee says.

At eight miles an hour we finally reach the Skinker exit. Lee pulls the car over on Skinker and stops.

"There's an extra empty wheel in the trunk." Lee tells me. "I'll put that on the right side. That'll at least even things up."

We jack up the car and change the wheels, get back in and proceed down Skinker. No one is behind us a few blocks north.

Lee tromps the gas pedal to the floor. The steel wheels grind away on the concrete pavement, throwing a huge shower of sparks 50 feet into the sky and at least that far behind the car.

"Wow! Did you see that?" Lee asks. "I had to look at it through the rear-view mirror. Man, what a sparkler display!"

"Yeah," I said, "I never saw anything like it. And we were only two days away from the 4th!"

We continue on toward Wash. U. Lee says:

"I'm just gonna keep goin' to Vernon. That'll be the quickest way to get back."

We rumble along at about 20 miles per hour. At Vernon, Lee turns left, heading west. When we reach Pennsylvania Avenue he continues on Vernon.

"Hey, you shoulda turned at Pennsylvania!" I tell him.

"I know…but watch this!!"

Vernon Avenue is a new stretch of concrete in front of recently erected tall apartment houses. Lee puts the Plymouth in first gear and pushes the gas pedal to the floor.

"Whee!! Look at the sparklers!"

The sparks from the steel wheels grinding away on the concrete fly 75 feet into the sky and at least that far behind us. The noise resounding in the cavernous hollow formed by the apartment buildings is simply deafening! Windows fly up with people looking out to see the source of the terrible racket!

When Lee reaches Midland, he turns the car around and repeats the process in the other direction, until we are again at Pennsylvania Avenue. Then Lee drives up that street to Cornell and takes me home.

We sit in the car only a few minutes talking when a U. City cop car pulls in behind us. The cop gets out and walks over to our car. He looks in at Lee.

"I thought so! I figured I'd find *you* up here, Lee!"

He held his flashlight on the rear wheels of the Plymouth. "Yeah… it *was* you raisin' hell down there on Vernon." Lee laughs – "Well, it's only 2 days til the 4th. I was just makin' some 4th of July sparklers!"

"Yeah, well the people in those apartments didn't seem to appreciate it!"

The cop was one of Lee's family's friends.

"Now listen to me Lee…I'm only gonna be on duty for another seven or eight minutes. The guy who comes on after me – if he catches you raisin' hell down there on Vernon – he'll give you a ticket for peace disturbance, destruction of public property, being a general nuisance and – maybe a few others I can't think of.

You've got just enough time to take this car home – and leave it there until you can get some tires on the back of it! And try to drive making as little noise as you can. Okay?"

Lee nods. I get out of the car and start walking to my house.

The cop is gone. The Plymouth rumbles on down the street. As I look up in the night sky, someone has set off a bottle rocket, probably down near Heman Park. It explodes into beautiful colors. I go into the house.

Two days later it is the 4th of July. But that year…I do not even get on my motor scooter and ride down to watch the community fireworks display at Heman Park. One night of super-sparklers had been enough!

A Bad Connection

1/22/12

Billy 'Hambone' Hamilton was one of those 'hangers on' at Combrink's filling station just two blocks down Balson from U. City High School. You could always tell when Billy was at Combrink's after school, because his 1929 Essex four door sedan would be parked right out front.

I had been in the same class with 'Hambone' ever since kindergarten. We were friends, but not extremely close. By our junior year in high school, we each had different groups of friends that we traveled with. Billy was the outgoing extrovert – a little guy like myself; but he was the only boy cheerleader for the U. City athletic teams. Our only common interest was antique cars. He had that nice '29 Essex and I had my beat-up old '29 Ford Tudor sedan.

Occasionally, on my way home from school, I would stop in at Combrink's station when I saw Hambone's Essex parked there. I'd go in and chat for a few minutes before driving the three or four blocks up Midland to my home on Cornell.

It was one of those afternoons when the Essex was parked out front as usual and I pulled my Model A in on the large rear parking area. As I walked in the station's side door I could hear a conversation in process. A delivery truck driver was talking with his dispatcher on the payphone near the front door. Billie was behind the counter with Combrink. They were both giggling, trying to hide their laughter. Hambone waved to me and put his finger to his lips, I just stood there.

"Yeah," said the driver, "that's what I tol' yuh. I made that second delivery up there at Peeroo and Ballstown." Whadayah mean there ain't no such streets! Guess I oughtta know – why I jus' come from there five minutes ago. Yeah! Peeroo an' Ballstown. Hey, speak louder. I can hardly hear yuh. You know I'm hard a' hearin'. An we got a bad connection."

I was about to go up to the driver and tell him that he really meant Perdue and Balson, but Billy shook his head and motioned for me not to do it.

Just then my buddy Larkin, having seen my car parked there, pulled in with his gray ghost; as his father referred to it; a 1937 Hudson Terraplane sedan in primer.

When Larkin walked in, I cautioned him to remain silent just as Billy had done to me. Again, all of us listened.

"Yeah, I *did* ask 'em here at the station, but they don't know where the street is for that third delivery. Naw…they say it's someplace up north a' here. Where'm I now? Hell, I tol' yuh. Right down from Peeroo an' Ballstown."

"Well look it up on yer map. Yeah, Peeroo Avenue…You can't find it… well look in that city directory. Aw, don't tell me it ain't in there. You ain't spellin' it right. Wait a minute. I think I kin see the street sign on the corner; I kin almost read it if I move a couple feet closer t' the door.   It says Ballstown an' Midlin. Yeah, it's kinda hard t' read from here; looks like M-i-d-l-i-n."

"That's not in there either! What kinda directory you got there anyhow? Look, I'm 'bout one mile west a' Stinker Boulevard. I come offa there from highway 40. Yeah I went west on Vermin Ave."

By now Larkin and I were fighting to hold back our laughter.

"He means Vernon," Larkin whispered.

"I know."

The dispatcher checked his maps again and made another comment to the driver.

"What street off forty? Why it's *Stinker*! Stinker Boulevard. I took it all the way, 'bout a mile north off highway 40! Yeah!"

"Oh…I mean Skinker…like a skink? Yeah I know what they are; we got lots of 'em down home."

"Okay, you know where I am now…I should keep goin' west to Handy Road an' go right. It's not Handy, it's Hambly? Hansy? I can't get what yer a' sayin'. We got a bad connection."

"Okay, I go right at the T intersection…all the way to…what's that, National Fridge? Is that the name of the street? Sounds t' me like some brand a' icebox. It's what…it's Nashville Ridge? No? Aw hell, I'll jus' ask somebody when I get up that way closer."

I giggled in a whisper: "It's supposed to be: Hanley to Natural Bridge!" Everyone laughed.

The delivery truck driver hung up the receiver and pulled down the brim of his cap. He shook his head in exasperated disgust.

"That dispatcher – he's about as hard a' hearin' as I am. An' he can't even read, neither!"

Hambone chuckled with his usual saucy cynicism: "Yeah, *somebody* sure can't read!"

"An'" said the driver as he walked out the door, "On top of it all, we had a bad connection!"

Larkin looked at me and winked. He pointed to his head and laughed: "A *very* bad connection!"

The Gridiron

3rd Rewriting 12/10/22

It was on a motor scooter trip when I was sixteen, where I had been up in that tall fire tower in the Ozarks. There was only a light railing along its open staircase which must have been up 200 feet high at the top. It was created so that a forest ranger could see out for miles and miles in all directions.

The wind near the top of that tower was so strong that it felt like it was going to blow you off! I had gone up in that fire tower to try to cure my great fear of heights. As you probably suspect...it didn't work!

But there was one other option which occurred to me a year or two later: THE GRIDIRON! Anyone who is familiar with professional type stage work knows what the Gridiron is: it's an open grillwork of steel angle-irons hung directly above the top of the performance stage from which certain lights or other stage equipment can be placed or hung down. But because of its extreme height, perhaps 100 feet, it is rarely used.

The access to the gridiron is from wall-ladders, first to the "fly gallery" about 25 feet up, and then the rest of the 75 feet straight up the wall to the gridiron! I had been part of the stage craft class at the University City High School, and it gave me access to the stage on many days.

I had decided to try to cure my fear of heights by going up to the gridiron! First it was up the wall to the fly gallery (and don't look down). Then, not hesitating, another 75 feet right on up the wall to the gridiron. (And obviously, don't look down!)

I got to the top, eased my way out onto the gridiron just as the modern dance class was beginning on stage. For the next half hour, I watched, fascinated by the way people moved and walked when seen from directly above. As the class ended, I eased my way over toward the wall-ladder and slowly descended. At the fly gallery I began to shake a little. By the time I'd descended to the stage, I could hardly walk from the shaking – the realization of how high I had been up!

One of my classmates came on the stage to retrieve something for the class.

"Where you been?" he asked.

"Oh," I tried to reply casually, "up in the gridiron."

"What! The gridiron? Why that's *dangerous*! Man...the *gridiron*!"

I was shaking so badly I couldn't continue the conversation. I walked over to a corner of the stage and sat down on a pile of prop clothes...closed my eyes.

You know something – some intense fears must be there for a purpose – even if we can't determine that purpose. Maybe it's just better to accept the fear than to try to overcome it and chance causing ourselves great harm in the process.

It's been over 70 years now since I went up to the gridiron and I've never tried to do it again. And I haven't the slightest regret!

Did You Hear About...?

1/3/13

Mister Krasser, our music appreciation teacher at Hanley Junior High was a mousy-looking little man about five foot seven in height. He wore round, wire-rimmed glasses, which with his delicate build, made him appear even mousier.

Although Mister Krasser tried very hard to instill some appreciation for good music in all of us students, I think that had he been question in private as to how well he was succeeding, he might have admitted that he was *not* having great success – in fact, far from it.

My music class was at sixth hour – not the most auspicious time of day for *any* class – with students anticipating to be soon released from tehri daily "pedagogical prison". Somehow, Obren Koprivica had been placed in my music class at sixth hour.

Obie, even at sixteen was a veritable "mountain of a man", already over six feet tall, and he weighed at least two hundred and fifty pounds! And he was not all fat, either. He had such a powerful physique that it gave him the strength of a sumo Japanese wrestler.

Ordinarily, Mister Krasser would subject his students to listening to only the best pieces from Broadway musicals or from operettas. But for some reason, one particular day, he put on a twelve inch, 78 rpm recording of the aria from Verdi's Aida. Wisely, he put the five minute record on only five minutes before the end of class. By then there was already a typical hustling of papers and books, some low, murmured conversations and certainly a general lack of attention to the rather intense female operatic voice emanating from the turned-up volume of the record player.

As the record proceeded, nearly everyone in the class seemed to exhibit a sizeable degree of disaffection for it – if not outright dismay – having to listen to that unending, ear-piercingly shrill vocalization.

Obie stuck his fingers in his ears, stood up and laughed loudly. His seat was in the row next to the top of the upward sloping tiers of desks...and he was so huge that hardly anyone could avoid seeing this giant in the upper tier of seats. Obie's pal, Big Joe, sitting next to Obie, also stuck his fingers in his ears. General pandemonium ensued.

Then the class bell rang. Everyone attempted to leave at once, but since the door was at the lower, inner end of the music room, the thirty-five students had to file out only two at a time. Obie moved to the outer aisle next to the music room windows, which covered the entire west wall.

Mister Krasser walked over to where Obie was waiting for the rest of the class to clear out.

"Obie," he said, "I am *not* going to tolerate your creating a disturbance like that again. Do you understand?"

"But I didn't do nothin', Mister Krasser...I just stuck my fingers in my ears so I wouldn't hafta listen t' that woman screamin' on the record." Obie gave a light laugh.

"Obie, that is *not* screaming – that is a fine operatic singing performance!"

"Well...I didn't like it!"

"You need to learn to have some appreciation for the fine art of opera! You can't create a disturbance like that. There are other students who like opera and want to listen to it."

"Yeah? Who?"

Obie laughed longer and louder.

"Wh...wh...why...!"

Obie had called Mister Krasser's bluff. The big guy stood there gloating.

"Obie," Mister Krasser fumed, "Just...*what* kind of music *do* you like?"

"Uh...Spike Jones an' His City Slikers 'n' the Hoosier Hot Shots."

Obie laughed and laughed, knowing his answer would further enrage Mister Krasser.

"That's *not music*. That's just metered *noise!*"

Mister Krasser was infuriated. "Get out – just get *out!*"

He tugged at Obie's massive arm, but the gentle giant wouldn't budge.

"I'm going Mister Krasser. The bell already rang. I'm goin'...but you oughtta go first. After you!"

Obie bowed graciously and indicated with his hands.

"Get out! You hear me?" Mister Krasser yelled in a mousy voice. "Or I'll report you to Mister Baker's office!"

Amid peals of laughter from the students still left in the room, Obie grabbed Mister Krasser by his belt and with the other had on the men's coat collar, lifted the music teacher like a rag doll and gently slipped him through the fully cranked open window next to them.

As Krasser dropped to the ground only four feet below the window ledge, he was unhurt and virtually unruffled, though rather seriously compromised in pride!

You know...I never did hear whether Obie got reported to the principal's office. But I don't think I recall ever seeing him back in that music class again – and for weeks afterward, anytime two students met someplace, their first comment was: "Did you hear about Obie throwing Mister Krasser out the music room window?"

Memories of Lewis Park

1994

It was right down at the beginning of the block where we lived – on seventy hundred Cornell, just across Pennsylvania Avenue. That's where the entrance walk was, with its sign: 'Lewis Park'.

When I first crossed the street and walked up to the little park with its goldfish pond and tennis courts, I was only six years old. The park was tiny in comparison to what you would normally think of as a park. It probably comprised of less than half a city block. Long before he ceded the park to University City, Mister Lewis had developed the park area as a part of his personal estate.

His late Victorian mansion still faced Princeton on the private place that was just to the east of the park. I used to enjoy walking along the flagstone lined pond to watch the goldfish. There were so many different colors of them. Usually the water was clear enough to see easily into it – and I was amazed at how large those fish were compared to the tiny goldfish in my own aquarium.

The park was a gathering point for neighborhood boys. Older boys played tennis and we younger kids watched them, or wandered around the pond throwing pebbles and skipping rocks. One day, some boy got the idea to try to catch goldfish. He brought a pole and some bait and managed to hook a few.

We were all truly astounded at the almost unbelievable size those fish had achieved – as much as ten to twelve inches in length. That inspired all of us to bring poles and try to catch them. But whatever we caught, we always threw back – they were too large for our fish bowls. And although goldfish are just fancy carp, they were too pretty to eat.

On one of the rare occasions that a city maintenance worker visited the park and observed our piscine activities, we were summarily instructed that fishing for goldfish was prohibited – or fishing for anything was prohibited, for that matter – for frogs, or old bicycle inter tubes, or dead tree branches – all of which we occasionally pulled up, but we could still look at the fish from the bank if we wanted to…

There were other things at the park, however, to which a young boy could turn his attention. Along the east edge of the park, a thicket of large saplings, bushes and vines hid the back of the mansion from view. That wild hedgerow attracted me like a magnet. Birds, squirrels, rabbits – even box tortoises found a refuge there – and I also found a refuge there with my wild animal friends. Our communication was silence; our mutual understanding was in our silent communication.

The elderly man and his wife, the caretakers, would venture outside less and less. Finally, I noticed that the mansion doors and windows had been boarded up, weeds overgrew the entire property and when we realized that there was no longer anyone living there, many of the boys, myself included, began to cautiously investigate the inner sanctum of the mansion grounds.

Vandals eventually broke open the doors on the mansion and the carriage house and thieves soon stole the copper water pipes and brass gas light fixtures. Some doors still hung by only one or two screws in their hinges.

One day, a couple of older boys managed to pull off one of the huge carriage house doors and dragged it through the brush over to the pond. They cut saplings to use as push poles and spent the rest of the afternoon floating around the pond on their ready-made raft.

The rest of us were excited and jealous. Some of us came back the next day with crowbars and hatchets to make our own door rafts and push poles. Soon the pond was filled with boys on rafts traveling to imaginary far-off lands in our "sailing ships" fighting pirates and buccaneers.

For two delightful, autumn afternoons this amazing adventure went on, but by the third day the park officials had learned of our nautical journeys and they collected up all the doors, loaded them into a truck and thus ended one of the most joyful events of my boyhood.

Soon after that, the mansion itself was torn down and all the wild hedgerow along with it.

As I got older, I spent less time at Lewis Park. There were no great attractions there any longer – except in the winter. The hill up to Delmar Boulevard was so steep that it made a sled trail, which though short, was extremely fast.

Large rocks had been placed into the hillside as erosion barriers, but we removed enough of them to make two narrow sled trails for winter snow fun. After the snow became packed solidly into ice on the sled trails, it was possible to sled all the way to the pond – and when the pond was frozen thick enough, you could often coast all the way out to the middle of it.

The greatest sledding I ever had was when I was in sixth grade. A lot of the kids were in the park sliding down that steep hill – really enjoying it. Patsy Jacobson, a pretty, petite girl from my school class had brought her sled. Even though she lived not far down the street from me, I seldom saw her except in school.

I really liked Patsy – but even if we had been old enough, I would have been too shy to have ever asked her to go out with me. Sledding, though was different; that wasn't like a date. All Saturday afternoon we went down the hill together – both of us on her sled – laughing and really enjoying each other's company. The next summer her family moved. She left the school and I never saw her again. I still think about her sweet, smiling, pretty face – her blonde hair and blue eyes and that afternoon laughing and holding onto each other as we sledded down the hill in Lewis Park.

Ice skating was another winter sport on the Lewis Park pond. I tried out my first and only pair of ice skates on the pond. Other regular skaters always built bonfires, skating for hours, warming periodically by the fire. It was fun and good fellowship – if your ankles were strong enough. After two tries, I decided mine weren't.

Today, Lewis Park is still there. Still much the same they say, as it was when I was a boy seventy years ago. Whether it still attracts youngsters the way it used to do – I have no idea. I've passed by the park many times as I would travel Delmar Boulevard…but it's so hard to look down that steep hill into the park. Even if I could – and saw nothing, I would still at least have wonderful memories…of hedgerow wildlife…of boys on rafts…of blazing goldfish…of ice skating and sledding.

And especially, I would have memories of sledding one afternoon long ago with a laughing, pretty little girl, who, had circumstances been more favorable, might even have become my girlfriend.

The Long Ride

3/8/23

There were only a few more brush strokes to finish the bright orange-yellow paint I had been applying to the little two foot long trailer box I had constructed to pull behind my 1940 Powell motor scooter. My father opened the door from the front hall and looked into the garage where I was working.

"What's that?" he asked critically.

"Uh…just a little trailer…to pull behind the '40 Powell."

"Why do you need a trailer?"

"Well…see, there just isn't room to carry anything on the scooter… like a blanket roll or extra clothes or some tools that I might need."

"So where are you going that you'd need to have all that?"

"Uh…Kansas City…actually, Saint Joe."

"KANSAS CITY!!! SAINT JOE!!! DO YOU KNOW HOW FAR THAT IS?"

"Uh…yeah…it's 250 miles to Kansas city and another 50 miles to St. Joe."

"THAT'S…CRAZY!! To try to drive that piece of junk that far… it'll never make it!!"

"Well, I made it all around down in the Ozarks this spring…and I only had to push it up a couple of mountains."

"Yeah, but…Kansas City's a lot farther than that. Guess I oughta know…I've driven it many times – at 60 miles per hour. And it takes me 5 hours! You'll get halfway to Kansas City and that piece of junk'll throw a rod! Then you'll expect me to drive there and get you!"

"No," I said, "I had the engine apart and the crankshaft and rod still look like new…and the engine still has pretty good compression."

(My father was a "yeah, but" guy) "Yeah, but that scooter is eight years old…anything could happen. And why do you want to go to Sanit Joe Missouri anyway?"

"There's a school friend I haven't seen in a year and a half who moved there."

"So take the Greyhound Bus, it'll only cost probably 35 or 40 dollars for the round trip."

"But my scooter gets 50 miles per gallon! 600 miles would take 12 gallons at 25 cents per gallon, that's only six dollars!"

"Yea, but look how much time you'd save."

I slipped the toy wagon axel through the holes I had drilled in the plywood box, placed the wheels on it and bolted on a hitch made of steel straps.

That night, I went to bed early, got up at 6 and fixed myself something to eat and lunch to take along. With a full tank of gas, I went putting down the street and out to the highway.

The route to Kansas City was fairly level in many places, allowing me to putt along at 25, sometimes even 35 miles an hour. When I would hear a large truck approaching, I would move to the paved shoulder until it had passed – then go back on the pavement.

During the 11 hour drive to St. Joseph, I had plenty of time to consider my reason for going there. It had started over 11 years before on the first day in kindergarten at Jackson Park Elementary School. That was the day when I first saw Virginia Poppe as we 5-year-old children played our games in the large kindergarten room. For me, it was love at first sight the moment I first saw Virginia Poppe. She had a pretty face – though not extraordinarily beautiful – but it was her charismatic personality that was so attractive.

And I was not the only one charmed by her. (I recall many decades later having mentioned to former classmate Donald Gallap at a reunion about my fascination with Virginia, he said to me laughing "Oh, all the boys were in love with Virginia Poppe!!" Maybe, he was right! I will never know!! But my own fascination lasted 11 years. And that was the reason for my long scooter trip. I *had* to know if there was any mutual feeling by Virginia toward me.

Actually, in 9th grade, Virginia Poppe and I were in the same Modern History Class together. I wanted to impress her with my "intellectuality" so I studied our Modern History books assiduously. I would answer every question our teach would ask the class. And I did manage to impress our teacher Mr. McKee (he gave me an A) but it did not seem to impress Virginia Poppe. Ah well.

By 5:30 in the evening, I had reached St. Joseph Mo. I looked up Paul Poppe's address in the phone book and received directions. The Poppes were in a new subdivision in the east edge of town. I drove there, parked my scooter in the end of the drive and went to the door.

Virginia's father answered. He recognized me from my many visits to 'hang around' after school.

"Is Virginia home?" I asked.

He called to her: "Hey Virginia, there's someone here to see you – one of the boys from St. Louis!"

"I'm dressing for the big pre school dance tonight" she called down from upstairs.

"How'd you get here?" Virginia's father asked.

I pointed to my scooter parked in his drive.

"You rode that all the way from St. Louis? That's amazing!"

"Yeah…it took me all day…"

"Say, we're just about to eat dinner. Would you like to have dinner with us? Nothing fancy, but if you like corn on the cob we've got plenty."

"Oh sure – that'd be great!"

"Listen," Virginia's father said "we don't have a spare guest bedroom, but if you'd like to sleep on a cot in the basement you'd be welcome to it."

"Yeah, that'd be wonderful!"

I was shown the cot in the basement and where I could wash up. As I came up the stairs, Virginia, half dressed looked down "How'd you get here?" she asked.

"My motor scooter. Hey, Virginia would you like to go to a movie with me tomorrow night?"

"I can't – I already have a date!"

"Guess I'd need to get a reservation in a week or two in advance!"

"Yeah...I'm always busy."

At dinner both of Virginia's parents were extremely friendly.

"Virginia's a very popular girl." Her mother said.

"Yeah, I know, she always was." I responded.

The next morning, Virginia slept late. Her mother fixed me breakfast and packed a lunch for me to take along (what wonderful in-laws Virginia's parents would have been! Especially compared to those I eventually had!).

I rode the scooter on out to the highway and headed east over a generally level prairie route.

I had driven about 50 miles, near Chillicothe when one of the trailer wheels began to lose its tire.

By the time I had gotten into town, there was very little left of the trailer wheel and the bearings on the opposite wheel were rattling around, ready to fall out!

A large junk store was located right at the edge of town. "I BUY ANYTHING" (except your old man or old woman).

I went into the store and explained to Mr. I BUY ANYTYHING what my problem was. We went out to my scooter and trailer.

"How far did you come on those wagon wheels?" he asked me.

"Well...from St. Louis."

"From St. Louis!! Why that's 175 miles from here! It's nothing less than a miracle you made it that far with toy wagon wheels!"

"But I came the other direction." I said "it wasn't 175 miles, it was 350 miles!"

"I just can hardly believe that!" he responded. "You've had luck like no one I ever heard of."

We went back inside and he told me that he had no wagon wheels, but that he had a set of pneumatic tires on wheels that would do very well. They were hanging up on a wall and he used a hook to retrieve them.

They were truly excellent wheels, tires and axel. I asked him how much he wanted for the set.

"Ten dollars – no less! These are fine wheels and tires!"

I looked in my wallet. I had only 13 dollars left.

"All I've got is $13 left to get home to St. Louis. That's still 175 miles from here!"

"Three dollars'll buy you all the gas you need to get back." He said. "And these wheels and tires'll last almost forever!!"

I paid Mr. I BUY ANYTHING and he helped me enlarge the trailer axel hole for the new axel, then put a clamp on it to keep it from turning. I started up my scooter and hooked the trailer on it and was again on my way.

Mister I BUY ANYTHING was right – I had no further trouble with the trailer wheels or tires. But my progress was slow on the narrow highways. By the time I neared St. Louis, it was already beginning to become dark. The scooter's headlight was poor – too dim to identify street signs.

When I reached north St. Louis (Florissant), I could not recognize any major street. Somehow, I entered a subdivision and could not find my way out. I wandered from one subdivision into another, and into another. For over an hour I was hopelessly lost and unable to find even an open filling station where I could inquire.

Finally – I somehow came upon Lindburgh Boulevard near Lambert Field (the St. Louis airport) and from there I drove south to Olive Street Road, then east to Midland and up Midland to Cornell. I was home!

It was now ten o'clock. My dad was preparing to go to bed; my mother was already in bed reading her copy of Colliers. I used my key and unlocked the front door, went into the garage, opened the big door and rolled my scooter in.

Then without disturbing anyone I went to the downstairs "maid's room" where I usually slept and fell into a dreamless collapse on my bed.

There were some important lessons from that grueling trip: the most obvious was that a 16-year-old boy simply cannot carry on a relationship with a girl 300 miles away - even if she had been fond of me – which she obviously was not. Another lesson was that at 16, you don't know as much as you think you know and should seek the advice of those who are more experienced in life.

I never saw Virginia Poppe again. And I soon realized that some things are simply not meant to be – no matter how much we would like for them to be – or no matter how long or how intensely we dwell on them.

A year later, I met Marjorie Frank through a friend and neighbor Leslie Cohen. Somehow, I thought that Marjorie Frank reminded me of Virginia Poppe. How absurd! They were nothing alike!

And I fancied myself in love with Marjorie in spite of the fact that she really was not very good looking (according to the photograph which I still have of her). I guess that I have always been quite good at fooling myself. But life does have compensations. Sometimes those compensations are a little hard to understand or to recognize. But they *are* there if we look for them.

I had been working during the year following my graduation from high school. I was officeboy and general flunky at my uncle's paint store, still intending to marry Marjorie Frank. She had other plans – higher education and was no longer interested in me. We had little in common anyway. I began an intense relationship with Marjorie's classmate Judy Wasserman – another badly fated disaster. But there were compensations. The most obvious was that I learned to be a writer from Judy.

Life is full of disappointments. And perhaps a few good compensations.

The question is whether you can effectively dismiss the disappointments so that you can embrace the compensations. And I'm not always so certain that can be done. At the age now of almost 91, I find that life is less certain – both my own life and that of the rest of the world. I no longer try to predict anything – merely to survive from one day to the next.

Addendum for The Long Ride

Once, many years ago, I was told by someone (I can't even recall who it was) that one of our classmates, Ron Henges had organized a Jackson Park Elementary School reunion...and that Virginia Poppe came to it.

I had never received an invitation to the reunion – I do not know why. Although I no longer lived in St. Louis, my father was still listed in the St. Louis phone book and Ron knew his name (the same as mine).

Perhaps an invitation had been sent but was somehow "lost in the mail". I had remained in contact with Ron Henges usually a couple times each year by phone. Each time I talked to Ron on the phone I always wanted to ask him about the grade school reunion – who attended, and if there were a picture that had been taken. But every time I spoke with Ron, I would forget to ask. Finally Ron died unexpected at age 88. I had tried calling his wife Anne whom I had met, but the phone was no longer in service. A letter to her was returned as undeliverable. And she may not have known much if anything about the grade school reunion anyway.

Such is life. There are simply things we will never know. No matter how much we might like to know them...And does it really matter? Well...perhaps...but perhaps not...

Telephone Romance

This is based on a true happening to a close friend, Fred Summers, in the 1970's.

For Ferdie Gonifman, back in the 1970's, a Saturday evening without a date was so peculiar – such a social rarity – that he could hardly recall ever having been in a similar circumstance.

As he sat looking out the window at the driving October rain, he felt almost glad that the lady had called, too ill to make their evening engagement.

Ferdie continued sitting – and wondering just what he should do with the coming unoccupied evening hours. That book he had been reading was still in the car – and since the rain had not been predicted, he had, naturally , left the car parked in the driveway. He would definitely *not* try to retrieve that book, at least until the rain stopped.

Finding another date at the last minute – with a girl worth dating, was almost out of the question on a Saturday night. But he picked up his address book and began flipping through the pages, just to let his mind try to toy with various ideas. Finally, he put the address book down and went to the kitchen to fix himself a drink. He topped it with a shot of his favorite alcoholic anodyne for social ills.

Ferdie Gonifman, went with a calm directness back into the living room, sat down in his most comfortable chair and drank the entire contents of the glass he'd carried in with him. He savored the warmth of the room and the coolness of the drink.

Then…he began fidgeting with a key chain, and then, looking at the clock. After that, he started examining the patterns in the rough plaster of the 1920 style walls of the old house. With another spurt of nervous frustration, he walked out to the kitchen and fixed another smaller version of the same drink as before, but with an equal amount of the distilled spirit.

The added intoxicant seemed to stimulate bizarre crevices in hidden retreats of his mind. Ferdie picked up his little black address book again and began looking down the list of names.

"Let me see, " he thought, "now which one of these girls would probably *not* have a date tonight?"

His finger stopped at the name Mabel Schmuckenheimer. Lost in thought, he sat unmoving for several seconds. Mabel *was* a bit fat – not bad looking, but obnoxiously loud-mouthed. She would probably be home…but no – she would never do for his planned amusement. She had had a crush on him a couple of years before which he had successfully discouraged. If she recognized his vocal disguise, there might be trouble.

"So who else?"

Ah – at the end of the list he found her: Zelda Zitnik! Yes, she would *surely* be home. She was a large framed, overweight woman in her late twenties; very plain-looking and not overly bright. *She* would be the one to call.

Taking the telephone from it's stand, Ferdie sat back in the chair again with the phone on his lap and dialed up Zelda's number.

Zelda: "Hello! Hellooo…"

Ferdie (in a throaty, hollow – almost mechanical-sounding voice)
    : "Uh…is this Zelda?"

Zelda: "Yes it is…so who is this?"

Ferdie (as Bernie)
    : "Uh…uh…Zelda, this is Bernie. Bernie Schwartz."

Zelda: "Who?"

Bernie: "I'm Bernie Schwartz, I'm a friend of Ferdie Gonifman. You remember him?"

Zelda: "Oh sure. I haven't seen him in a few months. I haven't been going to very many parties. That's where I usually run into him. Ferdie's a really funny guy – always joking around. He's a panic!"

Bernie (choking back a laugh)
    : "Yeah, that Ferdinand – he's full of bull!"

Zelda (laughs)

Bernie: "Well he told me about you, so I thought I'd call you up and introduce myself."

Zelda: "Okay, so how do you know Ferdie?"

Bernie: "Ferdie and me – we used to go to school together. But I moved out of state – hadn't seen Ferdie for a long time. Then when I moved back to town again, I ran across him at a party."

Zelda: "So you've been away a long time, huh?"

Bernie: "Yeah, I've been living on the west coast. I was in the sardine business. Imported 'em. Some people think it sounds kinda fishy."

Zelda (laughs)
    : "Is that the truth?"

Bernie: "Not exactly – I worked on a fishing boat on the coast. But I had some health problems that made me quit."

Zelda: "So what was that?"

Bernie: "Aw – you know…like the stench was so bad it made my nose run. And it ran so fast I couldn't catch up with it."

Zelda (laughs)
    : "That's ridiculous!"

Bernie: "Yeah, it is, isn't it?"

Zelda: "Well, you sound like an interesting guy."

Bernie: "I am. But speaking of interest – what are *your* interests? I mean, do you have any interest in seeing movies or going to plays?"

Zelda: "Oh sure, I go to movies a lot. But plays – gee, I guess it's been years since I've been to one."

Bernie: "Well, maybe you'd like to go to a play with me sometime – I mean, if we could find one we'd both enjoy seeing."

Zelda: "Yeah – probably be fun. You know, you were saying you and Ferdie were in school together...was it high school?"

Bernie: "Yeah – high school, but grade school too. We started the same year in grade school. And then we went to the same college. But we were there only a year and we both got drafted."

Zelda: "Oh, that's too bad."

Bernie: "Yeah, Ferdie, he got a stateside assignment, but me...I got sent overseas...ended up in Korea."

Zelda: "Ooo...bet that wasn't any fun."

Bernie: "Nawh...it never was good; but it really got bad one time when they bombed us."

Zelda (with morbid curiosity)
    : "Ugh! So what happened?"

Bernie: "There were five of us in a kind of shelter when the bomb hit. It killed three of the guys outright, but me and another guy – we were injured pretty bad."

Zelda (her morbid curiosity more aroused)
    : "What *happened* to you?"

Bernie: "It's kinda hard to explain everything – but I'll try."

Zelda: "Okay – gee, I hope you didn't get hurt too bad."

Bernie: "Yeah...well, see that explosion crushed all the bones in the top of my skull, so they had to take 'em out and put a metal plate in my head."

Zelda: "Oh my God! That's *terrible*!"

Bernie: "Yeah, it was terrible. Now, sometimes I ublgu... (silence) uggl gub...

Zelda: "Bernie! Bernie, what's the matter? Are you okay?"

Bernie: "I'm alright now. Sometimes, if I get too excited it affects my speech."

Zelda: "Isn't there anything they can do for it...something that can help you?"

Bernie: "I just have to calm down for a while. What the doctors did – they installed a little light in the top of my head. Then that light comes on whenever I get too excited and someone can tell me and I can go laydown and rest for a while."

Zelda: "Oh my God! A light! Oh no!"

107

Bernie: "If I get really – really over-excited, then the light starts to flash. But if I have to wear a hat, then that hides the light and so there's an automatic device that starts a whistle going."

Zelda: "A whistle! Oh my God! Oh my GOD! Oh my *GOD*!
     Click.

Von Machinson Meets Kookie Otto

Figgus Figwort knocked at the door and announced his presence. As soon as he walked into the tiny two room apartment, the first words out of his mouth were:

"What's that screeching noise?" He pointed upwards.

"Oh, it's just Kookie Otto testing his new violin," I said.

"Well, somebody ought to tell him to take it back where he bought it and get his money back!"

"He can't do that."

"Why not – it sounds *terrible*!"

"I know, but you see, he didn't buy it – he *made* it."

"Huh…that's even *worse*!"

"It is, but I can't tell *him* that."

Figgus raised his eyebrows: "Well *I* can.   What's his phone number?"

With a quick stride to my telephone, Figgus looked up the number in my address book laying there and punched it in. As the phone upstairs began to ring, the violin's discordant scrapes and scratches ceased.

"What a relief!" Figgus' eyes rolled in exasperation.

"Hallo? Yah…iss dis Otto, d' great fiolin maker?"

Figgus then heard:

"Uh, uh…I'm Otto. What do you want?"

"I am d' renount Heinrich Von Machinson, dealer in fine stringt hinstruments.   Hit hass komt to mine hattention dat you haf chust completed a fapulous new fiolin, unt I vould like fairy much to hear it! Ist possible? Yah?"

"No." replied Otto. "I'm not ready yet to let it be heard publicly. It needs more refinement…and adjustment. Perhaps in a few months from now – after the instrument has had a chance to settle."

"Aach! I am dishapointed! But perhaps if you voud permit me, I could come offer to your place und you could gif me chust von or two minutes uf your time – zo dat I could hear dis great hinstrument wit mine own ears. Hokay?"

"No. I don't even know who you are."

"Look – I'm tellink you – I am Heinrich Von Machinson – renount dealer in fine stringt hinstruments. Surely you haf heard of me...yah?"

"No. Please leave me alone."

Click.

Well, now what?"

Figgus thought carefully for a few moments. Then the squawking and squeaking of the violin upstairs began again in unsubdued intensity, the ancient apartment's floor boards resonating the sound without any insulation to inhibit it. The tones were of no discernable melody and with the skill of a completely untrained musician.

"Ill wait just a few minutes," continued Figgus, "Like I've come from a distance somewhere, then I'll go up and knock on his door."

"*This* I've got to hear."

After several minutes of sitting with his fingers in his ears, Figgus Figwort stood up in exasperation.

"Doesn't this *ever* quit?"

"Yes, when he goes to bed – or for a few minutes while he makes some adjustment on the violin."

"Well, take those earplugs out of your ears and come out in the hall so you can hear me. I'm going up there!"

Figgus quickly traversed the long, steep flight of stairs to the third floor apartment.

"I'll stay down here out of sight." I said.

"Better watch, this'll be fun!"

A heavy knocking at Otto's door was the next sound. Immediately the squawks of the violin stopped as Kookie Otto opened the door just a slit, at the same instant slipping on the chain. Figgus pushed his shoe inside the door's slit before Otto could close it again.

"What do you want? What do you want?"

"I am Von Machinson!" Figgus announced in a heavy staccato voice dripping with German accent.

"Go away!"

Otto held his violin in his right hand at arm's length back from the door.

"Fiolin! I vant dat fiolin!"

Van Machinson's hair had been shaken into disarray over his eyes: he stomped the floor with his right foot while maintaining his left in the cracked door.

"No – no – go away!"

"I must haf dot fiolin – I pay you tventi-tousant!"

"No!"

"Fifti tousant!"

"No!"

"Half million!"

"Go away!"

Suddenly Von Machinson shivered and shook bouncing against the door and the jam, finally letting his foot slip away from the door bottom. He fell to the floor, thrashing and pounding the floor as if in an epileptic fit. Otto stood looking through the chained door, frightened, but fascinated by the acrobatic activity.

"Aach! Look vot chu haf done to me! I am haf a conniption fit! Aggh!"

In just an instant Figgus was again on his feet reaching through the opening in the door in an attempt to grab the violin out of Otto's hand.

"No – no…leave me alone!"

Kookie Otto stepped back from the door, pulling away from Von Machinson's grasp and out of reach. Van Machinson slipped and fell back away from the door, which Otto kicked shut with a loud slam.

"Fiolin…I must haf dat fiolin." Whimpered Von Machinson as he lay on the floor, pounding and kicking like a child having a temper tantrum. Slowly, he raised himself and trundled down the stairs. He came back into the apartment and sat heavily into a chair, looking exhausted, but smiling.

"I don't hear anything yet!"

"No…maybe you succeeded…for a while."

The 'while' lasted the rest of the afternoon and long after Figgus Figwort left. The quiet went unbroken until late in the next morning. At noon, Kookie Otto's feet could be heard on the steps – just as I was entering the hall.

"Hello," he said.

"Hi. You know, I heard some commotion up on your floor yesterday – what happened?"

"It was horrible! Some crazy man tried to take my new violin. A German-sounding lunatic. But he didn't get it. It was just horrible!"

"Oh, that's too bad."

I did not indicate which part of Kookie Otto's comment I thought was 'too bad'. But he might have gotten the idea later – when I recorded his violin sawing and played back hours of it to him on a speaker attached to the ceiling underneath his floor.

Ott on the Hot Pot

A true happening from 1971

I cannot remember why I happened to be in a hidden alcove at the rear of the second floor hallway, but I remained there listening to the incredible interaction between Lloyd Stomphouser and "Monkeywrench" on the floor above. Not too long after that 1971 incident, I wrote out what I had heard to the best of my memory.

"Gimme that torch, you mother fucker!"

Monkeywrench laughed and grabbed the small propane torch away from Lloyd Stomphouser who stumbled and nearly dropped the can of beer in his left hand.

"Ain't you never learned how t'sweat a pipe joint yet? You ain't got enough solder, for one thing. Here…squirt some more flux on it y' stupid son 'a bitch!"

"I'm stupid, huh?" Lloyd shouted back in a slurred response. "I wuz smart enough t' buy this apartment building wasn't I? What'd *you* ever buy – 'sides a six-pack of beer? And *that's* not very often! Call *me* stupid…"

Lloyd muttered his last sentence as he watched Monkeywrench sweat the joint. Then, as he started to step over the box of copper fittings for another elbow, Lloyd tripped on a pipe wrench on the floor, falling hard against the hot water tank and dropping his can of beer.

"God dammit – sonovabitch! That one had some hooch in it!"

"Oh…I wondered why y' wuz nursin' it so long. Y' got more y' kin put some in *mine*?"

"Ok, yuh stupid motherfucker – gimme another can outta yer six-pack an' I'll spark it up."

111

After Monkeywrench had handed Lloyd another can, Lloyd opened it and added a small shot of whiskey from a bottle he slipped out of the pocket of his overcoat. He began drinking from the can.

"Okay…me too, here!"

Monkeywrench was insistent, and Lloyd complied.

"Don't pay yuh enough, huh…I gotta share my goddamn hooch with yuh too?"

Lloyd's last comment was loud enough to be heard all the way to the first floor apartment. Mrs. Twiggy opened her door:

"Will you two stop shoutin' at each other? Sounds like you're havin' a shoutin' match!"

"See there yuh loudmouth son 'a bitch. Stop yer shoutin' like the lady says."

"Agh…you ain't no better. Okay when y' get that last elbow on, we can check it for leaks. Wait a minute – yuh got that hooked up on the right one? There's three pipes come out along the wall here. Now why they got so many pipes?"

"Probably usta have the third floor front apartment hooked in here."

"Yeah. Okay, follow this pipe up t' the sink. Kin yuh see?" Which side's it on?"

"Right side – that's hot, dumbass…supposed t' be anyhow."

"I know that, y' dumb son 'a bitch."

Lloyd was beginning to show the effects of his 'hooch'. "Ok, I turned it on. See any leaks?"

"No…I tol' yuh, when I sweat a joint, it don't leak."

"Yuh got a match?...Yer lighter? Take yer lighter an' start the water heater goin'. Y' push down on the red control button 'til the pilot starts, then twist it t' the right."

"I know that! Y' think I never lit a water heater before?"

"Aggh…hurry up!"

Monkeywrench got up after watching the gas flame for a few seconds. He looked at the dust-covered top of the water heater.

"Hey, there's no safety pop-off valve on this tank!"

"Arggh…I bought one yesterday but forgot t' put it in the box with the fittings. We'll stick it on there t'marra. It'll be ok for now."

"Alright…let's get d'hell outta here!"

As the two largely inebriated men clattered down the long flight of steps, Lloyd confided loudly to Monkeywrench:

"I tol' Ott I'd get the hot water hooked up right away when he took the apartment way back eight months ago. Least I'll have him off my ass now. First thing outta his mouth ever time I'd see him was: 'where's the hot water?' What a relief it'll be not t' hear *that*!"

"Yeah, I'll bet! He even ast me about it a couple times. Well it's done now."

Later that morning, when Ott arrived at the hallway bathroom for his usual mid-morning relief, he was pleasantly surprised by the sound of the blazing gas under the hot water tank.

He sat down on the old elephant-trunk commode and allowed his own internal plumbing to cleanse itself. Then he tore off some toilet tissue and wiped at his posterior orifice. But before he arose from the commode, he felt another urge. He sat solidly again and reached over twisting the handle on the tank.

With an explosive whoosh, a massive burst of steam and hot water came billowing out of the toilet – in every possible direction – but primarily underneath Ott's posterior extremity.

Just which of his private parts had been scalded, Ott was somewhat uncertain; but he *was* certainly frightened out of his wits; and came tearing down the hall steps as fast as his legs could carry him, hampered as they were by his pants still pulled to his knees.

"It exploded! Do you hear? It exploded! Help! Help!"

Joy Boy, the itinerant loafer, stuck his head out of his second floor apartment door.

"Whatcha mean, Ott? What happened?"

"It blew up when I turned the handle. I need some burn ointment!"

"Blew up? What did?"

"The toilet!"

"The toilet?"

"Yes – the toilet!"

"You gotta be kiddin'! That's *impossible*!"

"I don't care if it's possible or not. It happened! Go see for yourself!"

Joy Boy ran up the stairs and looked at the still -steaming bathroom. He examined the hot water heater and noted the high flame and lack of a pop-off valve. Then he turned the gas control down to its lowest position. After testing the hot water faucet on the sink and finding it cold – and the cold side producing hot water, he went back down to his apartment. Ott was still standing in the doorway.

"See what I mean?"

"Yeah...that drunken stumble-bum – that beer soused idiot Lloyd" laughed Joy Boy, "they hooked the hot water heater into the toilet supply. Then they turned the goddamned flame all the way up!"

Joy Boy was by now almost beside himself with laughter. He stumbled around his apartment laughing to the point of tears as he looked for a little first aid box with burn ointment. When he had found the box and handed the tube to Ott, his face took on a sheepish look.

"I'm sorry, Ott" he said trying to sound apologetic, "but this is the funniest bunch of goddam' idiot nonsense I *ever* heard of. I can't help laughin'. I know you probably don't think it's a bit funny."

"Definitely not! Ott offered with solemn dignity, "But I'll have plenty to say to Lloyd about it when I see him tomorrow."

The next day, Lloyd Stomphouser arrived early at the apartment with the new pop-off valve in one hand and a pipe wrench in the other. An unopened beer can protruded from the lapel pocket of his overcoat. He knocked on Ott's door, standing there until it opened.

"Lloyd!"

"Yeah, Ott...so how do you like your new hot water?"

"I would have liked it much better if I had not been scaclded by it."

"Oh...uh...I bet that damn Monkeywrench turned the gas control the wrong way. I let him do it 'cause I was too in..., uh, I mean I was afraid to bend over that far."

"Yes, I see...and I got scalded when I sat on the toilet!"

"Uh oh...I wondered if we had that hot water pipe hooked up on the hot side."

"Now, you know. And I also want you to know that I'm moving out!"

Lloyd stood there stunned.

"Listen Ott, I'm really sorry that happened to you. I'll make it up to you. Take half off your next month's rent. How's that?"

Ott contemplated before he answered.

"Well, okay." But he knew that it was highly likely that by the time next month's rent was due, that Lloyd would either have forgotten about his offer, or be too drunk to remember it. He thought he would suggest to his landlord one last piece of advice.

"Now look here, Lloyd, don't you think you could do a lot better with plumbing if you didn't mix it with alcohol? Haven't you learned that alcohol and that kind of water just don't mix well?"

Lloyd thought about it.

"You're right, Ott," he laughed, "alcohol and water don't mix well; y' gotta mix alcohol…with more *alcohol*!"

The Boiler

4/4/23

Still early in the evening when I just happened to be going by the street where my friend Figgus lived. I thought I'd stop in and say hello.

Figgus Fignewton was in one of his telephoning moods.

"Who should I call? He asked me.

"Oh… I don't now – I've heard of a boiler maker," I said.

"What! A *boiler* maker! How ridiculous!"

Then Figgus thought about it for a few seconds. "Hmmm… hmmmm… yeah, yeah… what's his number?"

We look up the number in the phone book and Figgus dials it.

"Hallo! Hallo! Ezz zis Meester Kilsi'grew?"

"Yes it is – but my name is pronounced Kil'sigrew, with the accent on the first syllable – but that's not important. What can I do for you/"

"Fell, mine name Vosnikide Rascovicovitchnik. HI ham hrepresent home for hretirement pipple of country: Mouldivina. You haf heard uf us, yes?"

"No, I'm sorry, I haven't. My knowledge of minor European countries is rather poor, I'm afraid."

"Fell…HI hexplain to you. Mouldavina between Gasnicovia hand Blustrovica – habout fife hundred mile from Adriatic Sea. Now you know far izz?"

"No, I'm sorry, I still don't know."

"Fell den HI tellink you, fe har niddink new poiler for home. Old fun over fun hundred years hold. Leaking bad! Fery bad! You can make new fone, yes?"

"Well… I don't know…"

"Fhy you don't know?"

"I would need more information."

"Fwhat chyou niddink know?"

"Well, for one thing, whether it's a steam or a hot water system. And I need to know the gallonage of the system. I'd really have to examine the unit in order to determine that."

"First hiss halso himportant izz, can you makein Baroque style?

"I'm not sure what you mean by that."

"Must *look* Baroque."

"Why do you need it to look Baroque?"

"Must make happy old Mouldivian hresidents!"

"But Mister… I… I'm sorry, I've forgotten your name – Mister…?"

"Vosnikide Rascovicovitchnik! Fwhy you cannot hremember simple name like tat?"

"Well, it *is* unusual!"

"Not in Mouldavina"

"Yes, but this isn't Mouldavina."

"You here making me mad – fwhy you argue fwith me?"

"But, sir, I'm not trying to argue with you: I'm just trying to get important information about your boiler."

"Ta poiler must be Baroque!"

"I understand that. But that's just the external appearance. We need to know the pressure and the gallonage!"

"Fwhy you not come here hand look for yourself?"

"Well, how do I get there?"

"Zimple! Go highway 29 fun half mile to t road. Den numper 17 zix mile highway '39 two miles to hexit, den vour miles – fill be on left. Every large Gothic pilding fwith turets hand gargoyles haround eaves on roof! Can't miss!"

"Sir, I'm not sure I understand where you mean that you're starting from."

"Fwhy you not sure? You not hlisten to me? HI tell you hegain. Pliz hlisten: take highfay 110 to t road14. Turn right on highway 4, go 12 miles to exit, den left. Izz on right."

"But sir, that's *completely* different from what I wrote down before!"

"Oh… fell… I zendink you map. Tat fay no mistake. Yes?"

"Yes… okay. Anything else?"

"Fell… halso fery himportant dat poiler must hafe fun quarter hinch thick tubes, made high strength steel. Like old poiler!"

"One quarter inch thick tubes! That's *extremely* heavy! I've never heard of a boiler using tubes that thick It would take a long time to heat up the water! And I'm not even sure I can get tubes a quarter inch thick. Three sixteenths inch is the heaviest I've ever heard of anyone using!"

"Must be like old poiler!"

"Why?"

"Hizz tradition. Must follow."

"Sir, that's crazy!"

"Fwhy you say tradition hizz crazy?"

"I didn't say tradition is crazy! I said... I said..."

"Fwat you say?"

"I said... I mean... I..."

"Hyou don' know fot chu mean!"

"No I don't – you have me confused!"

"Fell, you should call me fen you are not confused... if da tizz hever!"

"Now listen, you... you... God dammit... you..."

Click.

Figgus hung up the receiver and laughed.

"That was *mean!*" I said.

"Oh, he'll get over it. And at least he isn't going on a wild goose chase."

"I don't know about that. He might try to follow your directions."

"Well, if he does, he won't go very far – it'll just lead him in a circle!"

"Don't you think we should have told him it was just a joke?"

"No...this way he'll have a great story to tell all his friends for the next few months. Why spoil it?"

I shrugged, got up and began walking toward the door. "I'll stop by again when I'm in town, Mister Rascovicovitchnik."

"Hey... you actually got that name right!"

"Sure... I wouldn't want to insult such an upstanding person from Mouldivina!"

Dogs Do Talk

Dogs do talk. Did you know that? Yes, they really – *really* do talk...not in the same way that you and I talk, obviously, but they do have "words" of sorts – and even though these words may vary a great deal from individual dog to dog, there are some distinctly formed sounds.

But everybody who's been around dogs much, already knows this. They also know that dogs communicate with their eyes and with body language. Until you've been around those canine creatures a very great deal, however, you probably never fully realize the *depth* of what they try to communicate.

Human intellectual pursuits are certainly enjoyable; they enhance, they entertain, they enrich our lives with a diversity that a dog's mind simply isn't going to be able to grasp. But maybe a dog doesn't have to grasp this; maybe in his less complex thinking he doesn't have the *need* for all that enhancement; maybe there's already enough fulfillment in his emotional life that he doesn't require anything more – so that when he speaks, it's the full expression of the depth and breadth of his emotional existence. I wonder if we ever think about something like that?   I know I tend to be a lot more emotionally conservative than a dog when I talk – though I wouldn't want to suggest that I know how anyone else approaches it.

And then in addition to talking, there's the matter of being the "faithful friend". You know something – very few people have ever been betrayed by a dog, on the other hand, plenty of dogs are regularly betrayed by people.

We humans are at best, a fickle lot. Thinking about the faithfulness of dogs makes me wonder how many people and dogs I may have betrayed, knowingly or unknowingly, at various points in my life. The worst betrayal could be the unrecognized one…because then there's no means to try to correct it – to compensate for it – to make amends.

Actually, I can't ever remember being betrayed by a dog – unless you think that possibly a dog being so careless as to allow himself to be struck and killed by a car is some kind of betrayal…I don't know… it might be…in a quirky kind of way. You could probably say the same thing about people who smoke or eat themselves into an early death too, though.

Now I put the question to you: is it worse to be betrayed by your dog who allows himself to get run over and killed by a car, or to be betrayed by your wife (or husband) who lets herself or himself get run over by the wheel of obesity or junk-food self-destruction?

If you don't have a ready answer for that – maybe what you ought to do is consult your dog. Remember, dogs…do talk.

118

Apple Trees

10/6/93

He watched the October sunset explode like a fireball behind the blackened silhouettes of trees, then slowly dim. The fading of summer merged with the fading of the warmth of day. As the chilly air rolled through the hollows and up on the hillsides, the torrid love affair between sun and forest abruptly ended.

From the upper branches of an apple tree, the Boy could see the gray waters of the pond's dark reflections... and shadows of trees mirrored by the final unextinguished flames of sun.

The sack of apples was heavy. He bunched the open end and jammed it into a fork so that the sack lay across the trunk of the tree. Apple trees were nice, not just for the fruit but for the way they branched – so easy to climb... and for the way they danced and swayed in the stiff breeze of autumn. The trees caressed you and the wind embraced you.

The only thing that might be better was climbing a sapodillo tree once when he had picked fruit in the tropics. But here, at least, there were no chiggers – no sand flies – no fire ants. Only a couple of months of intense heat. In two months, the intense cold would make him long again for the tropics, though. Everywhere you went there were trade-offs.

He was dreaming in the top of an apple tree and the night air became more chill – the light more dim.

With the strap of the apple sack hooked over one shoulder, the Boy slowly eased his way down the tree, hugging its trunk, feeling for lateral branches in the darkness. On the ground, he stood there waiting in the silence – as if to hear a goodbye.

The trees were friends – mute and immovable, but friends. They were there before he came and might be there long after he was gone. Trees were good to have as friends; they never argued with you or fought with each other... or complained. Who could say whether they had thoughts? Perhaps... perhaps? He cared, even if no one else did. There were so many people who cared so little about each other or about trees – too many people and not enough trees.

The Boy Reached into the sack, grabbed a large apple and bit into it. Life, he thought, could be like a dream in the top of an apple tree... if only you didn't ever have to come down from it.

Vegetable Soup

Rewritten 12/5/2022

There was an audible "click" as Brother Grady slid the latch bolt on the heavy front door of Harmony Hospitality House, locking it securely. He turned, but before he could walk away, a light tapping sounded on the door. Grady pulled the cover back from the small observation window and looked out. An enormous figure of a man stood before the door.

"Yer too late! We're already locked up!" Brother Grady called out through the glass.

"Aw …lemme in! I come a long way. Da snow's deep…an' I got nowhere else t'git dinner."

Grady relented. He opened the door and Big Benji stumbled in.

"Now look, I'm doin' this fer ya this once, but in the future, if ya see that the weather's gonna be bad like this, ya beter plan ta leave early enough so y'get here before six. That's when we close the door. Okay?"

"Yeah, yeah."

Brother Grady eyed Big Benji "I don't think I seen ya here before, have I? Well, come along – follow me." Benji left a trail of alcoholic breath behind him.

They proceeded through a set of swinging doors into a large dining area.

"Go get yerself a tray an' then go over 'n' stand in that line by the servin' window."

Benji complied, with the weather inclement as it was, the dining area had filled almost to capacity.

Obviously, Benji was the last in the line to be served. He stood before the servicing window with his tray as the man inside placed a dish of rice and another of black beans on it. Then the server plopped a bowl onto the tray and ladled a large scoop of vegetable soup into it.

"Is dat all?"

"No, we still got some soybeans left, lotta guys don't like 'em though."

"Soyerbeans! Wha' yuh think I am – a Chinamanese er sump'm. I don' want no soyerbeans!"

"There's more soup, if ya want a refill." the server said. Big Benji nodded and walked over to a table nearby which had an open space. He did not sit on the stout wooden bench, but set his tray on the table and then picked up the bowl with the rice, holding it to his mouth and dumping in the contents. After a few seconds of chewing, he gulped down the entire mouthful. Then he repeated the process with the bowl of beans.

The soup seemed cool enough for him to hold to his face and drink from the bowl. He slurped down half of the contents, frowned and then carried the bowl back to the serving window. The server stuck his head out "Ya want more?"

"Nah...where's da meat? Where's da meat, huh? I want *meat!*"

"There ain't no meat t'night – maybe t'marraw! Hey, all we can do is t' give you guys what the grocers give *us*. Ya know beggars can't be choosers!"

"I ain't no beggar! Ya son-a-bitch!" Benji heaved the half full soup bowl defiantly at the server. The bowl slammed against the frame of the serving window, shattering and falling to the floor. Big Benji then pulled a small whisky flask from the inside pocket of his coat and took a couple of large swigs from it.

Quickly, Brother Grady responded. He sprinted over and took Big Benji by the coat sleeve, pulling him aside.

"Now see here, me boy, didn't you read those signs we got all over the place sayin' no alcoholic beverages permitted? An' ya can't be makin' a commotion in here either! I'm sorry, but yer gonna hafta leave!" Benji resisted "Agh leave me alone!" Immediately, three very large men at nearby tables came over, standing, in front of the recalcitrant Benji. Seeing himself outnumbered and outweighed, the big man began meekly following Brother Grady to the door.

As he escorted Big Benji to the door, Brother Grady shook his head in disgust. "I hate doin' this to ya on a night like this, but I got no choice." He slipped the latch, opened the door and Big Benji walked through it into the snowy night.

"Listen," Grady called out, "There's a place over on the main street a couple blocks from here called "The Hangout". It's a bar and grill with sleeping rooms over it. If ya want me to, I'll call 'em and have 'em save ya a bed – we'll pay for it."

"I know dat place!" Benji shouted, "It's a bedbug flophouse!"

Grady sighed "Well, that's the best I can do fer ya."

"Wait a minute! Here, take this dollar bill I'm gonna toss to ya an' go to some all night coffee shop an' just keep buyin' cups of coffee. At least that way you'll stay warm."

As Benji took another step, to pick up the dollar bill, he slipped and fell into a snow bank. "Ahh yer harspertality house ain't harspiterable!" Moving a bit further through the doorway, Grady called out to Big Benji "So what is it ya don't like about us, huh?" Big Benji pulled himself up and started walking away, he turned his head back and yelled, "Arrgh – VEG'ABLE SOUP!!"

A Hamburger Eater

6/7/95

"Y'see! Wha'd I tell yuh? Now am I right or not? I'm telling you – it don't make a damn *bit* a' difference what you do or how you live...when your time is up – that's *it*! Yer gonna die! It's just that simple. It's fate. When your number comes up..."

"Oh Merven, *stop* it! That sounds so disrespectful. He was your own *brother*!"

Sarah put her hands over her ears in a feigned display of protest. Lifting one of his massive arms, Merven wiped perspiration from his brow.

"Now look, Sarah, I really did care about Jonathan. He may have just been my half-brother...an' he might have acted a little crazy at times – the way he lived 'n' how he ate 'n' all – but he *was* my brother. And I *do* care what happened to him."

"Well, then you ought to *act* like it Merven. I know he cared about you. Wasn't his fault anyway, that a tree limb blew off in that sixty mile an hour wind and killed him!"

With a momentary expression of what seemed like contrition, Merven glanced down at the floor. Then he reaffirmed his position defensively.

"You know, you *could* say that if he'd a' been as smart as you always say he was, that he shouldn't a' been out in a storm like that in the first place!"

"Now, Merven, you *know* that storm came up so sudden-like, lots of folks were caught out in it. Jonathan was running, tryin' to get back home!"

"You say he was so healthy – hell, he couldn't even outrun an ol' tree limb. Ha!"

"Not with a sixty mile an hour wind behind it!"

"Aw, he just shouldn't a' been out there in the first place. Look at me – I was smart enough t' stay inside 'n' just sit here watchin' it on TV!"

"There you go again, Merven – see, you're still mad at John for trying to get you to change your diet. And you know that Doctor Wallace keeps tellin' you – that you gotta lose weight – an' about all the fat you eat. Don't he keep tellin' you the same thing John did – t' eat more vegetables?"

"___?__, Jonathan was just what I'd call a crazy *extremist* – with ___?___ raw fruit 'n' vegetables! Scrawny little guy – couldn't even outrun a tree branch. All his preachin' to me about how I'm gonna die from what I'm eatin' an here, *he's* the one that dies! Just look at me – I'm *strong*! I can take them hundred 'n fifty pound axels at work 'n' lift 'em over my head 'n' pile 'em up on the shelves. John couldn't a' done that!   He needed t' eat hamburgers 'n' French fries like me! Ha! I'm a hamburger eater! See – I'm *strong*!"

Tri County Tribune   Monday, May eighth
   Two days ago the Tribune printed an account of the tragic death of Johnathon Slimtrim of Folsom, during the storm last Friday in which tornadic winds uprooted numerous trees and blew off several roofs. Mister Slimtrim was struck and killed instantly by a large tree limb.
   It is now our sad duty to report another tragic death in the same family. Merven Hulkheimier, younger half brother of Johnathon Slimtrim was pronounced dead on arrival at Memorial Hospital yesterday. He died at 2:45 pm. Of a massive heart attack. Merven, aged forty six is survived by his wife Sarah and a son Clyde of Loosealot, Nevada. Funeral arrangements are as yet incomplete.

The Woman at Lock and Dam 11

1995?

   It strains the very core of the shabby car's strength to negotiate hilly streets that seem to angle almost straight into the sky. There is no point in continuing to the top of the hill because the Old-Guy can tell that he is off his route. Backing the car into a driveway, he turns it around and faces downhill holding hard against the brake pedal.
   The street takes a 45 degree angle turn to the left. Victorian mansions are sprouting from the steep hillside like highly decorative flowers in a rock garden. Granite cobblestones still pave some of the narrower, winding side streets, but the Old-Guy is barely aware of the exquisitely preserved architectural flavor of this ancient river town. He finds the main route north again, stops for gas.

Already, it is late afternoon; he has been driving all day from southern Indiana. And the car seems tired – and he *is* tired…groggy – even sleepy from too many hours behind the wheel. Far enough for one day. The melon plantings in the Dakotas will wait. What the hell, planting time waited in Indiana when he was in Florida didn't it? Experienced farm hands are always in demand – so long as they get there by some reasonable time.

Driving toward the north edge of town, more hills appear. There might be a local park – somewhere close. Likely – very likely. He heads toward the river, knowing that this area at least, will be fairly flat. Traffic is merging into a main route going north. The Old-Guy follows it.

At what seems to be a couple of miles from town, the road ends abruptly into lock and dam #11. Built like a park, it appears to have been designed for public access – to watch the tugs move barges through the lock.

The parking area is great! Very few cars. He picks a spot near the most distant end, where he can stay for the night. There are even restrooms. Perfect! Heat of the day has dropped off. And it is always cooler near the water.

A tug with 6 barges waits for the lock to empty. After emerging from the restroom, the old-guy wanders over to watch the barges enter the lock. It's his first experience seeing the process of lowering and raising of a lock.

Along a public walkway, a woman is standing alone watching the lock fill. Suddenly the Old-Guy is conscious of how grubby he must look after 3 days sleeping in his car and not changing clothes. He walks past the woman, who smiles pleasantly but says nothing, her long gray hair gently flopping along the middle of her back in the river breeze. He makes an embarrassed nod as he walks past her, avoiding the direct gaze of her eyes.

She must be near 60, he figures – not a great beauty now – probably was in her younger days. But she is still pleasantly attractive – slender and well preserved for her age. An aversion to facing the difficulties of a first encounter elicit the Old-Guy's natural shyness.

As the lock begins to fill again, he walks to where he can be as close as possible to see how the lock operates. He is also positioned where he can look at the woman with the long gray hair, whenever he turns to see the front end of the barge fleet.

A stocky middled-aged man walks over from the direction of the men's room, stops and engages the woman with long gray hair in conversation. The Old-Guy turns away again, assuming this is her husband. For the next 15 minutes, they all continue to watch the barge move through the lock.

The Old-Guy leans against the steel railing; in a dream reverie watches the lock continue to fill to the top. Thumping of a barge against the side of the lock jars him back to reality. He looks again to where the woman with the long gray hair was watching the barges. She is gone. The man is still standing there in the same place, his attention focused toward the river.

With a panoramic glance, the Old-Guy turns to see the woman with the long gray hair walking toward the line of parked cars. It is now obvious that the man standing with her was not her husband. She gets into her car and starts it. In a quick sprint, the Old-Guy dashes to his own car, throws the door open and fumbles the key into the ignition. The woman with long gray hair drives past revealing an out of state license plate which passes too quickly to be read.

The Old-Guy does not start his car; he can think of nothing logical to say to the woman, even if he could catch up with her. Perhaps, he thinks, her smile at him was only because she thought he was funny-looking. The car window is open; in dejection he looks at his face in the side mirror, rubs the gray growth on his chin. "What an ugly old beat-up looking bum you are, bud! Really think she'd have anything t'do with the likes of you? C'mon – get real..." There is a long silence in his mind as though he is actually expecting to hear himself answer. "Some things are simply not meant to be," he thinks, this time out loud. "It was just that she looked like such a warm, sensitive, real kind of person and... and?"

The last touches of evening sun form a fringe of orange highlights around the gray-blue center of clouds that almost curtain the eastern sky. Heaped up like mountains and trees and bizarre faces, the clouds gently flow from one form into another. Leaning back against the car seat, the Old-Guy watches with half closed eyes relishing the cloud formations. Eventually there is a silhouette. He can almost imagine that it resembles a woman... a woman with long gray hair.

The Girl in the Red Sport Car

8/31/93

A Conversation at a stop light between a slim young girl in a red Triumph and a paunchy middle-aged man in a yellow MG.

He: "Nice car!"
She: "Yeah, I like it."
"Must have set you back quite a chunk."
"No…no, it was a gift."
"You're lucky to have such a wealthy…boyfriend?…husband?"
"Nope – my dad."
"Still lucky."
"I guess…but not for his gifts. What's that you're driving?"
"MG Midget."
"I like yellow convertibles."
"Trade yuh for your red Triumph!"
"That's not what I had in mind."
"Would you consider going to a sport car rally with me in your Triumph?…In my MG?"
"Not what I had in mind either."
"Well, how 'bout dinner and a movie, then?"
"I think you're a lot faster than your car."

The light changed – she was half a block away before the MG hit second.

The Treasure Hunter

1/3/00

"Bennie! Com'on! Git'cher butt on in here! Hurry'up!"

"What, Momma?"

"Don'chu 'w'ut me, boy. Ah'm *mad*!"

"But Momma – I didn' do nuthin' – honest!"

"Yeah – well, that ol' white-haired lady down th' block, Mrs. Griffin… you know who she is – she called me a little while ago, said you was diggin' through her trash burner again. An' she seen you a diggin' in it a couple days ago, too! She jus' don't want nobody t'git cut or nuthin', so stay out of it! Y'hear?"

"Aw, Momma – I found a penny n' a dime."

"So? I know fer a fact, if y'd go over t' Mr. Wilson's an' cut his grass, he'd give yuh a *quarter*!"

"Hey, that's no fun."

"No, it ain't fun – it's *work*! That's how people have t' git money in this world."

"But Momma – if somebody *loses* money, ain't it better if somebody else *finds* it?"

"Maybe. But it ain't sumpthin' fer a ten year old boy like you t' decide! I'll bet yer one a' them boys mister Hughes told me was scatterin' his trash, diggin' through it!"

"But Momma – that guy that fixes stuff – th' big man with th' beard – he gives us money for things we find in th' trash – anything he kin fix."

"So, you were with them boys! Bennie, wachya wanna be a hobo when yuh grow up? Jist a ol' bum?"

"Oh, no Momma – I want to drive a bus like Uncle Clyde!" "Well, yer Uncle Clyde don't dig through nobody's trash! Y'know if I tell yer papa 'bout what y' been doin', hell whop yuh up side ta' head!"

"Aw, Momma…"

"Hey, look over there – that guy walkin' up with th' red bindle… ain't that 'Trash Burner Ben'?"

"Sure looks like him – yeah… hey Ben, come on over n'warm yerself by th' fire. We got plenty a' stew left, so grab a can!"

Fire feels good, 'Night train'…kinda nippy out t'night."
"The 'boes ain't seen yuh fer a while, Ben, been doin' any good?"
"Naugh – just found a penny n' a dime tonight. That's about it."

The Dumpster King

Revised 8/99

The ragged station wagon limped its laconic way around to the rear of the Cosmic Super Store. It wheezed, then coughed out a muffled gasp when Dumpster King shut it off.

"Hey, look at that, man!" Dumpster King nudged Novicio as he pointed to the enormous dumpster. "Every time I come here, seems like they got a bigger one – must be 20 feet long! Super store, super waste!" He shook his head cynically.

With a clunk followed by a continuous squeak, the car door swung open, Dumpster King almost leaping out. Novicio trailed after him – slowly, more fascinated by the way the late afternoon sun stretched the Dumpster King's shadow so that it looked as though it was from a distorted giant.

"Common – this time of day, we got a lot to do. Discount grocery like this is even more wasteful than a regular chain store. Look, there's a smaller dumpster, so let's do it first and I'll show yuh what they're like at most'a th' stores."

Standing next to the smaller dumpster, which itself was eight feet high, Dumpster King made a springing leap, catching the tip of his right foot on the dumpster's middle seam and at the same instant grabbed the top edge. In another second he was balancing on the narrow ridge at the top. Then he was over and down into the garbage.

Novicio spotted a pallet and carried it over to the side of the dumpster. He climbed it like a short ladder and looked down at Dumpster King. "Hey, man – how d'helld' juh do that?"

"Easy, pal – just takes a little practice. Here, grab this sack a' potatoes when I throw it out. Yuh got it? There's three more sacks – I'll pitch 'em up to yuh." Novicio caught and lowered the sacks to the ground. "Watch it, I'm comin' out!"

It was like watching a huge grasshopper, Novicio thought, as the Dumpster King leaped high, hooked his fingers on the top edge and hoisted himself up and out.

"See – nothin' to it!"

"Yea right – well I ain't no spider monkey, man!"

"Agh, it's not as hard as it looks – like I said, just takes a little practice, that's all."

As they were loading the sacks into the car, Novicio scrutinized the potatoes. "What's wrong with these?", he queried.

"Oh, we'll have to pull out one or two rotten ones from each sack and maybe wash a few that were next to 'em. They're just too lazy to do it in the store – or it might cost 'em more in labor than they could get out of what they'd salvage. And then y'know that almost everything's prepackaged now, so there's probably no bin for loose potatoes anyway."

After pulling the car over close to the side of the large dumpster, and climbing up on the front fender, Dumpster King made a leap to the top edge, slid his legs over and sat there. "See – the sides are just as tall on this one, but the top edge is four inches wide, so you can't get a good enough grip to pull yourself up on it. But as long as you can get your car next to it, you're ok. Guy like you – you're probably tall enough, you wouldn't have any trouble gettin' up here from the top of that pallet – but a little shrimp like me – I'd never make it."

Novicio dragged his pallet over, climbed up and peered in, as Dumpster King dropped down inside and began quickly gathering together boxes full of a mixture of oranges and apples, celery, carrots, beets, cabbage and lettuce. Each of the heavy boxes Dumpster King lifted up to Novicio, who carried them down and packed them into the station wagon.

After filling two final boxes with more fruit and balancing them on the wide top edge, Dumpster King climbed out where the trash had been piled high in the dumpster. He jumped to the roof of the car and then to the front fender. "God damn – we got enough stuff to feed half the poor folks in this country!"

"Hey, it's not polite to call us po' folk any more – we're the 'economically deprived' now, or we're 'disadvantaged', or 'disenfranchised'. How y'like them big words I read in a magazine?"

Dumpster King gave a slight laugh. "Yeah – big words from big turds! I'm not sayin' this t' insult you, Novicio, but it seems t'me, most of the time I hear people with a lot of big words comin' *out* of their mouths, it's t' cover up the fact that they don't have a lot of big thoughts *inside* their heads! Oh well – can't argue with what you said. Guess a guy's gotta be politically correct...."

Surveying the load of food in the car, Novicio offered a comment of amazement. "Y'know sumpthin' – those apples just got tiny little bruises and the oranges, all's wrong with them is they got a few brown specks on 'em. Bet every one of 'em's gonna be ok."

"Sure, that's why I been gettin' this stuff. None of it looks real pretty, but even the lettuce and cabbages – they just need to be trimmed up."

With a nervous glance around him, Novicio plopped himself down in the car and closed the door. He and the Dumpster King continued to converse through the car window. "Hey, man – we got enough of a load now?"

"What's th' matter, Novicio? Yuh act like yer scared or sumpthin'."

"Well – what if somebody comes out and sees us?"

"Agh, don't get so nervous. Sure once in a while that'll happen. I think outta the hundreds of times I've been dumpster-divin' over the years, maybe a couple dozen times someone's come out. If they tell me to get out – I don't argue with 'em. Just get in the car and drive away. Then lots of times I'll wait til they're gone and come back. Depends on what I was gettin'. I remember one time some smart-ass kid came out 'n got real nasty. Had to give him a lecture on our American waste economy. I don't think he liked it too much – didn't even listen. Most people in this country – they don't even know what's goin' on – the amount of waste. But they wouldn't care anyway. If any number of 'em *were* really concerned, things wouldn't be the way they are."

As a fly landed on his chin, Novicio swatted at it and seemed to shake himself back into the conversation. "Well – I still don't get it. Why are they throwin' this stuff out? With all the hungry people out there – and lots of 'em not able to even afford to buy fresh food like this – why don't they just *give* it away?"

Dumpster King peered in the car window at Novicio, his voice dripping with caustic cynicism. "They don't give it away, 'cause they think if they did, everyone'd stop buyin' the perfect lookin' stuff... an' then wait til it *all* got spotted like this so's they could get it free!"

"Aw, that's *nutz.*"

"*I* know it – an' *you* know it, but you can't make the store managers believe it! Besides, they build in the cost of loss like this into the price everyone pays inside the store, anyway. Y'know sumpthin' – just about everybody in this country's livin' in la-la land! Well, we better quit gabbin' and get rollin'."

As Dumpster King reached up to try to lift down the last two boxes, a deep voice roared from behind the car at the back end of the dumpster. "HEY – you can just put it ALL back in there!" Stan Machoman, the store manager stood there with his hands on his hips. He was scowling. His black bushy moustache was scowling. All two-hundred twenty-five pounds of his muscular six-foot two inch frame seemed to be scowling.

Suddenly in a confrontational mood, Dumpster King shouted back to him. "Haven't you got the message yet that it's a crime against humanity and a crime against planet Earth to waste – to waste anything still usable?"

"Look punk, YOU'RE PUTTIN' THAT STUFF BACK – *UNDERSTAND*?!"

"I understand that you don't own this dumpster – and the only one who has any right to tell us to get out of it or put anything back into it, is the one who owns it!"

"Listen, bud – I'm not gonna put up with no more a'yer bullshit! Didja' hear what I said to yuh? PUT THAT STUFF BACK! If I gotta come over there and put it in myself, I'm gonna put *you* in with it! Got that?"

"Yeah – ok – ok. I heard you – loud and clear. How could I help from hearin' it?" With that last response, Dumpster King reached up and swiftly grabbed the last two boxes, setting them down on the hood of the car. In almost the same instant, he jumped down, swung open the car door, reached for the key and gave it a twist as he slid inside. Amazingly, the engine started instantly and at the same moment he pulled the car into drive. Lurching forward, the momentum forced the two boxes on the hood to slide up close to the windshield. With his head out the window to see around the boxes, Dumpster King glanced back at his antagonist.

Machoman stood with his hands still on his hips, but his scowl had been replaced by a look of astonished disbelief.

"What're you gonna do now?" Novicio asked.

"We'll just pull around front and stop in the parking lot and stick those boxes inside. I don't think he'll try to follow us."

They were moving slowly, looking for an empty parking space. Without warning, a car backed out directly in their path. Dumpster King jammed on the brakes. The car came to a stop, but the two boxes on the hood didn't. The other car's driver, a young woman got out and came over to them.

"I'm *terribly* sorry! Really, I just didn't see you. I...I don't know why..."

"Neither do I," Novicio muttered under his breath, laughing. "Nobody's used to seeing a rollin' vegetable box!"

By now the two scavengers were standing in front of their car viewing the spilled oranges and apples, some of which were still rolling away.

"Here, let me help you gather up the fruit." The woman offered.

"Oh, don't worry about it – that's ok. We can take care of it."

As her emotionality eased, the woman gained some perspective on the scenario. She looked again at the boxes and the spilled fruit. "I don't understand – say... where'd all this fruit come from? And those boxes... how'd they get..."

"Lady... even if I tried to explain it to you," Dumpster King offered, "you'd never believe me. So let's just say that it was 'manna from heaven' that missed its mark a little bit."

Radio Man

9/2/93

Mr. Odmann raised his eyebrows, smiled slightly and shrugged his shoulders. "You never met Walter? You know he died...Walter was an electrical genius! Almost another Nicole Tessla. Why he..."

Kent shook his head. "No," he interrupted, "can't say I ever met him. At least I don't recall..." He wasn't really concentrating on what Mr. Odmann was saying – thinking how silly his expression looked. "Oh wait...wasn't that the old guy you introduced me to a couple of years ago who lived in the basement of his sister's house down on 20th street? I just couldn't bring his name to mind."

"Sure; I knew you'd remember." Mr. Odmann smiled broadly. "You wanted to buy all those old radios he had down there."

Kent nodded. "Yeah, and he kept saying to me: 'You collect radios? What do you want with those old battery sets? You don't know how to make them work, do you? Wait 'til I'm gone and then you can probably have them.' I got a fairly good look at some of them – there were several very rare, super valuable sets. Tubes were still in them – just needed cleaning up."

Mr. Odmann clasped his hands piously. "Poor Walter – he was an unrecognized genius…that man could rewind any motor you brought him – and he was an expert on attempts at perpetual motion machines. But such an unhappy person, living alone all those years that way. I didn't even know he'd died until a couple of days ago. It's been almost a month. But you know I don't read obituaries; a friend told me about it. Guess you'll want to go and see his sister, right?"

"Right…but – it's been so long since I was there, I doubt that I could find the house again. And then I never met his sister, either. How about meeting me there? You know I'd take you in the car, but you won't ride in cars – that's pretty far for you to walk."

"Oh, I've waked it many times before – but I'll put on my roller skates. I can skate 8 miles an hour. Then I can plan to meet you there in about 40 minutes."

"Tell me," Kent inquired, "you know his siter pretty well – what do you think she'll want for those radios?"

"Oh, I don't know – not very much.   Maybe 15 or 20 dollars apiece…"

"That would be great if you could talk her into not over twenty each."

Kent was waiting in his car when Mr. Odmann skated up to the driver's side window and pointed down the block to a typically narrow, two story Victorian brick house. "It's the one with the green shutters and brown trim. I'll take off my skates and walk over with you."

The elderly woman who answered the door appeared frail and tired. "Hello, Mr. Odmann – why how nice to see you!"

Mr. Odmann clasped his hands piously. "First I want to say that I'm so sorry I didn't get to the funeral, but I just heard about Walter passing away two days ago."

"Oh that's alright – I understand. You know we didn't have any announcement in the paper…there's so little family left. Uh…who's your friend?"

"This is Kent – he was down in Walter's basement apartment once and talked to him about buying those old radios Walter had down there. Walter didn't want to sell them then, but…"

"I'm just wondering if I could possibly buy them from you now." Ken interjected. His eyes had already flitted around the room and spotted a 1925 Synchrodyne reposing on top of a bookshelf. The case was still good and the three dials were intact. He walked over to the set and lifted the lid. There was dust inside, but all six tubes were in it. "What about his one?"

"That old thing? That's one Walter brought up here for my mother to listen to…must have been back in 1935 – before I even left and got married. I don't think it works and never could figure out how to hook up all those wires. You can just take it, if you want it."

"Well…thanks very much, ma'am. That's very kind of you; I appreciate it…uh…what about all of the other radios in the basement?"

"That old filthy stuff? I want to tell you – when I went down there a few days after Walter died and tried to look through the piles and boxes and shelves full of dirty, moldy old trash, I started sneezing and coughing so bad I thought I'd never get over it! Oh, it was horrible! You wouldn't have wanted such awful junk, believe me. I gave it all away to a junk man out in the alley."

Kent Atwater's eyes fell and his jaw dropped so far it looked dislocated. Mr. Odmann looked at Kent. He stepped back, raised his eyebrows, smiled slightly…and just shrugged his shoulders.

Preface for "Mineral Man"

It was probably in early 1959 when I first met Rudi Brumenshenkel at a Natural Hygiene convention in St. Louis, Mo. Besides Natural Hygiene we had a great deal in common – organic gardening, a love for antique cars, obscure philosophies and technologies. But the one thing that Rudi knew about that I didn't know, was soil mineralization. He had already met and spent some time talking to Albert Carter Savage.

How Rudi Brumenshenkel met "Dr." Savage, I am not quite certain; possibly through having first met John Lyle, "Dr." Savage's field man, who was always out and about dealing with local farmers, making soil tests, etc. Rudi is now (At this writing 7/2/21) 94 years old and very hard of hearing. I would find it very difficult to communicate a question to him about his introduction to "Dr." Savage, so I will probably never know the answer to how they met. Rudi may have told me years ago, but if he did, time has managed to erase that information from my memory.

At some point, probably in the 1940s, "Dr." Savage, interestingly, established the Albert Carter Savage Foundation (primarily for the promotion of and dissemination of literature for soil mineralization). The foundation still exists and can be found listed on the internet.

Mineral Man

6/30/21

A brief memory of Albert Carter Savage and those associated with him, partially recopied from a fragmented paper dated: 3/24/1979.

From his first step down the rock-strewn, mud-rut road, I knew there was something – perhaps esoteric about him – a wisdom, a curiously subtle finality to so much of what we seek. He was a slightly ragged epitome of the "Kentucky Colonel", with goatee, black string tie and black jacket.

He was standing at the edge of a field, tall, erect, white hair to his shoulders – smiling with the serenity of great age. And he greeted me like the prodigal son.

We talked as though we had been friends for all my short life. And the days and weeks of his generosity revealed a wealth of knowledge about the soil – about minerals that make good plants, good animals, good people – about life and the purpose of life.

One day, I asked him "Why are we here?" "I can't answer that," he replied, "Only *you* can – someday."
I never knew if he were being evasive or brilliant. Perhaps he was playing a little game with me.

I thought about it as we walked to the great spring that flowed from the cave on his ancestral Kentucky farm – and I thought about it later as I was helping in his garden – and I thought about it watching him milk his goats – and in the evening as he played an ancient fiddle – watching the summer sun dropping slowly, like a glowing ember in a campfire; time seemed to have stood still there.

Once, with boyish curiosity, I asked him how old he was.

"Quite old – yes, quite old…" he said.

Later, I calculated that he must have been an astonishing 85. He did look old, but nothing like *that* old.

He drove me to town in his battered 1948 Hudson to get books he recommended from the University of Kentucky library. "They don't like me there," he offered. "They read books, I write them"

When we returned, the soft humming of the locusts in the warm night was strangely incongruous as was the ramshackle farmhouse with his "lab" in the attic and the "test mice" that ate different amounts of various wheat sprouts raised on varying mineral mixes. The mice ran free in and out of the woodwork – confusing and a little frustrating…answers that were never definitive – only with the results.

Once in his reference to his discovery of the importance of "minimum mineral standard" soil supplementation, he said to me, "The doctors gave me up to die at 40. But now they're all dead and I'm still alive."

"President Roosevelt's personal physician came here in the 1930s to learn about minerals. They had given her only 3 weeks to live. She ate from my mineralized garden, went home and made her own mineral garden – lived a long time."

Once, when we were walking along the entrance road to his farm, "Dr." Savage pointed to a series of long stone steps that now led to nowhere.

"My family had one of the 7 original land grant colleges here. Those steps led to the university buildings that occupied this entire long field. The buildings were all made of wood – frame construction. Back in the mid 1800s there was a disastrous fire that burned all of the college buildings as well as the dormitories located just a few feet down the hillside. Everything burned except part of one of the dormitories at the farthest end. That's where I was born and raised. My family decided not to rebuild the university since by that time there were already other colleges and universities established nearby in much more accessible locations. Those steps are really all that's left of the original Savage Land Grant College."

He seemed neither sad nor regretful just a mood of acceptance for that which had occurred before his birth.

More than once, I can recall Albert Carter Savage stating in reference to a biblical quotation about "God breathing the breath of life into a handful of dirt." That "It couldn't happen today – most soils now are too mineral deficient."

Albert Carter Savage had a truly brilliant mind, but his writing style left much to be desired. His books were merely booklets. And one must realize that the man was born into the Victorian era; his writing style reflects that era and is difficult reading - not clear and concise. Listening to him speak in person about soil mineralization was a much clearer and more informative method than trying to read his "books".

Although the photographs in one of "Dr." Savage's booklets did show clearly the difference in the bones taken from animals raised on different soil types, it was not as convincing or compelling a reason for soil mineralization as actually holding these same bones in one's hands.

There were three sets of bones – all femur bones from the same type of cow, raised on different soil types. The first which "Dr." Savage showed me was from an animal raised entirely on the typical mineral-depleted Kentucky farm soil. It was noticeably small and felt light as a bird's bone from all of the porosity throughout the length of the bone shaft.

The next bone I was shown was from the same kind of animal raised on grass and grains from a farm in Deaf Smith County, Texas (the "county without a toothache"). The Deaf Smith bone was somewhat larger, *much* heavier and with relatively little porosity in the shaft.

But the final bone that "Dr." Savage showed me was from the same variety of cow raised on mineralized soil in Kentucky. That bone was only slightly larger than the Deaf Smith bone, but was even heavier and with hardly any of the porosity of the other two bones. It was the extreme density of the mineralized bone (its difference in weight) that was so convincing when you held those bones in your own hands.

Albert Carter Savage spoke moderately fast and emphatically: "For more than a century, the farmers here have been taking out of the soil and not putting anything back into it – or at least not enough. Their crops are often ravaged by insects – the soil is so mineral deficient, don't you know."

He continued: "Right here in Kentucky we have three of the four mineral rocks that I use in the minimum mineral standard recommendation program. The first is what I call "black rock" – it's a dark mineral-rich shale with streaks of yellow sulfur. It can be found in many parts of the state exposed in highway cuts. The second is a form of limestone also rich in magnesium and many of the minor and trace elements. I call it "cave rock" – it's full of fossils like brachiopods and crinoid stems."

"The third rock I call "potash marl", which is a soft, greenish shale-like material with its own list of beneficial minor and trace elements. It's also called: "greensand". The fourth rock has major, minor and trace elements to complement the first three. It's called "phosphate rock", or we can use what they refer to as: colloidal phosphate. It has the advantage that it doesn't need to be ground up in a hammer mill. And it's minerals are in an available form – it doesn't have to be composted like the others, don't you know?"

"Then we take the recommended amount of each rock type, as determined by a flame-photometer soil sample analysis test, compost the powdered rocks in a compost heap with organic residues and both aerobic and anaerobic bacteria. That's so that as the bacteria begin to break down the organic residues, they create humic acid, which dissolves out some of the minerals into a soluble, available form that the plants can use immediately. Of course, most of the mineral content stays in reserve so that the mineralization will last for many years, don't you know?"

"Although each plant has it's own particular mineral balance preference, which can be and often is different from all other plants, we have to create an average balance where the minerals are present and then let each kind of plant absorb whatever it needs."

"Also, the mineral mix that we create is based on a study of the mineral content of human remains done from the mineral content of people worldwide. We, of course have to base our work on averages. So if an individual has a dietary need for a certain mineral predominance, then we recommend that their garden plot be mineralized into four sections, each with a predominance of one of the four mineral rocks. That way they can plant across the mineral rows and choose whichever vegetable or fruit seems to taste best to them. Now, am I making myself clear?"

I nodded "yes", but in fact, I was still somewhat confused. But I knew that later, I would get it all figured out.

At times, Albert Carter Savage seemed to give the impression that in some small way, by trying to teach the essentials of soil mineralization, he was in effect continuing the Savage Land-grant College of two centuries past. I and a few others were his "students".

The "'doctor' of sick soils" could talk longer than I could listen. And some of his words seem to still be bouncing around inside my head, like forever echoes that never diminish.

I can remember "Dr." Savage's wife – a slender, pleasant-featured woman several years younger than her husband, but then, also in her 80s. I cannot recall her name, though I probably knew it, but I can picture her yet with long hair that still had lots of black streaks in it. She was always congenial to me, but stayed very much in the background, so I never really got to know her.

On my second visit to the Savage farm (about 1967), I was driving a rather low slung 1948 Hilman and decided that the ruts in the Savage farm road were too deep and large rocks protruded too high for my car to attempt to drive in. I had parked my car near the county road and was in the process of walking toward the Savage house, when I met two other persons walking out. One was the well-known artist, Henry Faulkner and the other was his sister Lois. Henry was then 41 and Lois 52. Since Henry and I were both artists (painters) and had a love for Victorian furnishings, our common interest made us immediate friends. Lois Faulkner had a great love for and knowledge of early country music and became the one who   helped me develop an appreciation for and a strong interest in early country music (largely Jimmy Rodgers).

A year or two later, Louis Faulkner became an interesting and knowledgeable traveling companion when Rudi Brumenshenkel and I took trips to Texas and other locations. Lois remained a permanent fixture at the Brumenshenkel family farm in Ohio for at least a decade. After her brother Henry died in an auto accident at the age of only 58, Lois then went to California where she remained until her death, years later.

Before the third trip which I made to visit Albert Carter Savage, I was at the time living in my art studio which I had built from an old chicken's house on my parent's property in Crestwood, Mo. As I remember it, I was doing something with one of my antique cars in the parking area below the house when my mother called out to me that I had a long distance phone call.

I ran up to the house and picked up the receiver. "Hello?"

"Yes, hello. This is Albert! Calling from Nicholasville, Kentucky!"

I had never thought of him as "Albert", but I realized instantly who it was and I felt truly honored to be called by this great man! (He didn't even have a phone at his farm and had called me from town!)

"Why don't you come and visit me and we'll talk about building mineral gardens?"

Ah, how could I refuse? It was not a convenient time for me to make the 400 mile trip, but I left within a few days arriving at the Savage farm in late summer. I could understand why "Dr." Savage had called – hoping that I might be the one to carry on his practical and experimental work with soil mineralization.

Both of his sons were Christian ministers in their 50s and 60s and neither of them seemed to have the slightest interest in carrying on the soil mineralization work. John Lyle, his field man was dead. Rudi Brumenshenkel, though knowledgeable about mineralization, did not have the educational background to be able to write about it or to lecture on the subject. It would, then, be left to me.

And, "Dr." Savage knew that I had gone out of my way to visit other soil scientists, like the famous William A. Albrecht whom I had visited at his Missouri University office; obtaining volumes of his articles and other printed materials after a friendly, informative discussion about soil remineralization.

The third visit I made to the Savage farm, I brought along much of my painting materials, intending to stay again in the 2 room cabin that Roosevelt's physician had had constructed there. I was in the cabin only a day or two, sorting through a small filing cabinet that had been left there by "Dr." Savage's field man, John Lyle. (I met John Lyle only once, briefly during my first trip there and he had, unfortunately died from exposure to the cold while trying to live in an unheated rented room the next winter.)

The file cabinet contained dozens of soil analyses from various farms and the mineral recommendations which "Dr." savage had prepared for each field. I loaded the papers into my vehicle, since "Dr." Savage had another set.

I was prepared to stay for an extended visit, however, Albert Jr. learned of my presence and summarily "evicted" me. I then stayed at the nearby farm of Henry Faulkner, my artist friend from the previous visit.

The last visit I ever made to see "Dr." Savage was when he was 95. He had been recently kicked by a milk cow several feet across the barn and suffered 3 broken ribs. Although his eyesight and hearing were still good, he was much thinner than I had remember him being. He told me that his wife had died the year before. She had been induced to go into the city of Lexington to live with relatives in a much less harsh city life. When she was no longer able to have access to the mineralized garden produce and began consuming the SAD (Standard American Diet), it took little time for her to succumb to some "infectious" disease which the physicians treated with toxic drugs that ended her life. He seemed not as bitter about losing his wife as he was about the well-meaning relatives who had induced her to leave.

On that last visit, I was on my way to Florida from Ohio and it was already cold November or early December. "Dr." Savage invited me stay for the night, since it was already late in the day when I arrived there. I can recall trying to sleep on a couch in the "dining room" of the house, which was separated from the kitchen by a pair of multipaned glass doors. The only wood stove was in the kitchen and it served to warm the whole house. But even with the glass doors opened, very little heat entered the room in which I was sleeping.

That was in 1968 or 1969 and I was never able to take the time to try to visit "Dr." Savage again. By then, I had my own domestic responsibilities. About 9 years later, my friend Rudi Brumenshenkel, informed me that he had heard that "Dr." Savage had died at 104.

Now, I begin to understand "Dr." Savage's modesty about age, as I too view the cosmic clock a little more closely – a hundred years was just a laughable flash of a fraction of an infinitely tiny fraction of a second in the ticking of the cosmic clock.

But my question to him: "Why are we here?" still remains unanswered (unsolved). So I will never know whether he was truly brilliant or just smart enough to know that there was no way to know... perhaps that in itself *is* brilliance.

Addendum

At closing in on 91 myself, I have decided why we're here; it is simply to learn to love – to love each other, to love ourselves, to love the animals and plants – to learn to love truth – and beauty! And also, to learn discipline and to expect nothing, but to be grateful for anything.

There may be more, but at nearly 91, it has escaped me.

The Old Man and the Packard Limousine

9/1/93

We used to hide behind bushes along the sidewalk and throw tiny pebbles at him... not large enough to hurt anyone, just an annoyance. He was small and lean with a frozen, unemotional expression. It never changed... even when we got a resounding thud off his top hat. Both he and his chauffeur simply ignored us – the sensible thing to do, because it caused us to soon tire of the game.

But for years we would still watch him slowly walk to the car and be driven off. We never knew where he went or what he did when he got there.

Eventually old men always die. Sometimes their cars die too. But the Packard limousine reposed in the garage behind his house long after he was gone. It stayed there until a shopping center went up on the property. Years went by before I saw it again in an open fronted steel shed – not too much worse for all the passage of time. True, there was a lot of surface rust – and moths had eaten the wool upholstery badly in places. Windows were fogged and yellowed between the layers of safety glass. Running board rubber mats were hard and brittle and shrunken. So was the Pantesote cloth top – and it had pulled away from the body allowing light to stream through moth holes in the headliner.

But it was the same car, I was sure of it... I could tell from the odd tread pattern on the tires. I bought it and dragged it home. A neighbor helped me push it into the back of the barn and for a long time I had fond dreams of being driven around in that old limo. But I enjoyed just sitting in the back seat – enjoyed just looking at the car.

Someday my age will probably be the same as the original owner's was and I wonder if I will ever act like him – or maybe even look like him...?

Say... my grandfather's top hat fits me perfectly. Wouldn't that be the thing to wear when I sit in the back of that 1930 Packard...? You know what... one of these days I'm going to put a battery in the car and some gas in the tank and start it up... fix the flat on the left rear. Hey, I forgot there's even a complete chauffeur's uniform put away that I bought at a Salvation Army store years ago. Still my size. That would be just what I'd need if I drove the car around... right?

I'm thinking, though... if I did that... I couldn't sit in the back seat wearing the top hat. Well – you can't really drive a car from the back seat anyway, even though a lot of people try...

An Extra Chair, A Double Bed

2/08/08

It was with a smile and just a hint of lilting laugh that Judith offered her usual greeting to the start of another autumn evening. And then, singing in a half-hearted, rendition of an unknown nursery rhyme, she began walking with almost ethereal cat-paw footsteps toward the workroom door. She opened it silently.

Jacob Silberbaum sat concentrating on a nearly repaired German wall clock movement; the ticking of dozens of clocks sounded a delicate, almost musical tone somewhere between a symphony and a complete cacophony.

A few moments passed, But Judith's presence remained unnoticed until the elderly woman placed her hand gently on Jacobs shoulder, bent over and touched her lips to his cheek.

"I love you..."

That was her daily, simplistic and only verbal communication when she entered the room.

Jacob smiled slightly, reached over and touched her hand, continuing to watch the even release on the clocks verge.

"It's almost finished, " he told her with satisfaction.

"Oh good!" she replied, still with their hands touching.

The shocking striking on the hour of all the chime clocks nearly at once was like a pointed hammer piercing into Jacob's brain. He sat back, intently alert. Then he looked over at the large Ithica calendar clock; the big hand pointed to twenty-seven.

"September twenty-seventh! I forgot to mark off the day yesterday on the calendar! Would you cross if off for me Judith?"

She picked up a black marker and in motion that was like drifting – floating, went over to the calendar hanging on the wall and put a heavy "X" across the number twenty-six: then number twenty-seven.

"It's hard to believe," she said, "but 1987 is nearly over. Of course, one day is like another to me anyhow, you know."

Jacob returned his attention to the wall clock movement. He thought about the hour and stood up.

"Why, it's seven o'clock! It's almost time for my brother to come over."

"Yes, it's getting late, dear. Perhaps you should stop now. I'll put on some water and the two of you can enjoy a bit of tea. Would you like that?"

"I would. It's turning chilly earlier now and my brother will like it as well."

"Ill be out in the kitchen. Chamomile again?"

"Yes, that's fine."

"Alright... Oh Jacob... why do you call Bill your brother?"

Jacob's face took on a perplexed expression.

"Why... why... it's... uh... it's just because he *is*! You know we've been hanging around together since we were boys. We didn't need to have the same mother, but we're just as close as if we'd had. We grew up together; we have the same interests. I think we even talk alike."

"But you two don't *look* alike."

Judith delicately picked up a very old framed photograph of the two boys standing next to their bicycles. The two young men appeared to be in their late teens. With a flourish that was almost lost in its ephemerality, she carried the picture over to Jacob's work table, placing it in front of where he was standing. Then Judith laughed a silly giggle.

"See, he's *very* tall, with straight dark hair; those angular Scottish features...and you... ," she laughed again, "you're so short and you have sandy, wavy hair. And your features are like mine – Mediterranean – soft and rounded. But you're both *very* nice looking boys."

Silence ensued, broken only by the muted tick-ticking of the clocks. The sharp regularity of the clocks was in poignant contract to the dismal disarray of the dust-hung cobwebs that draped off curtains, window frames and even from the ceiling itself . Hazy glass panes with a thirty year film filtered the slanting rays of the setting sun. With a sudden altered attentiveness, Jacob listened for the footsteps on the porch.

"It's getting late, he offered", repeating Judith's observation. "I wonder why he isn't here yet. I'm getting tired, Judith. Think I'll lay down until he arrives."

"Oh yes," she agreed, 'you've ben working on those clocks nearly all day. I'll fluff up the pillows on the bed and you can sit up there and read for a while if you want to."

"Thank you, dear Judith."

The couple moved into the bedroom, where the woman placed both pillows against the double bed's headboard. Then she began unlacing Jacob's shoes as he sat on the edge of the bed.

"No – don't take them off. Just put a piece of this newspaper under my feet when I lie down there. Then I won't have to retie my shoes when bill gets here. He should be here any minute now. I can almost hear him calling out, 'Hey Jake!'."

When he had been propped up on the bed reading the newspaper for a few minutes, the old man slowly allowed his grip to loosen and the pages of the newsprint fell to the floor. Not even being conscious of having dropped the paper, Jacob lay with his eyes half open, mind only half-conscious of where he was or even who he might be.

Then he felt Judith's warm, soft, rotund body close to his own, He could even feel her heart beat next to his chest and he reached over to embrace the small female form that pressed in next to him. With his eyes completely closed now and his body and mind fully relaxed, the wiry old clockmaker's breast began slow, rhythmic pulsations. Judith smiled with her arm rising and falling. She giggled again like a little child.

"Mmmm, the delicious taste of being here…"

"Yes…" Jacobs reply was just above a whisper. "I'm feeling so comfortable with you here next to me. Nothing could be sweeter. I wish it could last forever."

"But Judith, even when we die?"

"Yesss… oh, yesss…"

The thought went through Jacob's mind that her voice was as light and soft as the rising mist of the dawn of a warm spring day.

There was a sudden thumping noise out on the front porch that jarred Jacob's mind back to reality.

"Bill? Bill… that you?"

But Jacob's inquiry went unanswered.

"It was probably just that shovel I stood up out there yesterday getting blown over by the wind. Judith, would you be kind enough to go look... and then go out on the street. Bill might have tripped an fallen. After all, he is getting old and perhaps a bit fragile."

Judith walked almost silently through the house with a feather-light step, until her footsteps were no more audible than the distant ticking of the clocks. There was an interval of ten, then fifteen minutes as the time distorted and jumbled his thoughts – until Jacob began seeing himself as a tangled, disjointed doppelganger, floating and fumbling – clawing – at the air when he tried to arise. Finally, he got up with such impulse of urgency that it forced him pounding to the door and then out into the fast darkening evening chill.

He began a sudden running down the street – looking from side to side – calling out both Judith's name and that of his friend. Frantically, the octogenarian ran through the streets of the town until he reached the cemetery at the edge of the incorporated area.

Although there were night-birds in the trees next to the paved path which Jacob traversed, not one avian call broke the deathly breathlessness. The massive tombstones seemed to reach out to try to impede the old man's progress; he felt as though he were trying to walk through a field of sticky taffy that hung on to each foot, making progress slow, if not impossible.

When he had reached a familiar massive pylon of a grave marker, he paused and looked up at the Star of David etched into the uppermost face. With a hoarseness derived of the near-exhausting run, Jacob spoke aloud the family name below the Jewish star.

"Wasser... it's Wasser!"

There was a surprise to his expression – as though he had never seen the marker before. Then he read the names on the row of individual headstones below the centrally placed pylon.

"Henry, Edith, Roger,... Judith. Oh, Nooo – Judith!"

Twice he repeated her name with an undertoned scream of horrified, desperate agony. Then he reiterated: "Judith... Judith..." again and again and again in whining, almost whispered gasps of regularity.

With a final half-crazed, tear-drenched, choking sob, Jacob bent down and read once more, as he had so many times in the past, the dates of her birth and death.

"Born April 22nd, 1913 – Died June 10th, 1959."

Jacob threw himself down against the ground in front of the headstone – flailing the air with wild gesticulations – pounding his fists against the earth. He accentuated his arm motions with piercing, unrestrained screams.

The wailing from his agonizing screams shattered the evening still like a sword being thrust through the heart of some unwary and underserving wretch. Still thrashing and screaming, the normally placid clockmaker moved a few rows over to another grave marker. He paused in a near stupor to read aloud the name and dates on that stone as well.

"William McLarkin! Born August 11th, 1907 – Died November 15th, 1958. Arghhh – aaghergh!!"

Jacob's screaming again exploded, penetrating the evening calm with a fierce intensity that invaded the home of the Spynstehr sisters. Emily breathed out a shocked, sudden expulsion.

"He's at it again! It's *terrible*, Lydia – just *terrible*!"

Her sister nodded – then looked sadly out the window toward the graveyard.

"Doctor John wants to have him committed." Emily offered her comment with a tone of approval.

"Oh, Emily, it wouldn't do him any good; really it wouldn't."

Emily's face took on an expression almost like a question mark. The large, dark eyes in Lydia's usually happy countenance welled up with heartfelt tears.

"I wish I could just go and put my arms around that poor old man. Maybe I could comfort him a little."

"And maybe he would kill you… *more* than a little."

"Emily! He wouldn't hurt me; he isn't hurting anybody."

Still shaking her head in a rejection of Lydia's appraisal, Emily raised her hands to cover her ears.

"Emily? Emily, you *know* he's just a frustrated, lonely old man – he can't deal with the reality of things. You and I can't even imagine what his daily life is like."

"Oh, I suppose I understand. But maybe they think he'll hurt *himself*."

"If he's going to hurt himself – well… he's already done it. Anyway, tomorrow he'll be alright."

"What do you mean?"

"Oh… just… never mind. Besides, if they took him away, then who would fix our clocks?"

"Lydia! It would be for his *own* good!"

Lydia's face forged an age-shocked expression of disapproval. "No, no, sister... I don't think you're right." There was a quaver in her voice - a quaver that extended beyond the vocal dysphonia of age. "Perhaps it's simply that he has to suffer a periodic agony of reality to be able to continue enjoying the ecstasy of his dreams."

"Well, I don't know if he – or anyone, for that matter is ever ecstatic."

Emily became silent as she watched Lydia move over to a chair with richly brocaded gold and red upholstery.

"Don't sit in that chair without putting a covering over it! Do you hear?"

Lydia ignored her sister's agitated, fierce caveat.

"What are you trying to do, Emily, preserve it for posterity? Would *that* be ecstatic?"

The two sisters stood facing each other, one smiling slightly, the other with a frown.   Emily's lower lip trembled – just perceptibly before she spoke.

"They say it's all God's plan – ecstasy, misery – isn't it?"

"Emily... how can anyone dare to have the audacity to attempt to speak intelligently to the most arcane, obscure issues in the entire realm of earthly human existence?"

"Oh, stop being a college professor, Lydia... you know I can't *stand* your lording your education over me!"

"That's *not* what I'm trying to do. It's just... this struggle between life and death for Jacob Silberbaum. Death is pulling him apart... as though life could no longer exist in any form – after the dagger of death has severed life from its corpus."

Emily sneered: "Some claim to know that life continues on; some claim to know that it doesn't."

"Huh! Well, there are at least a few of us left who are honest enough to say that we don't know. Anyhow, the strength of someone's personality *can* remain with us after their death, in the form of various arts and achievements – as well as in our memories. At least it does for a while. If we're perceptive, we can avail ourselves of the remains of that expired personality – even if we're not in any way able to knowingly affect *it*. But maybe we wouldn't want to anyway."

"Lydia – this is all silliness – none of what you're saying makes that old man any less insane."

Lydia looked down again. "I guess not." She began to fidget with a rubber band.

"Anyway, at this age, I suppose it will all soon be a moot question. And then, no one will ever know what he sees or hears or feels."

"Well, they don't really know *now*."

"No, Emily, you're right. It's... the most extreme, horrible conundrum imaginable. And I suppose the great mystic Masters have had the last word: Nirvana."

"Oh nonsense! Some doctor could cure him." "No doctor could cure the disease of *severance*."

"Yeah, well nobody cut his *head* off."

"But they might just as well have. Now listen, Emily... tune your brain in to what I'm saying for a minute. You and I... we've lived out the existence of our puny little lives, seeing the world only through the slitted windows of our own narrow minds – never having to touch the obnoxious decadence of the humanity that surrounds us. We can hide from it: we can pull the blankets over our heads and pretend that it doesn't exist. And we'll probably do that all the rest of our lives – until we shrivel up with a prune of a soul – a spirt that has dried out into the dust of eternity!"

Emily's countenance relaxed. She reached over and touched her sister's cheek in a softened gesture of acquiescence.

"I don't know, Lydia... I don't know if you're right or wrong. I guess I don't even know what ecstasy is any more... if I *ever* knew. I wonder if there really *is* ecstasy in a dream."

"I suppose," Lydia began again, "that finding ecstasy depends on who occupies the castles in your dreams... or perhaps... it depends on whether you still dare to *have* dreams."

Epilogue:

This story does not have any kind of "moral"; perhaps not even much of a "lesson". It does, however, have a point – that point being our inability to distinguish the sometime subtle difference between the reality of external things and that of the reality within the mind – blending the two until there is no longer any way to understand the overlappings.

At first, I described this story as a psychological "horror" story, but perhaps it's more of a dramatization of the sometimes absurd, ironic paradoxes of human life.

Jacob is always a little "insane", but not enough that anyone who encounters him would realize it. Only when he becomes *completely* sane – forced into the realization of a brutal sanity – only then, does everyone believe that he is totally *in*sane!

Joaquin (aka "Backwoods Jack")

Bar Talk

11/27/93

"You been over to the theater yet?" the Folksinger asked his friend.

"Yeah – they got a gal by the name of Judy Collins coming there for the next two weeks. They say she's pretty good – even has a record out!"

The Folksinger's friend opened his guitar case, took out a beat-up instrument and strummed a few chords.

"You want to stay here at the Left Bank tonight?" he asked.

"I don't care – may as well. There's nothing at the theater – or anywhere else on the square I'd want to hear."

When the Folksinger took out his own guitar, they played a chorus of "Wildwood Flower" together, the Folksinger singing a verse with chorus. One person at the next table looked over. No one else seemed to notice.

"I'm going to the bar to get a beer." The Folksinger's friend stood up – then hesitated. "Want me to bring an extra glass?"

"Sure. As long as we're going to be here a while, it'll look better. If I'm going to have to drink it, just put about a half a glass in mine. You know how I hate that stuff!"

The entertainment was beginning with the spotlight glaring on a six foot young amazon with long blonde hair. She belted out a stream of ribald blues numbers in a harsh, throaty, sexy voice. Her blues guitar accompaniment was brash and simple.

The Folksinger and his friend listened throughout the set.

"How would you like to have a girlfriend *that* size?" the Folksinger's friend asked him.

"Can't even imagine it! I don't know what it would be like. Bet she could teach me something about singing, though."

"Maybe... she sure has power – gotta say that."

The Folksinger's friend had finished his beer and switched his empty glass with the still half full one. They stayed, waiting for the next set. The Folksinger took out his guitar and played and sang. Again no one paid attention. His friend began playing a few chords.

"Hey," the Folksinger interrupted, "try G7th' instead of G in that sequence. I know the tune you're doing and that needs a G7th going into the bridge."

"You sure?"

"Yeah I'm sure. If you try *singing* it as you chord... you'll see what I mean."

"Hell – you know I can't sing."

"Okay, just *hum* it, then."

"I'll take your word for it; you know so much about all this... but what I can't figure out is why you don't ever get up there and play on the stage." The Folksinger's friend made his comment with an inquisitive look on his face.

"Well... just don't think I'm good enough yet."

"Hey – your guitar work is better than some of those paid professionals."

"Thanks, but I get kind of flustered on stage and my voice gets all choked up."

"I sure know what you mean about the voice – that's why I decided to only be an instrumentalist."

They sat through another set without a second beer. It was nearly eleven.

"We better leave."

The Folksinger looked over to the door where a group of movie-goers had just come in.

"We're taking up space for paying customers. Anyway, it's late."

"Can you take me part way home?" the folksinger's friend asked.

"Yeah, I guess so."

"Thanks, you know I appreciate the lift, but can you wait for a minute? I want to get something to eat. Seventeen's coming down the block."

The Folksinger sat down on the steps and picked a chorus of 'Freight Train' – then he sang a verse as seventeen's bike rolled up.

The imaginative peddler had his bicycle basket piled high with items wrapped in white paper and covered with a blanket.

"You lookin' mighty *cool*, sebenteen!" he said, "Ah gots shrimp 'n' ha'd bo'lled aigs!"

"Yeah, we're cool, seventeen."

The Folksinger's friend walked over and bought a small bagful.

"How come yo' fr'en' be done settin' out heah playin'. He soun' good 'nuf t' play inside?"

"I don't know – he's just that way."

The next night, the Folksinger and his friend joined the barflies and hangers on at the theater, nursing their usual split bottle of beer through Judy Collins' first two sets. During the break, they went to the restrooms downsairs.

Sitting in the restroom lobby waiting for his friend, the Folksinger took out his guitar and played a couple of old ballads. He was singing the final verse to 'She's Like a Swallow' when his friend walked out of the men's room. Judy emerged from the ladies' lounge at almost the same moment. She stopped and listened until the Folksinger finished the verse.

"Well what d'ya think? Terrible?"

"No, no – really, your guitar work is pretty good. I liked your singing – but just don't ever try to sing opera!" she laughed as she bounded energetically up the steps.

They squeaked another beer through the next set. Folksinger's friend nudged him:

"Why don't you play a few numbers during her break? That last guy really wasn't very good."

"Ahah… I can't go up on stage here – there'r too many people in the audience. Besides, me follow Judy Collins? C'mon, get real! And you heard what she said about my voice."

Judy Collins had been gone for a week when the Folksinger made an assertation to his friend:

"You know what I need to do? I need to go out to a bar someplace else – in another part of town where nobody knows me and I don't know anybody. Maybe that'd give me enough confidence to get up on stage."

"Yeah, maybe you're right. It's worth a try."

Thursday evening at Joe and Jerry's County Line Restaurant and Lounge was always slow. The Folksinger had never been in there before, but he walked through the door with a degree of new-found confidence. As he sat down at the bar, Joe, the bartender came over to him.

"What are you goin' t' have, pal?"

A broad smiled flashed over his fleshy features and he smoothed his dark hair with his hand. Joe's instant friendliness was obviously a large part of the bar's success.

"I really don't want anything, but... I just wondered if you'd mind if I waited here for a while. I'm kind of expecting to meet someone."

"Why – that's perfectly okay, kid. I'd even try to get you to play your guitar up on the stage, but the microphone went out the last time we used it and I haven't been able to get it fixed yet."

The Folksinger breathed a sigh of relief.

"Well, I might just try playing a little here at the bar, if you think anyone would want to listen."

"Sure, that'd be great, kid – go ahead."

With an improved degree of accuracy in his fingering and an unfaltering resonance in his voice, the Folksinger played through what amounted to a full set. The people at the bar were neither silent, nor overly talkative; just the right mix.

When the Folksinger had finished, two well-dressed middle-aged men got up from their table next to the bar, picked up the bill and proceeded to the register to pay. One of them came over to the Folksinger.

"Say... I just wanted to tell you that I really enjoyed your music. Here, you can probably use this."

He pulled out a five dollar bill and handed it to the Folksinger.

"Thanks – thanks a lot! I'm glad you liked it."

The second occupant of the table came up to them:

"I had some change when I paid the bill – do you want it?" he held out four ones and a few coins.

"Sure... thanks again to both of you."

The Folksinger had been packing up his guitar in its case and turned to leave.

"You know, I'm wondering," the first man said to him, "if you've ever considered studying voice – opera."

The Folksinger stood there too stunned to answer at first.

"Well, not really. I just don't have the ability to project – or to sustain those long notes. Besides, I'd never be able to afford it."

"You're wrong about projecting and sustaining. That kind of ability is something that can be learned. That's part of technique. What you have is a natural vocal *quality* and that's something you can't be taught.

The Folksinger still stood there.

"Here's my card; call me at this business phone Monday and I'll arrange to get you professional voice lessons. It won't cost you anything."

Saturday night, Folksinger and his friend were in a bar in Gaslight Square.

"So this guy wants to pay for singing lessons for you?"

"Yeah, that's what he said."

"Michael Berger, industrial machinery? What's a guy like that know about opera? If what he said is true, don't you think somebody else would have told you the same thing by now? And remember what Judy Collins said to you about trying to sing opera? Listen, those guys were probably half-drunk. If you call him Monday, he's not even going to know who you are. That was just... 'bar talk'!"

The Folksinger picked up the card from the table – looked at it for a moment. Without raising his eyes, he crumbled it and dropped it in the ash tray. There was a momentary look of fragile wistfulness and sudden betrayal on his face.

"Yeah – I guess you're right... it was just 'bar talk'."

Hobo

Revised 5/1/23

Across the track, down a deep ravine
Where the woodland giants grow
There are trails to the secret, dark retreats
Only elves and the animals know

In sylvan silence, close to the ground
And high where the trees flag their leaves
There are earthly delights and arbored flights
And the child-like mind believes

In endless moments of pensive thought
And timeless visions of love
As lost in the ageless anals of time
The plaintive call of a dove

The trains roll along, and the hobo's song
Is heard ore the din of life
And I listened near as the sound so clear
Played a concert of human strife

Sonoreal strains touch the infinite car Of
the living breathing earth
At the end of the day, who would say
That the effort was more than its worth

And who would say that the lonely 'bo
In memories of days gone by
Is erased from the common, cultured mind
As he hops an old freight on the fly

Jam Johnson's Third Wife

1/17/01 completed: 3/7/08

Prologue

Although the plot of this story is partly fictional, the personalities of the main characters are based on individuals I have actually known. I could never have "invented" either Jam Johnson – or Jake Rubblestien. I've made the Jam Johnson in this story perhaps a bit more conniving and crafty than his real life counterpart – but only a degree more so. Jake Rubblestien is a combination of Old World Jews I knew as a boy. Those Jewish, immigrant junk-shop owners with their strong Yiddish accents, now, are all from an era long gone.

The radically and ethnically accented dialogue is stereotypically 1950's… and even though that era of racial and religious intolerance may be in the past, the remnants of it still linger. I've tried not to let my awareness of this inhibit the real and human warmth of expression that I once knew in the characters I've depicted.

Their dialogue may offend some 21st century readers, whose racially and religious equality consciousness has paralyzed their inherent sense of humor – but, if that is the case – then, so be it. All I can say is: don't read the story.

The plot in this story, I have taken from three partial real story lines which are linked together. I have taken some liberties by connecting them in order to bring continuity and cohesion to the plot, but essentially, much of the story comes from real life.

Part One: It's All Relative

There were just a few steps from the street to the front porch. Jam had ambled the distance slowly – as though he were actually trying to play the part of some comic strip character. Well, you see, he looked the part of a caricature – a caricature of the well-dressed, middle-class entrepreneur. And it was totally unintentional; that gangling, half-stumbling gait; the necktie pulled loose and twisted off to the side. Even his dragging, too-long pants legs with their carefully, hand-stitched repairs to various small tears… and, of course, the shine – that inevitable, over-pressed, rayon shine.

His hair, what little there was left of it, had been carefully and closely trimmed – which seemed to force your attention to the slight, almost perpetual smile at the corners of his wide mouth. Altogether, he gave the appearance of being rather pleasant, if not somewhat silly.

Jam had already spent much of the morning trying unsuccessfully to pursue door-to-door sales with his catalog of "stupendous" sundries. Although the prices of his merchandise were a bit cheaper than the local Woolworth's, the quality was cheaper as well.

During the previous evening, he had passed his catalogs around at the local tavern, where he often made a few sales to some of the patrons… after they were feeling happy and uninhibited – and perhaps with less cautionary discretion than usual.

But last night, he had allowed himself to join in the alcoholic revelries and quickly lost touch with his pecuniary purposes. He was quite sober by morning, but his suit was not. It still reeked form its own "hangover" where a drink had been spilled on it by one of the tavern's overly uninhibited patrons.

The next house that Jam approached seemed familiar. He recognized it as the home of a friend of one of his wife's relatives. An older lady answered Jam's light knock and eyed him suspiciously

"Well?"

It was *not* a friendly tone. Jam assumed that she did not appreciate the dark color of his skin – most people in this largely white Midwest town didn't. But he was used to it, so he gently advanced his reason for being there. Before he pulled out his catalogs, however, he would try a different tactic.

"Uh… ma'am, ah thinks you knows my wife's great aunt Thelma's mother-in-law… that's Mamie Bogglehead – they's on my wife's side 'cause… see, Ah…"

"Whut!! Wait a minute, now – you better run all that back by me again, mister. I don't know whut t'hell yer a'talkin' about!"

The elderly woman's scowl deepened as she waited for Jam to continue. Her scowl seemed as though it were going to droop as much as the rest of her half-melted figure.

"Well, see, ma'am – it's kinda like this, see… my wife got a great aunt, see…?"

"Yeah!"

"An' her name is Thelma… see?"

"Yeah, yeah!"

"An Ah thinks mebbe y'all knows wheh her house is – an' dat's why…"

"Wait a minute – yer a'tellin' me that this here woman yer a'lookin' fer is a relative – an' yuh don't even know where she's a'livin'?"

There was another massive scowl on the old woman's face. Jam swallowed quickly and his big eyes bulged.

"Well, er, uh – uh… see, we's usedta live a long way outta town, so das a distant relative. Yuh get the drift a' whut Ah'm sayin'?"

"Yeah, I get the drift of it, alright – just like the smell a'driftin' in from the brewery this mornin'! Humf! Now ain't you some kinda comedian?"

"Sorry, ma'am, Ah didn't mean t' be makin' no joke er' nuthin'." "Oh yeah… well, whut are yuh, anyway, a derelict from the Amos n' Andy show?"

"Now listen, ma'am, Ah wuz jus' tryin' t' get a li'l information."

"So why don't yuh just ask yer own wife?"

"Well… now, there's a long story to that, see, an'…"

"I'm sure there is… an' I don't want t' hear *no* part of it!"

It was already too late – everything had backfired. Jam realized that there was no point in trying to show the catalogs, nor would he get a lead on where his wife might have gone before he awoke so late. With one last apologetic effort, Jam tried to save face.

"Say… say, you *is* miss Mattie Bell, ain'tcha?"

"Nooo! Can't you see my name on the front door – plain as the big red nose on your face!? It *ain't* Bell! She ain't owned this house fer goin' on *two* years!"

Jam rolled his eyes. They were like a couple of big marbles floating around in his head. And whenever he rolled them, they bulged out even farther, so that it made him look as though he were doing some kind of turn-of-the-last-century vaudeville act.

"Ah'm sorry t' bother y'all, ma'am – Ah mus' be gettin' half blin'… er sumpthin'."

Jam stumbled down the walk and got back into his car. He kept wondering as he drove off, just how he was going to find out where his wife had gone. He could wait until she came home and ask her, but the whole scenario was already becoming too risky anyway. He had to keep track of her every move because he was walking a tight-rope. He was trying to do a delicate balance between maintaining two separate homes with two different wives, both in the same small town.

For several months, he had been very adept at keeping the two households going without having revealed even a hint to either wife of the other's existence. One night he would sleep at one of the houses, the next night at the other, telling each wife that he had been forced to work so late at his regular job at the junk yard, that he had simply decided to sleep there on a cot.

But Jam knew that no matter how careful he was – or how assiduously he kept track of each wife's whereabouts, sooner or later, he was almost bound to make some small mistake that would cause the elaborate ruse to collapse.

Lately, the matrimonial trickster had been having trouble sleeping; he had even begun to develop a slight nerve twitch in his jaw. He felt as though he were sitting on a time-bomb... waiting for it to go off – but without any idea of how or when it was going to explode.

An Incident at Gawkins' Grocery

There were the usual neat stacks of canned goods and boxes of cereal intermingled with shelves lined with rows and rows of bottles of everything imaginable. It was all carefully categorized and neatly arranged – every speck of dust and dirt removed daily, if not by the stock boy, by Blusterford Gawkins, himself; he was such a fastidious man. He personally greeted many of his customers, suggesting weekly specials and inquiring as to the health of the customer's family.

Good customer relations, after all, was a tradition in his family's grocery – a tradition in this store which he had inherited from his father. Gawkins would glance with a kind of quiet pride around his well stocked, neatly arranged grocery store. He could never have foreseen, or even imagined, what was about to take place when two of the largest women he had ever laid eyes on walked into his store within minutes of each other.

With a smile and a nod, Blusterford Gawkins greeted Lotta Johnson as she pushed a grocery cart past him.

"Good evening," he offered pleasantly.

Lotta nodded back and proceeded to a shelf where she began loading can after can of spaghetti into her cart. Only moments behind her, Vidallia Johnson was trundling another cart along the same aisle.

She reached the section where Lotta was still pulling off cans of spaghetti. Vidallia waited until the other was through. With irritation, she put the only two remaining cans into her cart.

"Boy, you really do like spaghetti!" Vidallia quipped.

"Yeah – I guess so!" Lotta laughed. "Maybe that's why I'm so fat!"

Trying to smooth over Vidalia's obvious irritation, Lotta introduced herself.

"I'm Lotta Johnson. What's your name, honey?"

"That's really odd… 'cause my name's Johnson, too. I'm *Vidallia* Johnson."

"'Course Johnson's a real common name," Lotta offered, "anyhow, Johnson's my *husband's* last name. His first name's Jam."

"Jam… not Jim? Hey, do you have a *picture* of him?"

Lotta proceeded to open a pouch in her purse where several photographs were kept. She pulled one out.

"Here, you can see what he looks like."

Gape-mouthed is not quite an accurate way to describe Vidallia's expression. There was a pounding, boiling anger suddenly frothing in her to the point of explosion. Her normally pale white skin became a livid red.

"Wha… what? What ta' *hell*?"

Lotta cringed.

"So do you think there's something *wrong* with a white woman bein' married to a black man? I know it is unusual."

"That has *nothin'* to do with it… 'cause *I'm* married to the *same* black man!"

Vidallia stamped her heavy foot down. There was no one else on whom to vent her wrath.

"You… bitch… you thievin', free-loadin' bitch!"

Vidallia swung her umbrella viciously at the other portly woman. It grazed Lotta's arm.

"Why you God-damn circus fat lady – try this on yer head for size!"

Lotta had picked up a huge ripe tomato from another nearby customer's cart and heaved it at Vidallia. The tomato smashed across the other woman's forehead, dribbling down her face.

"Fat lady, huh – well, see how hard a circus fat lady can whoop yuh up side t' head with this here umbrella!"

The umbrella caught Lotta full-force, breaking off at the handle. The injured woman let out a loud wail. By now, all of the store's other customers had gathered around the battling behemoths. Lotta grabbed a can from the shelf and threw it at Vidallia. Vidallia ducked and the can struck Mrs. Ryan on the shoulder. Mrs. Ryan thought that Mr. Dingle, next to her, was trying to get fresh... or steal her coat. She smacked him across the face with a banana. He, in return, threw the banana back at Mrs. Ryan, but it missed an hit Miss Prissell on the back of her head. Suddenly cans, bottles, fruit, eggs and occasionally fists were flying everywhere.

Blusterford Gawkins was quickly on the scene to try to become the oil on troubled waters.

"Ladies – LA-DEES!!" he screamed, PUL-LLEEZE... restrain yourselves, or I shall be forced to call in the police!"

Having recovered her composure a bit, Lotta Johnson walked over and shoved Vidallia Johnson, who stumbled into Mister Gawkins and then fell to the floor. Vidallia's elephantine weight had pushed Mr. Gawkins against the store's courtesy coffee maker, sending it crashing to the floor. The wiring shorted and blew the fuse for the lights in the back half of the store. In the ensuing darkness, full pandemonium broke loose, amid screaming, crying and flying fists, with bottles and cans whizzing everywhere.

Several women yelled for the police. The stock boy brought a flashlight and helped Mr. Gawkins up. He quickly restored the lights, just as a husky young police officer arrived on the scene. The police response was so quick, Blusterford Gawkins could barely believe it.

"What's going on here?" the officer of the law asked.

"Well," said Gawkins, "we've had a little trouble – it's these two women." And he pointed out Lotta and Vidallia, the latter of whom still sat on the floor, unable to raise her enormous body to a standing position without considerable help.

"You see, they had an... uh... argument... about something. Anyhow, if they'll both agree to clean up the mess they've helped create, then I don't want to press any charges."

Officer Toughchin looked over the mess and put his hand under his head thoughtfully.

"Well ladies, what about it?"

Both of the women nodded their heads in agreement and were soon supplied with brooms and mops. Gawkins had surveyed the store and determined that very little was actually broken. Mostly, the cleanup was a simple matter of re-stacking cans and bottles in their proper places on shelves. And, he was not anxious to loose even two of his customers to the larger grocery chain-stores in town. It all became just part of an evening's work – though a rather unusual occupation for the two women.

Placidly unaware of what had happened, Jam Johnson became hungry as he headed his big shiny '48 Olds sedan toward one of his homes.

"Ah mo stop at d' food sto' 'fo Ah goes back home," he thought to himself, "git me some jam."

He often bought several jars of jam when he went to the grocery – even though he would tell you in private that he "hated the stuff". But it was a clever way of covering the true source of his nickname.

As Jam Johnson walked through the door of Gawkins' grocery, he sensed that all was not as it should be. Though he hadn't any idea what the problem was, he was alerted by the peculiar way in which the people in the store seemed to be talking.

Jam's two wives had just finished cleaning and reorganizing the store and were near the checkout line with their carts.

"All these groceries," Lotta commented, "and I gotta walk 'em home in a cart. Worst of it is, I *got a car* – but I never get to use it."

Vidallia pushed closer to Lotta.

"You say you got a car... what *kind* is it?"

"Olds – a nearly new '48 Oldsmobile. And I made about seventy-five precent of the payments on it!"

"Is that '48 Olds you're talkin' about a two-tone brown and beige?"

"Yeah... why?"

"Well, that's *my* car! I guess it *ought* to be my car... *I* paid most of the payments on it!"

"Oooo... why that rat! If you paid for most of it... and *I* paid for most of it – what the hell did *he* pay?"

Jam was just returning to the front of the store carrying several jars, when he inadvertently passed the aisle where both of his whopping whales were standing. They all spotted each other at the same instant.

"There he is! Get him!"

"Hey, you dirty bastard!"

Vidallia threw an eggplant from her cart and it whacked Jam on the side of his head. He was barely able to duck as Lotta lunged at him, swinging what was left of her umbrella.

"You sonuvabitch!"

Jam leaped over a mop bucket in the end of the aisle and landed in part of the slick, wet floor. Even with his feet moving fast to try to maintain his balance, he managed to set the jars he had been carrying, down on the counter. His feet were still moving so fast that he looked like he was doing a tap-dance all the way to the door.

Once outside, he ran to the car, jumped in and put it in gear the instant the engine started. Driving as quickly as he could to his nearest home, he went into the apartment and first emptied Lotta's petty cash drawer into his pocket. Then he grabbed an armful of shirts and pants and a pair of shoes and a jacket from the closet.

It took only a few minutes for him to drive to the other apartment. There he repeated the process by removing Vidallia's change from the milk bottle where she had it stored. He also took a few more clothes and pulled his car title from under a couple of folded shirts.

The next stop was Jake Rubblestien's junk yard. He hoped Jake had not left yet. The old Jewish proprietor often stayed late, but it was already nearly seven o'clock. The door, however, was still open and the dim, bare bulb glowed through the office door glass – almost translucent from years of greasy smoke.

"Hey deh, boss man!"

Jake looked up at Jam and groaned.

"So vere vas you today? Kinda late now, ain't it?"

"Ah know, boss, Ah know…"

"Vy didn't chu call me ven you knew you vasn't comink in?"

"Ah know… Ah shoulda done it. Ah'm sorry, boss man."

"Sorry ain't good enough! See, Cham, vot's so bad habout dees ees, I vait too lonk for you – den I can't get no vun else."

"Ah know… Ah know Ah gots t' 'member t' call you. Say Mista Rubblestien… Ah's got troubles. *Big* troubles. Won't be able t' work fo' a while."

"Cham… you *alvace* got troubles. Zo vat ees it now? Hip bother you again?"

"No suh – wuse… it's *woman* troubles. *Big* woman troubles. My wife."

"Ha! Your vife? Vell, *vitch* vun?"

"*Bof*! See, Ah went to d' grocery sto', an' all a sudden – deh dey wuz – *bof* uv 'em… *t'getheh*! Ah don' know zackly whut happen, but boy, wuz dey mad! Ah means *really* mad… at *me*! Ah gots t' git outta town fo' a while!"

"An you need money for gas, ain't it?"

"Yassuh. See, Ah gots money in d' bank, but d' bank be closed now. If Ah waits 'til tomorra'… deh jus' might not *be* no tomorra'. Know whut Ah mean?"

Rubblestien nodded his head and laughed, then took a five dollar bill out of his wallet and handed it to Jam. The agitated conniver took the bill and grimaced with a pain – as though he had been stabbed in the back.

"Hey… zo vadd'ya' vant from me – *anyvay*? An' dat fife pucks – dat's a *hadvence* – not a *geeft*. Hunderstan?"

"Yeah, boss, yeah, Ah know. But Ah sure could use anotha' five – if yuh could see yuh way to it."

"Lessen loafer, las' time I gif you ten dollar hadvence, took you ten months to verk it off. No more! Be glad you got vot I gif you. Go out to dot cut-rate station on d' east edge uf town. Dot fife pucks buys you fifteen gallonce. Dot gets you fifti miles ofer into Hiowa. Far enough! Now lessen Cham. I got no son… but I'm tellink you chust like you vas mine own boy: vun vife… trouble enough. Two vifes… dot *ain't* no good!"

"Yassuh, Mistah Rubblestien, Ah knows… you right. But you gotta admit, dey's one thing 'bout havin' two wives – dey makes *twice* as much money as *one* wife do!"

Jake could no longer contain himself; he roared with laughter. Suddenly Jake picked up a fly swatter and began pummeling Jam on top of the head with it, still laughing.

"Sclemeel! Vot a sclemeel! Schlemeel an' a gonif!"

Jake sat back down in his grease stained desk chair and his tone became serious.

"You know, now dat you got to leave, you vill be turnink back into a hobo – a bum – chust like you vas ven you came to town two years ago."

"Boss! Hey boss… now you *know* Ah ain't go' be no *hobo*!" "Yeah, vell I know vot *else* you ain't goink to be. You ain't goink to be a fambly man vit *hroots*."

"Aw, boss man, now you gots me *all* wrong. Anyhow, Ah gots t' get outta heah. Hey, how bouts you looks through mah catalog real quick. Maybe yous could fin' sumpthun dat you needs fo' five dollahs…"

"Dot *chunk* I don't need. I got a whole yard out dere vots full uf chunk. See dot sign up dere… says Jake Rubblestien, chunk yard."

Jam looked truly hurt.

"Why dis here – what Ah'm sellin'; dat's good *new* merchandise!"

Jam grimaced as though he were going to cry. He stared to walk out, but turned back again to face the exasperated old Jew.

"Say, boss, jus' one mo' thing. Kin you let me have a wheel an' tire?"

"I chust let chu take a goot vun lest veek. Vot happened to hit?"

"Had a blowout on the rear. It's on there now. Ah don' got no spare."

"Oy, yoy, yoy!"

Jake threw his hands up in despair. He flipped on the yard light and walked out to the tire pile; then rolled back a wheel with a tire.

"Here, dis fits d' Holdsmobile. Not much tread, but hit's still up; hokay for a spare. Go on, you better get out uf here. Vere dit you say you vas goink?"

"Ah didn't."

"Goot. Don' tell me. Dot vey, ven dey hask, I can say: I don't know."

"Hey Ah 'preciates it boss. Really 'preciates it!"

"Aride. So try to stay out from more troubles. Hokay? Goot luck. Oh yeah, an' brink me beck dot olt veel!"

Jam put the spare in the Old's trunk and wasted no time in making a U-turn to go after gasoline and head out to the highway.

The big Oldsmobile soon glided up to one of the pumps at Skyrocket Discount Gas. Jam had the door window already rolled down before the pump jockey had walked out to the island.

"Whatcha need today, cool cat? The usual – two bucks worth of regular?"

Jam had been thinking on the drive from the junk yard, that gas might be higher out of state – or even out of town, for that matter.

"Naw, betteh fill it up. Wit' ethyl."

"Oooo, ain't we extravagant today! Where yuh headed, Daddio… a trip to the moon?"

Hipster Harry usually embellished his conversations with a little sarcastic humor, but today, Jam was definitely not amused.

"Listen, man, Ah ain't got no time fo' jawin'; jus' put d' gas in it so's Ah kin git goin'.."

"Yes *sir*!... sorry! First time I ever saw you in a hurry! You're not even gonna ask me t' look through your catalogs today?"

"Ah ain't got no time. Ain't got no time t' tell yuh *why*. Hey, do me a favor, man – anybody asts you wheh I gone – you don' know. Ok?"

"Sure, Jam. Why I never even saw yuh t'day. Must be your reflection I'm lookin' at. How can I tell someone where yuh went? You didn't tell *me*!"

"Yeah, an' tha's 'zactly why Ah *ain't* tellin' yuh. But it's mainly 'cause Ah don' even know myself."

As the numbers rolled on the gas pump meter, Jam watched and listened for the sound of the click-clicking as Hipster Harry topped off the tank.

"There yuh go pal, fourteen gallons even that's four dollars 'n twenty cents."

Reaching into his pocket, Jam pulled out the five dollar bill Jake Rubblestien had given him. He handed it to Harry, who gave him back the change out of the pump jockey's money changer.

"Eighty cents. Now don't spend it all in one place!"

"Yeah, man – like Ah might run some po' cat outta his whole stock a' hamburgers… huh?"

In a flash, Jam Johnson was peeling out toward the highway north of town. For over three hours, the Olds sped down the highway with Jam hunched over the steering wheel – occasionally listening to the radio, but mainly watching the highway signs. He continuously cursed himself for forgetting to ask Harry if he had a road map, though he knew that it was unlikely that the cut-rate station would have been that accommodating to its customers. The only thing Jam felt was important, was that he continued to follow roads with highway markers having the designation "n" for north. Not far back, the signs had changed to the word "Iowa", or the shape of that state.

With trepidation, Jam looked at the car's fuel gage. It showed an eighth of a tank. Ahead was an all night diner and gas station. When he reached it, he curved the heavy Oldsmobile over to the canopy area by the pumps and the car's headlights illuminated the figure of someone sitting against the station's wall.

After stopping the car next to a pump, Jam walked first to the men's room on the outside of the station. He passed the figure his car's headlights had picked out.

She was as large as a baby elephant, he thought, and probably just as heavy. As he walked past where she sat on a huge suitcase, back propped against a pile of coats padding the station's wall, he nodded politely. In a few minutes when Jam returned, the woman was wailing in a long, low, mournful sob of anguish. Jam crouched down.

"Hey, whut's d' mattuh, honey?"

"Aw... he done left me here stranded! She wailed. "Just took the truck an' went!"

Her words were punctuated by loud sobs between each phrase.

"I been waitin' for him t' come back now fer seven hours. He ain't comin' back. He's just plain *gone*."

Jam sat down next to her on a box of clothes.

"Co'se, ain't none a my business... but mebbe Ah kin hep y'all some way."

"Nobody's gonna help me – he's gone... he jus' *hated* me... left me stranded here in the middle of nowhere. 'cause I'm so *fat*. That's *why*! *Look* at me!"

Her eyes scanned Jam with an intense sincerity.

"See, when we pulled into this here station, I was sleepin', so he tells me that the truck started a bad grindin' noise in the rear end and he wanted to drive into town about a mile away and have a garage look at it. That was about three o'clock this afternoon. He said he had to have a hundred dollars in case the rear end needed replaced. So I gave it to him an' then paid for a full tank of gas."

"Well, mebbe dat truck broke down on the way inta town; mebbe he jus' *stuck* somewhere," Jam offered.

"Aw, there wasn't nuthin' wrong with the truck. I wasn't *that* sound asleep. I didn't hear *nuthin'*. Sides, he coulda walked a mile from town back here in *seven hours*!"

She began loudly wailing again.

"He told me he needed to take all my clothes out the back of the truck so there wouldn't be no problem when they was workin' on it. What a bunch a' bunk!"

Late evening dew was settling out everywhere; the island lights from the filling station had little halos of rainbow-colored fog around them. As Jam watched the subtle display of colors, his mind was going into high gear.

"Wheh's y' fambly at? Can'tcha have em' come an' git you?" "No.

They're all way down in Georgia! That's too far t' expect anyone t' drive... all the way here in Iowa!"

Jam thought for a moment.

"So you be from d' south, huh? Say, Ah bets you kin fix hog maws n' chittlin's n' corn bread n' collard greens!"

"Sure... why?"

"Oh, Ah wuz jus' wonderin'. Das all."

The big lady looked quizzically at Jam, then continued.

"Well, see, me an' my man, we come up here from Tulsa. He was headed for a job he said he knowed about in cedar falls an' since all he had was a little bit of a disability check each month, we needed the extra money. I give up my job doin' telephone sales. I wasn't even makin' two hundred a month most months, anyway. An' the company I was workin' for... they said they'd get me another phone sales job up here. But now, all I got is about fifty dollars left. That ain't enough t' buy me a bus ticket t' hardly anywhere n' eat 'til I get started again. I don't know what I'm gonna do."

The big woman started sobbing again.

"So, you still gots fifty dollahs, huh?" Jam muttered almost to himself, thoughtfully.

There was no response as the mountainous female began her diatribe again.

"Why, what that rat told me was nuthin; but a bunch of a lies. Jus' bold-faced *lies*! He had this planned all the time – he was gonna *dump* me when he found the right spot!"

Another long period of wailing sobs poured from Jam's new corpulent companion.

Jam picked up one of the woman's hands and looked directly into her eyes.

"Hey... whut's yo' name, honey?"

"I'm Amanda."

"My... dat's a purty name. Dey calls me 'Jam'. Ah's Jam Johnson."

"You from around here, Jam?"

"No... Ah... Ah's from a little town south a' heh. Wuz deh a couple yeahs, but now, Ah'm jus' travelin'... kinda hoboin', yuh might say. Y'know, 'Manda, Ah gots a idea, if you'd put some gas in mah O'semobile, Ah could take y'all on up t' Cedar Falls n' he'p yuh fin' a room someplace. Den you could get a phone an stawt yo' telephone sellin' again. What you think?"

Amanda looked down at her massive piano-legs and was again taken by the hopelessness of her situation. This time her sobbing was not very loud, but more bitter than ever.

"Ohhh... I don't know what t' do anymore. Men can't stand me 'cause I'm so fat. No man's *ever* gonna want me!..."

Jam Johnson put his arm around the big lady – around as much of her as he could. His face took on a wry smile.

"Aw, honey, now *dat* ain't true… what you sayin' 'bout yo'self – why *Ah likes* big women!"

"Backwoods Jack" aka "Joaquin"

Racoon In the Sweetcorn

4/8/99

"Claramae! CLARAMAEEE!!"
Claramae walked rapidly toward her husband at the other end of the garden.
"F'chrissake, what's wrong?"
"Look! Jus' look!"
"Wha…? Oh – those two ears of corn? Looks like a 'coon pulled 'em down last night – tore 'em up 'n' ate 'em."
"Yeah – an' them was the first two big ones! I was gonna take 'em t' eat *t'night*!"
"Well, I guess there ain't nuthin' y' kin do 'bout it now, Cecil. Y' sound jus' like yer ready t' cry over it – growed man like you!"
"Oh yeah… well, by God there is somethin' ah kin do 'bout it! Whar's ol' Mutt? Ahmo git her down here 'n' tie *her* at the end a' the row t'night! Next ears gonna git ripe in the end a' the same row. Betcha ain't no 'coon gon' mess aroun' with a dog tied next t' the corn."
The old hound dog had responded to her name and eventually ambled down to the garden. She pushed her head under Cecil's hand and he gave her a few friendly pats. Then he spoke directly to her as he crouched down to pull some weeds.
"You won't let no racoons come in here 'n' tear up my sweetcorn, will yuh girl? You know whut ah'm a'sayin', too don'cha?"

When the heat of the day began to bear down, they left the garden, but that night, as he had planned, Cecil drove a stake in the ground three feet from the ripest corn. He tied Mutt to it with enough rope so that she could reach any animal that might try to steal the next ripe ears. After pulling some straw from around the rows to make a dog bed, he gave her a hug and she responded with a sloppy lick on his cheek.

Silvery haze still blanketed parts of the morning hillsides where early sunlight hadn't burned it away. The two gardeners walked immediately over to the sweetcorn patch.

"Gawd damn! Goddammit!! Look at that! Would you b'lieve this? That racoon done come in here an' et' three more ripe ears with a dawg tied right next to 'em! Who'd a' thought that dawg 'ud sleep right through sumpthin' like that!?"

"Well, now, Cecil, you know she *is* gettin' purty old – I don't know... maybe she's a gitin' a little deaf? D'yuh think? An' then yuh fixed her sech a nice bed. Ah jest don't know... Ah can't figure it out neither."

Cecil was so mad he felt like he could spit nails – that is, if he'd been a spittin' man. All he could think of was how he'd been robbed of the wonderful taste of that first sweetcorn of the season. His ample gut was proof of how he loved to eat sweetcorn – and everything else too, for that matter.

"That's *it*! If the dawg cain't catch that racoon, guess Ah'll hafta do it myself! Is my shotgun still standin' behin' the door, Claramae?"

"Yeah, but Ah don't know where yuh put the shells for it."

"Don't matter – Ah'm a goin' t' go t' town 'n' buy me a box a' fresh ones anyway. Ah'll set down there tonight an' ah'll shoot that thievin' 'coon!"

Old Mutt followed Cecil over to the car. When he opened the door she squeezed in ahead of him and climbed in the back seat.

"You wanna go with me? Okay, gal – le's go. Hey Claramae – hey, you want me t' gitcha anything in town?"

"Aw... jus' some laundry soap, ah guess. That's about all Ah kin think of. You don't think Mutt'll git sick a ridin' in the car, do yuh? Y'know how she is sometimes."

"Naw – Ah didn' feed her nothin' yet t'day. She'll be okay."

Dust devils were beginning to spin in the dry heat of mid-day as Cecil returned up the drive. He stopped the car near the house, got out and put the box of shotgun shells down on the hood.

The familiar 'whump-whump' of the old ringer washing machine on the porch was already audible as Claramae came over to the car to get her washing soap out of the backseat. She started to reach in through the partly open window.

"Cecil – there's your racoon! It's in the backseat of the car!" Without
   thinking – with a leap, Cecil grabbed the box of shotgun
shells, then realized he didn't have the gun anyway. He spotted a large stick on the ground, picked it up and threw open the car door holding the stick threateningly.

"Why there ain't no rac… there ain't nothin' but the dawg…?"

It was all Claramae could do to keep from laughing! Don't you see that big pile of sweetcorn that your 'racoon' throwed up on the seat next to her?"

Cecil stood there dumbfounded… then he laughed:
"Damn – that's the funniest lookin' racoon I *ever* seen!"

The Evil Flywheel

10/8/12

When you've seen those episodes enough times, you get so that you can tell one even in the beginning stages.

I pick up the phone receiver and dial my neighbor Robert's number. He answers on the third ring.

"Hello?"

"Hi, Bob… I was afraid you might be working today, but I thought I'd take a chance and see if you were home."

"Naugh… I'm gonna be here; the union didn't call this morning. What's goin' on?"

"Gotta take her to Springfield again."

"Again?"

"Yeah… she's just starting – but I can tell."

"So… you want me to ride along?"

"I'd appreciate it. I'm afraid she might try to jump out again when we're doin' sixty. And you know I can't lock that car door from
the

inside."

"Okay… I didn't have anything planned anyway."

"Good, I'll be right over."

I hang up the receiver and walk out to the car. She's already sitting in the front seat of the old green Chevy tudor, staring vacantly ahead. I get in and start the engine.

"Where are we going?" she asks.

"For a ride."

"To Springfield; to Saint John's." her reply is a statement.

"Yeah."

"I... figured...," she says, resignedly.

In only five minutes, I've driven the mile and a half to Robert's house. He's standing outside waiting. He slips into the front seat and she slides over toward me. Bob rolls the door window down and rests his arm on the ledge.

"Gonna be a nice day; it's already warming up," he says.

"I know."

We drive back toward my place in silence. She suddenly spots a couple of engine parts on the floor under her feet.

"They're evil! They're evil!" she shouts.

"What's evil?" Robert laughs.

She looks at Robert wild-eyed. "They're evil... I tell you, they're *evil*!" she shouts.

"Well," I say, "there's sure plenty of evil out there in the world." In the next instant, she grabs a heavy flywheel from the floorboard, hoists it to shoulder level and heaves it past Robert's face out the car window. The flywheel hits the pavement alongside the car and goes rolling along for several feet before it finally spins off into the trench alongside the road.

"Why'd yuh do *that*?" asks an astounded Robert.

"It was evil," she replies dramatically.

"Hey... isn't that the flywheel that goes on the engine we're puttin' together for your Dodge?" Bob asks me.

"Yeah... but I don't want to stop for it now. I saw where it went in the trench. And it's right across from my own property. It won't be hurt lying there in the grass and weeds for a few hours. I'll get it later – when we come back."

"Okay... well, I guess you're right; it's not gonna get hurt."

The rest of the drive to Springfield is uneventful, I park the car in St. John's Hospital's lot and we all walk into the admissions office.

"It shouldn't take long," I tell Robert, "She's been here so many times before that they already have most of the information they need." But I'm wrong. The time drags on and on as we continue waiting in the admissions room. Hours later, Robert and I walk out, back to the car.

"Sorry it took so long," I tell him.

"Oh, that's okay; I didn't have anything to do anyway."

On the forty mile drive back home, we discuss details of the Dodge engine reassembly. When we reach the place where the flywheel rolled off into the trench, the autumn sun is already beginning to set.

"Bob, I'm just going to drive you home; it's too late today for me to look for that flywheel. I'll get it in the morning."

The next day, I begin searching for the flywheel in the trench alongside the road. Although I'm certain I know exactly where the flywheel rolled off, when I'm actually standing there... I'm no longer so sure. And... there is not just grass and weeds in the trench; blackberry and multiflora rose canes have begun to invade the bottom, making the search a great deal more difficult.

I search for an hour – then give up in disgust. Two days later, Robert and I both search the trench.

"Maybe someone saw it and picked it up." Bob suggests.

"How would anybody find it? Nobody could even see it when they're driving along the road... and nobody ever walks these roads."

"I dunno..."

"This is crazy," I tell him, "It's *got* to be here!"

Every day for the next week I search for the flywheel. Finally, I pull another flywheel off a junk engine. We assemble the engine and get it back into the car.

For the next year, periodically, I stop alongside the trench and make a brief search for the missing flywheel, never finding it. One day, I mention my continued searching to Robert.

"You know, Bob, I simply cannot understand how something as large as a flywheel could just disappear like that; it's not as though I were looking for a lost dime!"

"Well,' he laughs, "you have to remember... that flywheel *was evil!*"

173

The Painting Job

Rewritten 5/1/23

It was probably about 2008 when I was still in the process of trying to build the world's largest collection of hobo postcards. I had attended a postcard show in Collinsville, Illinois and was seated at vendor's space immediately next to that of a fellow by the name of "Earnie".

As I was looking through a display of hundreds of postcards, Earnie, a housepainter by trade, began telling a friend his experience in offering a homeless woman a ride. I could not avoid hearing the entire story and thought it was so interesting that I had to write it down as soon as I had an opportunity.

Earnie, of course told his story in the first person, which would have been an awkward way for me to present it   I have changed only the name of the cop and altered the ending slightly. Other than that, the story is exactly as I heard it.

With a final pull on the tie-down straps for the ladder racks, Earnie stepped to the door of the van, opened it, got in and started the engine. He looked at his watch. Eight forty-five – that would give him just enough time to get to the building at the other end of town, and leave a few minutes to look it over – get some idea of how to make his estimate before he met with the owner.

As he was driving alone, Earnie kept thinking about how much per gallon the titanium white was going to cost him with the reno price increase. When he reached the first main cross street, he turned right, heading east. At the first stop light two blocks up, it turned red just as he reached the intersection.

His van was next to a bus stop where a woman was standing with two suitcases. She appeared to be in her late 40's, dressed in somewhat shabby, out of style clothes.

Earnie reached over and rolled down the door window and called out to the woman:

"Hey – you need a life somewhere?"

"Yeah… I'm tryin' t' get to a couple restaurants 'bout a mile down."

"I'm goin' right past there." Earnie told her, "Open the back door of the van and put your suitcases in on top of the paint cans."

As the woman placed her suitcases in the van and closed the door, a cop car pulled alongside the van, lights flashing. Earnie looked over as the cop pointed to the curb, indicating that he wanted Earnie to stop on the other side of the intersection. The light turned green and Earnie and the cop proceeded across the intersection parking on the other side. The woman was still standing on the other corner.

Earnie already had the window rolled down by the time the cop had walked over to the van.

"Lemme see yer license!" the cop snarled.

Earnie got out his wallet and handed the drivers license to the cop. The traffic was becoming ferocious.

"Why'd you stop me?" Earnie asked. "What's your probable cause?"

The cop had to yell out to he heard about the traffic noise; "Soliciting a prostitute!"

"What!" Earnie yelled back, "Soliciting a prostitute? Why that's ridiculous! Anyone with any sense can see that she's just a homeless woman in need of a ride to get something to eat!"

The cop then walks to the corner and calls out to the woman, still on the opposite side of the street. He calls her by her name;

"Hey, Cindy, what's goin' on here?"

"Nothin'! Nothin's goin' on here! An' don't you call me a prostitute! I ain't no prostitute! You know that, you goddam' asshole!"

The cop goes back to his car to run the license check. In a couple of minutes, two more cop cars came screeching up with lights flashing.

The first cop then comes back to Earnie's van and hands him his license. At that moment, one of the other cops, a sergeant comes over and takes charge.

"Now just what's happening here?" he asks the first cop.

"This guy was getting belligerent with me – yelling at me," says the first cop.

"Yelling at you? Yeah, sure – the same way you were "yelling" at *me* to be heard over the traffic noise!"

The sergeant then goes across the street to bring Cindy back, the first cop is still standing next to Earnie's van.

"What's your name and badge number?" Earnie calls out to him, "I want to file a complaint against you."

"It's right here," he points to the name bar on his chest. "Adam Growler #127"

The sergeant returns and walks over to the van's open window. He speaks to Earnie in a subdued tone:

"Now listen, we know all about this woman. She does this all the time. She gets men to feel sorry for her and give her a lift somewhere, then she files a charge of sexual assault against him. We have to accept the assault charge since there were no witnesses against her word. Before it goes to trial, she offers to drop the charge if the guy will give her a hundred dollars. And he usually does because he figures it will cost him more than that to 'fight it in court'. "This woman may not have it all together 'upstairs', but she's definitely not stupid."

"And," continued the cop, "Growler may not be the most tactful cop on the force, but the streets would be a lot worse off without him. And he may just have saved you a lot of money."

"Yeah... well, I still think you ought to tie up your 'bulldog' for a while – or put him on a leash. Or feed him some milk instead of raw meat every day!" Earnie quipped.

"Well, just remember," the sergeant reminded Earnie, "he may have saved you a lot of money."

"Yeah, well, if I don't get to meet that guy on time for the house painting job estimate and I lose out on it, it'll cost me a helluva lot more money than that!"

"Alright, then just go on... "

Earnie removes the two suitcases from his van and takes off rapidly down the street. The cop walks over to the second cop car which is still sitting at the curb. He speaks to the driver:

"Do you know to take Cindy to a restaurant?"

"No, she doesn't want to go there. She wants to got to the precinct station to file a charge."

"What – sexual assault?"

"Yeah."

"Against the guy who just left?"

"No, against *Growler*!"

The Right Thing To Do

2/16/95

"Stop! There's a car stalled up there… in our lane!"

"I see it! Damn good thing I'm tired and was drivin' slow or I'd have gone right into the back of it."

The Small Guy brought his car quickly to a halt only twenty feet behind the stalled car ahead.

"Jeez – you'd a thought that even if the driver had a heart attack, his lights'd still be on!"

He yanked on the hand brake and pushed the flashers, then swung open the door.

"Get ready to pull up to the bumper – slow… and push it off the road! I don't know if the bumpers match, but we can't take time to check."

She slid into the driver's seat while the Small Guy raced over to the other car and threw open the driver's door. He took a quick relieved look down the interstate, finding no cars coming in the mile distance he could see. The stench of alcohol and urine hit him like a cloud from a battlefield gas attack.

With his head slumped on his chest, the driver still sat behind the steering wheel in a drunken stupor.

"Move over!" yelled the Small Guy. "Hey – you guys pull him over! Get him over! Hurry up!"

The other three scruffy middle-aged men in the car pulled on the disheveled driver as the Small Guy squeezed into the driver's seat, then slammed the car door.

"What's wrong with this thing? Why'd you guys stop?"

"Downo…" one of the slightly less inebriated passengers answered. "Downo..! Ch'ollie… why yuh stop? Huh?"

The Small Guy found the ignition lock, twisted the key and the engine started. He jerked the car into gear and moved it over onto the berm. As the car was still in motion his fingers fumbled around the dash until he found the light switch and turned it on.

They were less than a quarter mile from an exit; he drove up the ramp followed by his own car. Crossing over the interstate, they entered the parking lot of a twenty four hour truck stop and café.

After he had parked the car and gotten out, the Small Guy could feel a cold wetness in the seat of his pants and the distant odor of beer and wine again.

"Agh, jeez – what a friggin' mess!"

In a state of total disgust, he walked over to the café and asked a waitress for use of their telephone, explaining quickly the circumstances.

"Just need to call the state patrol," he told her.

Not wanting to contaminate a seat with his wet pants bottoms, the Small Guy stood for the fifteen minutes it took until a couple of troopers arrived. The waitress pointed out their protagonist to them.

"What's goin' on?" one of the troopers towering above the Small Guy queried in a hollow tone that seemed unfriendly and intimidating.

"Found a bunch of drunks stalled in the right lane out on the interstate – just sitting there without any lights."

"So you got 'em off or what?"

"Yeah."

"Well, what d'you want *us* to do about it?"

"I dunno – what *can* you do about it? Seems t'me that someone could'a run into the back of the car, sitting there with no lights. I just happened to be driving slow, you know there could'a been a helluva damn accident – somebody probably would've gotten killed!"

"Yeah, you're right. But there's nothing we can do now. We didn't *see* them – we don't have any *proof* they violated any laws."

"My God! – just go look at 'em out in their car! They're still almost dead drunk – especially the driver. Hey – *I* saw it!"

"Look," the trooper replied aggressively, "When we arrest someone, we gotta have probably cause – *and* something that'll stand up in court.

"So what'er yuh gonna do – just go let 'em back out on the highway again an' kill somebody?"

The trooper thought for a moment, then consulted with is partner.

"You got the car keys?" he asked.

The Small Guy handed the keys to the trooper who walked over to the waitress.

"Here," he told her, holding the keys out to her, "lock these in the cash register and when the day manager comes in, tell him not to give them back until the driver is sober enough to drive again."

With a newspaper he'd picked up in the café under his arm, the Small Guy went back to his own car. He unfolded the paper, put it down on the seat, then drove in silence out to the interstate.

"You know… I'm really wondering if I should have driven those guys off the highway."

"Whatd'yuh mean?"

"Well, tomorrow they'll be right back out on the road again with a fresh load of booze. The same thing may happen again – just somewhere further up the road. Maybe the cops *would* have found 'em tonight and stopped 'em permanently. Maybe all I did was prolong the problem an' somebody else is goin' t' get killed tomorrow night. It's hard to know what to think about it when you don't get any real cooperation. Those cops made me feel like I was just some kind of nuisance.

"You know what it was, actually… just a gut reaction when I saw that car. When you don't have time to think about something like that… and everything happens so fast. See, if I'd had more time to think… huh… who knows *what* I'd have done?"

"Maybe I should have just left their car parked on the highway's shoulder. The state patrol might have found 'em. On the other hand, the driver might have sobered up just enough to drive back out on the pavement and kill someone. How can you ever say what's really the right thing to do?"

"Maybe there isn't any right or wrong thing – maybe there are just several possible choices and you do what seems best at the time. Anyway, there are all kinds of freak possibilities that could wreck even the *best* planning." I shook my head in disgust as I drove on.

"Well… you just did what you *had* to do," she said with finality.

Just a Bunch of Daisies

9/25/93

He thought back about the last couple of weeks – that random act of picking up a copy of the 'Times' and accidently opening it to the 'personals' page… and then spotting her ad.

Not that it had said all that much – but there was something appealing about the ad. And then when he wrote her a note and got back a reply with her phone number… well?

So she did seem sincere, interested – interesting… But making that first phone call… it's something that's hard to make yourself do – because you're afraid that you'll screw up somehow – say the wrong thing – or say the right thing at the wrong time. Will had never enjoyed the prospect of making a call like this to anyone – particularly to a woman he'd never met and really didn't know anything about… and yet who could potentially become an extremely important part of his life.

He picked up the receiver and started to dial – then set it down and reread through her letter one more time. Finally, he picked up the receiver and quickly dialed the number. Her phone rang… and rang and rang some more. He let it go for a total of ten rings, then hung up.

Two hours later he tried again – with the same result. In the evening, he tried calling again, this time feeling more comfortable dialing – definitely more confident.

She answered the phone on the third ring.

"Hi – this is Will Goodhardt! I answered your ad in the 'Times', remember?"

"Sure – you were the one who was the vegetarian and tries to eat mostly raw food? Gee, it's nice to hear from you, Will!"

There was introductory 'small talk' for the next few minutes. Will couldn't seem to break loose of it. Finally, he picked up a handbill from the table.

"say, Gina, have you heard about the talk on environmental problems that's going to be given Thursday evening – by John Robbins? You know who he is? He's the author of 'Diet For a New America."

"Uh… yeah, I think so… I think I've heard of him. The name of the book kind of sounds familiar…"

"Gina, he gives such a clear and powerful statement in his book – the reasons for us as a nation to change to vegetarian diets… it's really worth going to hear him speak. Maybe we could meet there and get better acquainted."

"Yeah, that sounds like a good idea. Tell me where it's going to be and the time."

After Will carefully explained where the lecture would be held and the time, he and Gina batted the conversation ball back and forth for the next twenty minutes. It seemed to Will that he was initiating most of the conversation, but Gina's replies were very friendly.

"How will I be able to tell you from all the other girls in the crowd? he asked her, finally.

"Oh, Will, I'm not a *girl* anymore; I'm a thirty-five year 'old lady'.""

"well, that's not as old as I am; I'm forty-three." Will laughed a bit, "but actually, I look only forty two."

Gina tittered. Then Will continued:

"I'm a slim five foot eight and my hair is graying slightly at the temples. Oh, and I'll be carrying a small beige briefcase that I always bring to lectures."

"Hmm," Gina thought momentarily, "I'll just wear my old dark red summer dress… and I'll have a barrette in my hair; it's got a small yellow rose on it and I'm a brunette and I've five feet five.

Will gave a cheerful: "sounds good. And you have my phone number in my letter if anything would happen where you can't make it – right?"

Um hum… well, I'll see you there. Bye Will."

Thursday had been a typically hot 'July scorcher' and Will thought that the temperature alone would be enough to keep people away that night. He had told his next door neighbor about the Robbins talk. Surprisingly, the elderly woman was also leaving to attend as he walked down toward the street.

"Hi there Mrs. Weaknee – I really didn't expect to see you going out with the heat the way it is tonight."

"Oh, we older people have to get behind environmental issues too, you know."

"Say," Will observed, "your flowers are really beautiful. What kind of daisy is that, anyway?"

"Those? Oh, they're called gaillardia. They *are* pretty, aren't they? Listen, anytime you want to cut some, you just go ahead. There are *so* many of them."

"Well, thanks, maybe I'll cut a few right now. You see, I'm meeting a lady at the lecture, and…"

"Oh, I think that would be nice. Be sure you wrap them in moist paper and put them in a plastic bag."

The Unitarian Church building was designed to accommodate at least eight hundred people; that was large, Will thought, but not what you'd call enormous – just adequate, he reasoned. He arrived early and watched as the hall quickly filled.

Since there were entrances on two sides, it was difficult to see each persona as he or she went in. Finally, Will gave up looking for Gina, walked inside and was seated in the last row.

It was five minutes until seven, but more people continued to arrive. Helpers scurred to bring in folding chairs. Three more rows filled and still the people came. By the time the talk began, late comers had availed themselves of 'standing room only' around the edges.

Will's mind wandered – he looked around in the crowd constantly for a woman in a dark red dress and a yellow barrette.

After a time, the heat became intense inside the high domed hall. The small bouquet lay on top of Wills briefcase and inside the case was an old copy of Dr. Shelton's Hygienic Review that had a well written, simple article on basic Natural Hygiene. Will had also stuck a copy of Shelton's Hygienic System Volume II in with it... just in case Gina seemed open enough to the idea of natural health, that she might want further reading.

As the lecture proceeded, Will placed the briefcase and the bouquet of daisies on edge by his feet on the floor. The flowers fell off when the person in front bumped the case. After picking the bouquet up, Will opened the wrapping slightly. A couple of daisies in the front looked tired – *very* tired.

A few people were now beginning to leave because of the oppressive heat. When there was a question and answer session after the talk, even more people filtered out. Will positioned himself at a central point between the two exits that allowed him to watch everyone leaving.

When the majority of the audience finally dismissed itself, Will took another look at the daisies. They were almost all very tired-looking.

Nearly everyone had left except some of the those who had been among the first to enter. Mrs. Weaknee walked past. Will was eying his bouquet sadly.

"You couldn't find your lady friend? That's really too bad. But maybe she's still in here."

"Nagh... nagh – I'm sure now she wasn't here."

"Well, don't give up... keep looking. Someday..."

Some of the lights were being turned off as Will walked over toward the exit. A tall, hefty fellow with a janitorially hardened face was standing by a trash barrel along the door. He fingered a wide push-mop, obviously anxious for everyone to leave. Will walked over toward the barrel with the bouquet in his hand.

The big man's iron face cracked slightly into a smile:

"She didn't show, huh?"

"Nope... Aw well, these were just daisies anyway. She probably wouldn't have liked them. You know how some women are..."

Will took another look at his sad bunch of daisies.

"I just can't figure why she wouldn't have wanted to come to a lecture like this."

He had directed his comment to the big man with the iron face and the push-mop.

"Hey, bud – look at it this way; this place was packed tonight – right?   There   was   maybe   a   thousand   people   here. But how many people y' think heard the news releases about it on radio and TV or saw something in the paper. A hundred thousand?   A half million, maybe?   Why weren't *they* all   here?   I'll   tell   yuh   why: 'cause most people just don't give a damn! That's the simple fact of it. If everybody *did*   care about the environment, there wouldn't even be some guy havin' t' write an' lecture about it."

"I'm the same way – I'm the perfect example. *I* wouldn't be here except they're payin' me t' help clean up the mess!"

Will took one last look at his bouquet and without even raising his hand, dropped it in the trash barrel.

Addendum

We humans are very smart about creating ways to exploit our planet's natural energy resources – but very, very stupid when it comes to creating ways to prevent the need for the high, unnatured, abnormal use of that energy.

I cold hope to see some kind of vast, positive climatic and sociological change take place even in my lifetime were it not for the fact that the politicians who, unfortunately are the ones who make those changes, are often even less knowledgeable and dedicated than those average citizens who put them in their positions of power.

Preface for Just Another Lunatic

The following story is a true happening. Since it took place in 1966 and thirty or more years passed before I decided to write down the incident, nearly all of the original dialogue was lost far in the past.

My recollection of the dialogue hopefully retains at least some of the flavor of the original. There are certainly some conversations elaborated for clarity and a few conversations that I've added merely to provide both reader interest and plot continuity. But essentially, the story is probably quite accurate.

Just Another Lunatic

5/3/95

The turreted nearby towers, in an almost smotheringly intimidating Gothic permeation, gloom down on me as I drive past the stone and wrought iron gate house. The guard watches me with some suspicion, but makes no effort to stop my old rust-edged station wagon.

Above the graveled parking lot loom four ponderous stories of blackened red-brick, institutional – looking buildings. The edges of the walls and roofs of the massive sanitorium complex are delicately outlined in turquois corroded copper gutters, down spouts and filigreed finials, contrasting incongruously with the glowing life-filled brilliance of an early September morning.

After stopping, I swing open the car door, ready to give it the usual slam shut, but in an almost intimidated manner quietly ease the door until it clicks – as if I'm fearful of awakening sleeping spirits from a Victorian past.

As I walk into the gaping entrance hall, it is dank and dismal – reminiscent of the chill autumn nights. Going a little farther on, I encounter a dimly-lit office where a nun in the antiquated habit of some ancient order sits in attendance. Pleasantly, but without smiling, she looks up.

"Yes… may I help you?"

"Ah… I was wanting to see someone here… Edward Onward?"

"Let's see… Onward… Onward, Edward Onward. Strange name… hum… yes, he's on floor three in the west wing. Let me check to see if he has grounds privileges. Well, he's only been here a day or two so probably not. But… oh yes, he does have grounds privileges. Now

I'll look on the list to see if he signed out – it's such a nice day out there. Yes, he's somewhere on the grounds. Uh... are you a relative?"

"Why? What difference does that make?"

"There are instructions for only relatives to visit!"

"Oh... well, yes, I am a relative."

"Are you his brother? When I saw him yesterday I noticed he had a beard too."

"Uh... yes. Yes, we are brothers, indeed. Well, thank you very much."

I walked back through the depressingly somber hall and out into the sunlight. Just as I re-enter the world of light and warmth, Edward approaches carrying a paper bag filled with walnuts.

"Eddie!"

"Hi – hey, want some walnuts? The ground is covered with them out there! I'm going to take this piece of brick I found and break some open. I'll give 'em to the other people here. You know, the fare in places like this is not especially good..."

"But tell me – how... how did you know I'd be moved here? They just transferred me yesterday. And I have no idea why. I was going to try to call you tonight to tell you. It was my father behind it, no doubt. Whatever his reason, at least this place is far better than that prison of a state mental hospital in the city. At least here you can get out and see the trees and sky. But this is kind of quick for you to be coming back to see me..."

Ed's face takes on a puzzled expression.

"And how did you find out I was here? Certainly not from my father?"

"No," I tell him, "a friend of your sister called me. She said that when she found out you were here, she called this place and asked about visiting hours and was told you wouldn't be having any tomorrow. Then she asked why, because tomorrow is the only day she could get here with your sister. They told her you were scheduled for a shock treatment."

Ed stands in awed, near-disbelief. Then he slowly proceeds: "So... it wasn't just because of my complaints about the prison-like atmosphere..."

"Look, it doesn't matter whose idea it was," I tell him, " – or why; we've got to get you out of here *now*! Maybe not this minute, but *today*. That is, unless you want to stick around for whatever number of their brain-destroying barbaric shock "treatments" they have in mind

185

to subject you to. Come on, let's walk the fence line along the east side. That's heavily wooded, and I've already checked to see how close it goes to the adjoining shopping center's parking lot."

We walk casually toward the tree shrouded six foot chain link fence.

Ed shakes his head, looking vacantly:

"This is really hard for me to follow – shock treatments for someone who just walked a little too close behind a woman in the park – because I was near-sighted! Good Lord… what is this world coming to? The whole thing… it's so bizarre. I thought after the police arrested me, they'd just keep me there in the hospital for a day or two until they had a chance to look up my record. But not this… certainly not *this*. You know, it could have something to do with my participation in the anti-war rallies – my political views…"

"And the fact that you *look* like a hippie." I suggest. "And I suppose, when you get right down to it, you do *act* like one – not having a regular eight-hour-a-day job."

"Yes, and having no incentive to get a regular job, either. Ah yes… most people can never accept the idea that there's any other way to live besides "keeping up with the Joneses" – and living like the Joneses. I'd have to be crazy, wouldn't I?"

I respond thoughtfully:

"Sometimes… I wonder why they haven't targeted *me*. My beard's longer than yours – and I have shoulder length hair…"

"But you own a car – and you're not too near-sighted to drive it – and, I guess more importantly, you don't walk too close behind paranoid old women in the park…"

We both laugh sardonically.

As we reach the thicket where it begins to hide the fence, we begin walking along the line toward the main road. Then we see a large sapling growing next to the fence, I stop and point to it:

"This one might have strong enough side branches to let you climb up to head height so that you can step on the top edge of the fence and go over."

Ed slithers his lean six foot two inch frame up grasping the upper part of the tree without pulling it over. He puts both feet on the fence's top rail holding on to the tree.

"Okay," I advise, "now all we have to do is to mark this spot so it's easy to find again. Got something we can leave here?"

Ed pulls out a handkerchief and wedges it into the fence fabric: "There!"

"Good, let's go back and I'll meet you here at the fence just before dark. That way you won't be missed and the guard won't be alerted. Better bring a change of clothes and anything else you can stuff in a paper bag. It'll just look like you're going out to pick up more walnuts."

The sun is rapidly sinking and the ominous image of the levanthian edifice is heightened by the presence of a few bats flying after evening insects and a flock of raucous crows settled on the branches of a dead tree. After parking my car in the shopping center lot, I walk about a city block through an undeveloped brush-covered field to the point where Ed is to meet me.

"Ed – Eddi, you there?"

"I'm here – further down the fence!"

I walk over and reach up as Ed hands his bag over the fence to me. Then with a quick, nimble leap, Ed is up the tree, balancing momentarily on the fence fabric with its top rail, then over and dropping lightly onto the soft earth. He straightens with a smile of satisfaction and confidence, as I hand him the bag.

"Now what?"

"Come on," I tell him, "let's get out of here. Neighborhood dogs are beginning to bark."

We reach the car and drive off.

"Where are we going?" Ed asks delicately.

"Where do you want to go? Have you given it any thought? I guess you could stay with me... for a little while."

"That's not really practical. I still don't know if the police have charged me with something. And... I'm not about to try to find out. Maybe... I should go to the Trapist Monks in Kentucky. They take anyone in. I'll have time there to think about what I want to do. But I'll need transportation."

"Don't worry about that; I've already talked about bus fare with some of our friends. We already have it. But we really need to change your appearance just a bit... don't you think? Just to be on the safe side?"

"My beard?"

"You can grow it back later."

"Of course." Ed smiles, nodding.

We reach the home of a friend and are welcomed in:
"Hi guys – you had dinner yet?"
"Well… I have, I answer, but Ed here… he probably had to skip his. He certainly wouldn't have had much that was palatable there, anyway."
Our host chuckles and nods knowingly: "Well, look in the fridge. Hey, you guys want to clean up? You know where the bathroom is. Need anything?"
"Yes, a scissors and a razor," Ed laughs.
"Oh, sure – I'll get you a scissors. There's a razor in the bathroom."

A few minutes later, Ed emerges from the bathroom minus his beard.
"Hey – looks good!" I tell him, "But let me trim the moustache a little; it's too bushy. If we give you a pencil-line, you'll look like one of those English matinee idols from the 1930's."
We all laugh.

After helping Ed do the moustache trim, we stand back nodding approvingly as we give him a hand mirror. Ed look at himself, smiles slightly, but says nothing.
"Ed, I called the terminal and the bus for Kentucky doesn't leave for over two hours; we'll just have to wait here." I tell him. Then I hand him an envelope with the money that I've collected.
"Guys," our host says, "I need to get to bed. Have to wake up early. Just lock the door when you leave and throw the key through the mail slot. I have a suspicion you won't be back here for a long time, Ed, so… good luck!"
He shuts off the harsh overhead light and we sit in the dim glow of a night light, silently for several minutes. Ed breaks the silence:
"Ah… I'm afraid he's right; I won't be back for a long time…"

We look out the front window at the street lights and the brightly lit houses in the surrounding neighborhood.
"Sometimes," I say pensively, "this world doesn't make a lot of sense."

Ed smiles; "It makes sense to a lot of people. I just don't happen to agree with them... "

"And," I add, "the end result of where everything's going is desolation – the destruction of life – annihilation of beauty – decimation of truth."

"Do you know what the basic problem is?"

"I think so... but tell me."

"Too many with a little corner *of* the truth, who think they have a corner *on* the truth."

"So where does that leave us?"

"Just here... just, *here*."

Ed smiles again and places his hands under his chin, head supported by arm against hip. Again there is a long silence. Later, Ed gets up, walks into the other room and finds a straight pin.

"What's that for?" I ask. He jabs his finger with it and draws blood.

"Hold out your finger," he tells me.

I place my index finger in front of myself. Ed grasps it and instantly sticks it with the pin.

"Ouch!" I yelp.

"Now, let me have your finger." Ed presses the two blood spots together. "See, now we're blood brothers!"

"Well... you really *are* a little crazy," I laugh.

Then I look at my watch; "We need to leave soon to get you to the bus station with some time to spare. No telling how many will be in that ticket line."

We drive several miles to the bus terminal without conversing. After parking, we walk into the station and stand in line at the ticket window, still saying nothing. Ed buys the ticket and we go out to the bus, where passengers are beginning to board it. He waits trying to be the last one on.

"What do you think... " he asks me, "is this whole world somewhat crazy? It seems like it."

"Ah... well... you won't have any argument from me. But don't you think that most people are kind of... caught in a trap – that for them – well, there's just no escape from it?"

"That's because they've allowed themselves to be sold on a false sense of values." Ed looks intently at me.

"Yes, I know," I tell him, "even I'm caught up in a lot of the destructive craziness. It's hard to avoid. Just... driving my car..."

As the bus driver starts up the engine, we grasp hands in the "peace hand clasp" of the era, give each other a quick embrace and step apart.

Ed smiles with a wide-eyed myopic grin: "Peace be with you, brother!"

"Yeah... go in peace... brother."

He steps up into the bus, turns as I shout to him with a laugh. Then he reaches into his pocket for a scrap of paper and a pen and scribbles a note. He hands it to me through the bus window. It requests that his belongings at the sanitorium be released to the bearer of that note, naming me specifically.

A few days later, I enter the large, ancient sanatorium complex. With note in hand, I inquire as to who has been the doctor in charge of Ed's case. A few minutes later, I meet the white-coated man and hand him the note.

"Are you a family member?"

"No."

"I'm sorry, sir, but we can release a patient's belongings only to a family member."

"Why is that? Even with a note in the patient's own handwriting?"

"It's just the rules. You see, the patients in here are not rational."

"But who determines *that*?"

"Why... our staff." The doctor's comment is punctuated by a derisive laugh.

"Isn't this all subjective opinion?" I ask.

"Perhaps some of it is, but I and my colleagues determined that your friend was, ah... not quite rational, from his previous actions and responses in activity; everything that *anyone* does could be looked upon with subjective opinion."

"Well... don't you think you might *ever* be wrong about your opinions – that you might be misreading something?"

"Young man, this is a collective opinion; this is not the diagnosis of merely one person."

"And collective opinions are *never* wrong?"

"Hardly ever."

"But not *never*? Doesn't it mean anything that the man was clear-thinking enough not to want to be subjected to your barbaric shock treatments?"

"Now look – society at large sets the standards."

190

"But if the society itself is insane, then the standards it sets are also insane."

The doctor laughs cynically: "Impossible!"

"Yes," I respond with my own resigned cynical comment "of course... how completely stupid of me. How could a whole society *ever* be wrong?"

"Now you have it" says the doctor, "It's as I've been telling you. He acted as though he was becoming just... another lunatic."

Addendum

This amazing story actually took place during the mid 1960's. I changed only slightly the names of those involved, but other than that, the story is quite accurate.

When this incident took place, I was still young enough to believe that it was possible to reason with conventional medical minds. My experience, obviously, proved otherwise. Whether this has changed any now that 60 years have elapsed – I cannot say, though I seriously doubt it...

That huge, imposing Victorian building complex that housed the mental hospital run by the equally antiquated order of nuns, is now long gone, as are the west grounds surrounding it. All has been replaced by modern business offices and cracker-box subdivisions. The old Victorian structure was built during the late 19th century when modern insulation concepts did not exist and with cheap energy sources available, was of little importance. But in today's world the building became completely impractical.   Perhaps the imposing, intimidating appearance of it turned potential patients away as well, helping to lead to the closing of the facility.

But the absurdly barbaric concept of shock 'therapy' that was used there still persists. And though its use is less frequent, it is still part of conventional psychiatric treatment. And this is in spite of one of their own psychiatrists taking a man with a burned out brain around to their medical meetings to lecture them on the dangers of using electric shock treatments to calm agitated patients.

Certainly, almost everyone today realizes that particular aspects of our modern world change very rapidly. But there are other often absurd – sometimes destructive aspects that seem to hang on forever.

Whether the modern changes and the advancement in technology are actually good for humanity (and the natural world) is definitely arguable. Decades may go by before that is answered.

But the maintaining of destructive absurdities requires no time element for its evaluation. It requires only antiquated and absurd mentalities – of which there seems to be no shortage!

A Christmas Food Basket, A True Tale of Frustration & Disgust

The Frowning Old Man Looked up the phone number of his local CEFS office, picked up the receiver and proceeded to dial.

A friendly-sounding lady answered: "Hello, CEFS. What can I help you with?"

"I'm trying to find out where to get the application for the Christmas basket – you know, for low income families?"

"Yeah… well, I know we used to have them here, but this year they've changed things. They didn't tell us where the applications could be picked up. Why don't you try the fire department?"

"The *fire* department?"

"Yeah… they might know…"

"You have that number?"

"Uh… let me look it up. Yeah, here it is."

The woman read off the number and the Frowning Old Man copied it down. He dialed the number immediately. A young man answered: "Fire department!"

"Uh… hello… I was just told by the CEFS office that someone there could tell me where I could pick up an application for a Christmas food basket for this year."

"I'll ask around – I don't know. Just a minute."

In a few seconds the young fellow returned. "No one here knows – try calling City Hall." "You have that number?"

"Um… yep… I'll get it in a second here."

Again, the Frowning Old Man copied the number and dialed it. A woman clerk answered:

"Richfield City Hall, Janet speaking, Merry Christmas."

"Ma'am, I was told by someone at the fire department that you might know where I could pick up an application for a Christmas food basket this year."

"No, I'm sorry, we don't know. But you might try calling the Moose Lodge . Maybe they'd know."

"You happen to have that number?"

"No, I'm sorry, I don't. I know they'd be in the phone book, though."

"Okay, thanks."

The Frowning Old Man looked up the Moose Lodge's phone number and dialed it. A gruff-sounding man answered the phone after several rings.

"Ahh... Moose Lodge! Whatcha need?"

"City Hall told me you might know where a person could get an application for the low-income family Christmas food basket this year."

"Ah don' know... lemme ask!"

After about three minutes the man returned to the phone: "They're at the thrift store. Y'know where it is? They got 'um." "Yes, thanks I'll call there."

Again, the Frowning Old Man looked up the number and dialed it on his old rotary dial telephone.

"Thrift store," a woman answered, "Just a minute, I'm with a customer."

Several minutes went by. Just as the Frowning Old Man was about to hang up, the woman returned.

"Uh... I'm sorry. What'd you need?"

"I'm trying to get an application for this year's Christmas basket – for the low income – you know?"

"Oh... well we have them – but this is the last day."

"How late are you open?"

"We close at four."

It was already three p.m. The Frowning Old Man thought momentarily then spoke to her again:

"Listen, I'm ten miles out of town, I'll see if I can get my car to start and try to get in there before four."

"Okay – now, we close promptly at *four*!"

"I'll be there."

The warm, pouring December rain had soaked everything – it seemed to make no difference whether it was uncovered or covered. A fine mist was beginning to rise from the rain soaked landscape.

The Frowning Old Man twisted the key in his car's ignition switch and listened as the engine turned over. For a few seconds, it sounded like the engine would catch. Then it just spun over and over.

"Damn! What a sonuvabitch! Always when you really *need* it to start!"

He got out, raised the hood an began wiping off ignition wires with a dry rag. Then he got in and tried it again. This time it sounded more hopeful, but, in the end, it failed to start. After popping open the trunk, he removed a small tool box and carried it to the engine compartment, then he took out a wrench that would fit the car's distributor cap bolts, fumbled removing them and slipped off the cap. He looked at the inside of the cap... but there was no moisture.

After cleaning the inside of the cap, he took a knife and scraped all of the spark points on the cap and rotor. It took much longer to reassemble the cap then it had taken even to remove it. He got back in the car and twisted the key again. Instantly, the engine started. He looked at his watch. There was only another fifteen minutes before the Thrift shop closed. In less than ten minutes he had raced the distance and pulled up to the store with five minutes left before closing. He ran inside.

"I'm here to get an application for a food basket," he told the lady behind the counter, who was checking out a customer. She nodded, then made him wait a full five minutes before she brought over one of the application sheets.

"I'm sorry, but they've already picked up all of the applications" she advised him. "You'll have to take it to the South Richfield City Hall tomorrow."

"Tomorrow! Why that's another trip into town just to take in this application. Each trip I make costs me two dollars in gasoline!"

"I'm sorry, sir, but that's how they set things up."

The Frowning Old Man's face took on a thoroughly disgusted appearance.

"If they were having you hand out these applications all day, then why on earth didn't they just pick them up tomorrow!"

"I don't know, sir – we're not in charge of it here. This program is being done by a group of interested citizens. As I told you, we're just supposed to hand out applications."

"Well, so who could I contact to ask some questions?"

"I don't know."

"Surely they gave you people some kind of contact name and phone number."

"I don't know what it is, if they did. The manager might know, but she's not here today."

"Well… what's her phone number? Maybe I'll just call her and she can tell me."

"I don't have her number, but she'll be in tomorrow."

"What inefficiency! What tomorrow craziness. Nobody knows *anything*!"

"I'm sorry sir, we're closing."

The Frowning Old man walked out and back to his car. He sat there contemplating. Then he took out a pen and proceeded to fill in the spaces on the form. His income was less than half of the minimum required to qualify. He owned his own home, but the value of it was just a tiny fraction of their minimum value. He filled in his phone number and address.

When he came to a line indicating any food allergies, he hesitated. He wrote in the comment: I eat only fresh, raw fruits, vegetables, nuts and seeds. NO meat. That, he thought would cover almost everything.

The next day, knowing that the South Richfield City Hall closed at three o'clock, he drove in a half hour early. Of course… it was already closed. He found several things to occupy his time until seven p.m. when the Moose Lodge opened. As he walked inside, he spotted a bar maid and explained his purpose for being there. He showed her the food basket application.

"You folks here seem to know something about these Christmas food baskets. I tried to turn this in at the South City Hall, but it was closed even though it was supposed to be open!"

The woman looked at the application sheet and shook her head negatively.

"I don't really know anything about it, may be one of the men that comes in later will. I'll try to get it into the right hands for you. I've got a number that you might try to call. Maybe he'll know something It's some guy named John."

He thanked her and left. Then he forgot almost entirely about the food basket for the largest part of a week. Finally, hearing nothing from anyone about when and where the food could be picked up, he decided to call the phone number the barmaid at the Moose Lodge had given him.

"Hello," said a friendly-sounding voice, My name's John – what can I do for you?"

The Frowning Old Man explained his situation again and said that no one had ever called to tell him when or where to pick up his food – or if he even qualified.

"Well," said the man on the other end of the line, "we normally don't call, we just deliver the food. It's more personal that way."

"But I live way out in the country," the Frowning Old Man told him; and besides, I have a six foot chain link fence around my place. You couldn't get in to leave the food... and if you left it outside the locked gate, rain and snow might get to it before I found it... or, some thief could easily come along and walk off with it. That's *why* I have the six foot fence – because the people out here *are* so terribly dishonest ! And all the thieving hillbillys from town come over here to steal everything they can lay their hands on."

"We figured we couldn't deliver it," said the man named John, "so it it's behind the bar at the Moose Lodge. There's not much in it, though..."

"Oh that's alright. I'd rather have just a little of something I *can* eat, than a *lot* of things I *can't* eat."

The Frowning Old Man expressed his thanks and hung up. Later that day, he drove into town to get the food. Sure enough, there was a small cardboard box behind the bar. He took it out to the car and looked through it.

"What a laugh," he said to himself. "It's all either canned meat, or vegetables fixed with salt and sugar and city water!" His eyes fell on one orange.

"*One* orange... just *one* lousy orange!"

Two days later, he happened to pass the thrift shop. He walked into try to find a pair of shoes that would be more waterproof than those he was wearing.

He was approached by the same woman who had handed him the food basket application the week before.

"So, how did you like your Christmas food basket?"

He hesitated:

"There was an orange in it: the orange was very good!"

"One orange... that's *all*?"

"Yes, one orange – that was it."

"They used to have several oranges and applies."

"I know. But not this year. And that's in spite of my having written right on the application form that I ate only fresh, raw fruits, vegetables, nuts and seeds! The rest in the box was just a few cans of meat – which I wouldn't eat: it's not proper food for humans – and a few cans of vegetables with salt and sugar in them – prepared with city water, also known as 'chemical soup'."

"Well, what's wrong with all that? And we need salt, don't we?"

"Salt is not food; it's just ground-up mineral rock."

"Rock?"

"Of course. Most of it's mined, just like any other rock. And the cheap white sugar – that stuff is so nutritionally degraded, it's more of a toxin than a food! It's just about nothing but pure carbon – everything, all the other nutrients have been robbed out of it. Takes B vitamins that you got somewhere else just to burn it! And the city water it's packed in – I wouldn't drink that stuff if you *paid* me!"

"I've never heard any of this before," the woman responded.

"I don't know *why*," said the Frowning Old Man. "All of this about what's proper nutrition has been out there; it's been around for over a hundred and fifty years. It's been in books, magazine articles, occasionally even on radio talk shows. This is all available in libraries, book stores, health food stores; it's on-line. All you have to do is *look* for it!"

"But those canned goods," another grossly overweight woman store worker broke in, "All those canned goods – why that's what *all* of us eat!"

"Yes," said the Frowning Old Man, "and it's probably what most of you will die from... inadequate nutrition and chemical poisoning. Why, there was a couple of cans of soup in that Christmas box, actually had monosodium glutamate in them! That stuff's so poisonous I wouldn't even feed that soup to my dogs! I think too much of their health."

"Well," said the first woman, "I don't think my husband would like it if I fed him what you're suggesting."

"Probably not," the Frowning Old Man replied sadly. That's why most people die long before their time and often have miserably painful deaths. If I tried to live on what the rest of you people eat, I'd have been dead long ago like many of you, or I'd be stumbling around in some nursing home like most of the rest of you my age… or I'd be in a hospital room somewhere just waiting to die."

"I don't understand something," the Frowning Old Man voiced with fiery emphasis. "Just *when* are you people going to *wake up*? When are you going to *learn*? The information is all out there. This is the information age; no one can claim ignorance anymore!"

The fat lady offered a comment:

"Some of us just like being the way we are. We like our food fixed the way it is."

"What incredible *stupidity*!" said the Frowning Old Man. "You average Americans are completly *stupid* about what you put down your gullets. If you doubt what I'm saying, just go into any grocery – anywhere in this country and see the overwhelming amount of chemicalized and nutritionally degraded white flour and white sugar products people have put in their carts at the checkout line. And look at them! The people are as fat as human *pigs*! And that's an insult to the poor animals!"

"We have great food content, labeling disclosure laws. But in all the years I've been going into groceries, never *once*… not even *once* have I ever seen anyone other than myself read the ingredient list on a label of any product! That in itself ought to tell you woman *something*; but I'm sure it doesn't." And even the federal government agrees with about half of what I'm telling you. And that's remarkable in itself, because the federal government is controlled largely by big business – and the food processing industry is a large part of that big business!"

"Hey – I didn't *invent* this stuff! Like I told you, it's been around for a hundred and fifty years! So *wake* up ! *Do* something about it! You   know   that   once   you've   been planted out in the marble orchard, you won't *ever* again be *able* to wake up; you won't ever be *able* to *do* something   about   it!"

"Well… I just don't think my husband would like it," said the first woman with a heavy sigh.

"Mine either!" said the fat lady.

"We're sorry you didn't like the Christmas food," another lady offered. "Maybe next year they might have more of what you like."

The Frowning old Man looked intensely at the three thrift store woman who had gathered around to listen to his almost apocalyptic tirade.

"What an incredible waste of time, energy and money that Christmas 'food' was," he began again. "*One* lousy orange! That orange cost me six dollars in gasoline alone! And if I had just gone ahead an *bought* oranges in the grocery, even at their highly inflated prices, that six dollars would have bought me at least *eight* oranges. What inefficiency, incompetence, bungling and outright, downright lack of concern by the organizers of that food project!"

One of the ladies looked at the Frowning Old Man with obvious compassion; "I don't know what else to say…"

"Well, I know what else to say," he mumbled – "and I've already said all of it… except… Merry Christmas."

He spat out his words with disgusted sarcasm – and left the store without even looking for a pair of shoes.

Preface for The Unending Train Ride

The main characters in the following story are based loosely on the personalities of two of my mother's relatives; her 'Aunt Gertie' and Gertie's daughter 'cousin Tillie'. While my memory of the two of them is not extensive, it is, none-the-less particularly sharp. In my mind's eye, I can still see little, huddled over, old Aunt Gertie and tall, pleasantly plain, cousin Tillie – reserved to the point of being almost unemotional.

My parents and I visited them a few times at their tiny apartment just off of DeSalevre in St. Louis, back in the nineteen fifties. Both Gertie and Tillie worked at menial, secretarial jobs and their income was too low to permit them to live in anything but the lowest cost housing available. My mother felt sorry for them and always gave them a Christmas present of money.

Dad would park the car on the narrow side street just below DeSalevre and we would walk up to the second floor apartment in that string of ugly old relics of human housing depravity. As Aunt Gertie opened the apartment door from the second floor hall, then closed it behind us, the murky yellowish hall light filtered through the dirt stained glass in the transom above the door. It played onto Aunt Gertie's face in a way that exaggerated the age lines… and it emphasized to me how fragile she must have been in the twilight of her pointedly mundane and uneventful life. The same sickening yellowishness of that hall light gave a similar illumination of decadence and despair to cousin Tillie's visage.

Their apartment was so minute that all three rooms were partly lit by that macabre light from the hall – and it touched both my parents and me with the anguish of this ghetto-like encounter.

Through the eyes of a teen-age boy, I built relatively little memory of Aunt Gertie - I know that I met her two or three times when my parents and I visited them on Thanksgiving or at Christmas at their midtown apartment. But Tillie stands out in my mind; even though I saw her no more often than that, I have a very clear memory of her – face – fraught with depressingly sallow skin and a hopeless expression in her eyes – eyes that were clouded by a distant, distracted gaze.

It seemed to me that her washed-out, dark blondish hair was a bit long for a woman in her late forties. And her facial features, while not what one would call actually pretty, were remarkably pleasant in an almost indefinable way.

Without quite knowing why, I had a profound feeling – almost akin to empathy for Tillie; perhaps it was largely pity. Tillie epitomized the daughter who – for whatever reason, stayed with her elderly mother and gave up all thoughts of ever having a normal family life of her own.

The last visit we made there was when I was still only sixteen – very inexperienced in life. I had little understanding of my own emotions… yet I felt that deep pity for Tillie. I wished later, that I had been able to say something meaningful – something loving to her. But I was too young – too inept. I just stood there, and that was the last time I ever saw cousin Tillie.

It was not terribly long after that – we learned that aunt Gertie had passed away. Her life must have been heavily insured, because Tillie gave up the ghetto apartment, took a trip to Europe, bought herself a new car and some expensive clothes – and then was dead within a year… at her own hand…

The following story, The Unending Train Ride is completely fictional. The two main characters are very marginally based on cousin Tillie and Aunt Gertie – but only as emotional elaborations of personality – not on any factual happenings. I have merely taken personalities and placed them in a hypothetical situation that could have taken place anywhere.

The Unending Train Ride

2/8/04

It was as though the sunshine – and the whole world outside were trying to leap in and kiss everyone within that window. Helen sat with her book, left arm resting on the window sill carefully, studying text – so it seemed. Her eyes could be followed moving from line to line as she read down the page. But she would suddenly put the book down and close it without a marker, then pick up a newspaper and begin reading down a column in that.

A few moments later, Helen became aware of a presence next to her. She looked up nervously.

"Young man, would you please try to find the conductor and ask him why this train is not moving? I know that I've been sitting here for at least an hour and it hasn't moved an inch! I'd like to know what's wrong. My Aunt in California is very ill and if I don't get there soon, she might die before I can say goodbye to her!"

The young man in his green scrubs looked back at her pleasantly, smiling slightly. "Yes, ma'am," he told her tersely – but agreeable. Then he walked off.

Helen slid over, away from the intense sunlight streaming through the window and fidgeted in her bag, pulling out a pair of reading glasses. She opened the book to a new place and began to read again.

With her long hair brushed straight back and the glasses, she appeared very much like a school marm preparing for a new lesson. Even her English tweed lady's business jacket and matching skirt added to the illusion.

If one thing gave the truth away, though, it was the patches on the well-worn elbows of the jacket. And somehow, the great length of her greying hair seemed inconsistent with a pedagogical appearance.

Mable edged her wheelchair over, close to where Helen was sitting. As the elderly woman placed a gnarled hand on Helen's arm, she spoke softly; "Helen, honey, I just wanted to see how you were doing today. Just wanted to say hello to you…"

When Helen looked up, her eyes glanced directly out of the window: she seemed not to realize who it was that had touched her arm.

"Oh… conductor! I'm so glad you came. I'm so concerned about the long delay. I know that the train hasn't moved in at least an hour, because I remember seeing that same house out there when I started reading this book. And you can see, I've already read about a fourth of it this morning! Just *what* is causing this delay?"

As though listening to an unspoken answer, Helen sat in alertness, smoothing her hair with her right hand while holding the place in the book with her left.

There were movements around the room, murmurs, but no one spoke loudly enough to be heard.

"Thank you conductor, I appreciate your reassurance... and I *do* hope they are able to clear that accident away soon so that we can proceed."

Mable backed her wheelchair away from the window and sat there studying Helen for a few moments. She lifted a tissue to dry her eyes sitting in the wheelchair, Mable watched Helen from a distance. The long scar across Helen's temple that went down past her ear, seemed even more faint today than usual.

"Helen... *Helen*!" Mable called out, trying to get the younger woman's attention. "Helen, that accident happened almost fifteen years ago. Don't you *understand* that, Helen?"

Helen looked around as though Mable's voice had come from outside the building's walls somewhere... as though it might have been part of the rumbling of the institutions heating system.

"Accident? Helen reflected, "what accident? Where has there been an accident? I hope no one was hurt... oh I *do* hope no one was hurt!"

Mable sat in agonized pity wiping the streams of tears that poured down her face.

"Helen – oh Helen... please listen to me. This is your Aunt Mable talking to you. Helen!"

The weak voice of the tiny crippled woman drifted away into the distant corners of the room. Momentary silence gave way to the clatter of lunch trays being delivered in the hallway.

Mable again edged her way against Helen's chair and touched her niece's arm in another attempt to gain her attention.

"Helen, honey – oh honey, I really *do* understand how much you must have suffered those two years just drifting around the country, desperate – begging... not knowing who you were or where you were. All of us understand. You do know who you are now, don't you?"

There was a long suspended delay before Helen answered.

"Yes... my wrist tag says I'm Helen Severnsen... so I guess that must be who I am... "

"Helen – we've been in here together now for almost ten years and every day you're still on that same train!"

Looking straight ahead of her with eyes that seemed to penetrate right through Mable into a cosmogenic vastness, Helen acted as though she had not heard her Aunt. Then she answered softly:

"Yes, I know – I know..."

"Helen, honey – aren't' you *ever* going to get off the train?" Almost as if transfixed in a hypnotic gaze, Helen's mouth gently opened and formed words of caustically cryptic finality.

"No," she reflected, "I'm probably not... not even when I die..."

The Death Knell

Rewritten 5/27/23

A gust of wind carried the huge, brightly colored beach ball out of Tony's yard, bounding and spinning along into the adjoining graveyard grounds. The six year old boy went running after the ball, following it until it rolled up a hill and stopped against the side of a small mausoleum.

He grabbed his ball and then on tiptoes tried to look into the building's long side window. He could barely see the long glass case with the body of a young girl preserved in a vacuum.

As the boy was about to run back home, the grounds caretaker drove up pulling an antiquated five gang spread of reel mowers behind an ancient tractor.

Aldous Grimstone shut the engine off and confronted the boy.

"Whateryuh doin' over here!" he snarled.

"The wind blew my ball." the boy replied meekly.

"Well get th' hell outta here – an' don't come back! Next time the wind blows yer ball over here, leave it! Go buy a new one! I don't care if the wind blows yer house over here! Don't come over here! You got that? Now *git*!!"

Tony ran back to his yard and played with the ball inside his house.

Later, his mother asked the boy about the incident; "I saw you go after your ball and the graveyard groundskeeper talking to you. What did he say?"

"Aw… he just told me to stay out."

"Well, don't go in there; they say he's not a very nice person. If it's windy, just play with your ball in the house."

"Alright."

During that summer, Tony learned to listen and watch for the tractor as Mr. Grimstone mowed the cemetery grass. There would be a long period when the grass on the opposite hill was being mowed that allowed the boy an opportunity to run to the mausoleum and look in the window. On one occasion he walked past the end of the building and found that the door had been left open to air out the building when Grimstone had gone in to check the vacuum in the case.

Tony slipped into the small building and looked in the case, his height being enough to see more clearly from inside. The girl in the case was extraordinarily beautiful with long wavy hair. The boy stood there fascinated, but ran out when he heard the tractor leave the opposite hill.

Periodically, during the next few years, the boy would occasionally slip away into the graveyard to look in the glass case at the sleeping beauty.

When Tony was twelve years old, his parents had a talk with him about his education.

"Tony", his father started, "You know that we want you to have a high quality education. The first six grades here in our local school aren't too bad. But the upper grades here are just not what I'd consider good enough to give you a proper preparation for college. There's a very good boarding school in another part of the state with excellent teachers and a much broader curriculum. I'll leave it up to you if you want to stay here or go to the other school. We have plenty of time – so just think about it. Okay?"

Tony nodded.

Later that week, Tony told his father "Yeah… I think I'll go to the boarding school. I think you're right."

"Alright, we'll try it for a semester. If you like it you can stay – if not you can come back here."

Two years went by with the boy staying at the boarding school and spending summers at home. He was already fourteen that summer, riding his bike around, exploring nearby places riding the short distance to town. One day, he was out in the back and listened for the sound of the mower. It seemed to be far off on some distant hill. He rode his bike over to the mausoleum and looked in the window. The case was empty! Tony stood there transfixed, unbelieving. He was not conscious of the approach of the tractor.

Grimstone got down off the tractor and waked over to where the boy was still standing.

"Ha! Yer girlfriend's gone ain't she!"

"Wha – what happened?"

"Ha, ha… she just dried up an' blowed away!!"

"Why?"

Grimstone suddenly seemed to have a touch of almost embarrassed compassion.

"Ah… it was the seals on the case. I checked the vacuum every two weeks. Last time I checked it was still okay. Next time there was no vacuum at all. Must'a lost vacuum right after I checked it. Those rubber seals was seventy years old – that's 'fore they had neoprene rubber. They dried out 'n cracked. That quick, wasn't nothin' left but skin 'n bones. Had to cremate everything."

Tony got on his bike and rode away. He headed toward town.

The two spinster sisters Sarah and Clara had just left Doc Wittiingham's Drugstore and were walking home.

"Clara, that's the death kneel, isn't it? Two short rings and one long one?"

"Yes it is – but this is Monday! It's always on a Saturday!"

"Well, I wonder who died!"

"Parson didn't mention anything about anyone dying yesterday."

"But he should know."

"Let's go over to the church and ask him."

"You know he isn't here on Monday – he goes to Grubtown to see the sick and elderly."

"You're right… so who…"

"Let's just cross the street and go in the church."

The two women try the front door and find it locked.

"Maybe the back door's open."

They walk to the side of the church.

"Look the side door's ajar. Let's see if someone's in there."

"No one's in here Sarah – but look, the bell ropes still moving a little."

"Hello… hello… anybody in here?"

"See, no one's in here. They must have gone out and then went up the street into the one of those houses. But I didn't see anyone, did you?"

"No, sister, the only person I saw was a boy on a bicycle."

"Well, I didn't notice him – I was looking in my purse for my glasses."

"Oh, the person will know – we'll just ask him tomorrow.

"Of course – you're right."

A letter to the Rowen family who own a pet crematory..

Dear Friends,

To receive a condolence card for the death of one of my little dog-children is more than unusual – it is unique. It has never happened before.

"Ragman" was my only "outside" dog. He had lived with me for 4 years and 4 months and had been brought to me from a family in Missouri, where he had just wandered in, the year before. The people had other dogs and were tired of feeding Ragman (who had no name). They kept him tied up all day because he bit at strangers. He was about to be taken to the dog pound, where his chances of finding a new home were very slim, so I offered to take him instead.

I called him "Ragman", because his black coat was very ragged-looking; I guessed his age to be about six or seven years. He was definitely no youngster. But Ragman quickly attached himself to me and became the most obedient little fellow I had ever kept. He seemed only to want to try to please me – that was his greatest joy in life… and he had almost a telepathic ability to know, very often, what I wanted him to do even before I could verbalize it. Each day, for him, was full of the joy of living.

Since the little fellow was street-wise and large enough to take care of himself (I had had 4 smaller dogs killed by wild animals the year before I got Ragman), I simply let him have free run of my 23 acres and the adjoining farms. Most of the time, though, he preferred to stay close by me and sometimes watch the other smaller dogs I now keep in my fenced yard.

I suppose that I should be glad that I was able to give Ragman an extra 4 years and 4 months of healthy, happy life – but even the thought of this doesn't seem to make his death any easier to accept. Although Ragman was always a very loving little guy, for the week before he died, he seemed to have almost a premonition of his own death, because he just couldn't get enough petting and hugging. It was as though he somehow knew that he would soon be going away and we would never see each other again. Perhaps a dog can sense this…

I look upon all my dogs as my little children – they are like little human children who never "grow up". No doubt that is why they endear themselves to us so much. Our human children are little and cute and funny for only a few years; by the age of ten or eleven they have already matured enough to have left that stage of cuteness. But our dogs can live their entire 15 or 20 years and never lose it. And when I say "my" dogs, I don't mean that I "own" them any more than I "owned" my human child. We merely happen to live together; they "belong" to themselves and choose to live with me.

There is a picture of me at age 2 or 3, wide-eyed and a little frightened-looking, standing next to the family German shepherd, Buddy, hugging tightly onto him. Even when I was only in my 20's I can recall telling people that I liked most dogs a lot more than I did most people. I think that this is because a dog is honest. If he likes you he'll lick your hand – if he dislikes you he'll bite your leg. Dogs are never two-faced – they either like you or they don't.

I've kept a lot of dogs in my nearly 84 years. Most were 'cast-offs" that I adopted (like Ragman). A few wandered in. A few were purchased for me or I bought myself. But I can't recall any of them being as obedient or wanting to please like Ragman. He was still basically a wanderer, though, and it didn't surprise me when he began to wander again early this year. He would stay away for only a day or two, not going far, but the last time he must have found something poisonous to eat and a neighbor down the road found him dead laying between two hay stacks a few days after he disappeared from here. The memories of my other dogs have dimmed over the years, but I hope my memory of Ragman never does.

It seems the older I get, the more these deaths affect me. Ragman's death opens up old wounds; all those other deaths – dogs and humans – revisit themselves upon my memory. All my best high school buddies who were like extended family – brothers and sisters – now all gone, as well as all my beloved dogs. And somehow... new friends just never seem to be able to replace the old – those of our youth.

Where it all ends is, of course, the grave – eventually our own. And we all know this; but the great expanse of life is slowly eroded by death... and our memory is inexorably compressed into the obscurity of half-forgotten dreams.

"Hobo Jack" Sophir

How I Found Natural Hygiene

(Or Did it Find Me?)

This unlikely story started back around 1941 or 1942, when at the tender age of 9 or 10 I first became aware of that unabashedly "cute" little automobile called the American Austin. Cute it was – without reservation, but reliable it was not. Built from 1930 to 1934, it was a mechanical absurdity. A barely warmed leftover from its older British cousin, the Austin 7. The engine, when it decided to run at all, gave the diminutive puddle-jumper about as much power as a kid's pedal car trying to negotiate a hill in a show storm.

But I loved those little disc wheeled chariots of the uncommonly poor man. Above any other car, I wanted to own an American Austin. Whenever we saw one as we drove along the street, I would say to my father "Daddy, I want to drive an Austin when I grow up!" My dear old dad would humor me with an indulgent silence (what else could he do with a dumb 9 year old kid?). Because by the time I "grew up", nearly everyone who had an Austin – and still had any sense – *no longer* had an Austin.

In 1948, I was sixteen and had just earned my first driver's license. After a disastrous experience purchasing my first car, a ragged 1933 Chevrolet coupe, I wanted to try to find a restorable American Austin.

In 1948, World War II had been over for 3 years and gasoline rationing was long past. The junkyards had absorbed nearly all of the Austins (and later Bentams and even Crosleys) that had been reluctantly kept alive during the years of gas shortage. It was then that I began riding my 1940 Powell motor scooter around to used car lots in search of a restorable American Austin.

I searched... and searched... and finally, on the trade-in lot of a Crosley dealer – there it was! The car of my dreams – as big (or should I say as *little*) as life. Standing there in its glowing flat black brush paint job, with rusty aluminum-painted bumpers and a pitted chrome radiator shell was the outrageous relic of an American Austin. The price painted on its smog-fogged windshield was $65. Only $65!

I rode my motor scooter home like a madman, grabbed the bank book and called my pal, Lark. "Hey, Lark... I found an Austin for $65. Can you drive me there to get it?"

"Sure, be right over."

Almost lovingly, I stacked what amounted to half my savings on the dealer's counter for this first dream car of mine, unaware that I would someday corner the market on Austins.

With the key in the ignition, I pressed the start button – and by some unknown miracle, the engine coughed, sputtered and started up. Off I drove, amid the fanfare of loose nuts and bolts and the ever faithful bailing wire rattling in, if not actually *flying* into the breeze. On we roared with no muffler – spewing a cloud of blue oil smoke like a jet trail, until...

Halfway home part of the wiring burned up. Almost at the same instant the radiator boiled over, spouting water at every hose connection. The gas line was leaking a stream, the clutch slipped so bad at 15 MPG that it made you feel like you were going 90 – but the brakes barely stopped at 10. The headlamps were too dim to see by and three tires were going flat... the little engine seemed to take a last mighty gasp before it died – forever. I got out and as I slammed the door, huge chunks of rust fell from the lower edge of the body.

Lark used his car to push the deceased midget the rest of the way home. As we pulled up to the curb, my father came out of the house with obvious curiosity – which quickly changed to irritation. He took one quick look "How much did they pay you to haul that refuge from the bone yard off their lot?" "Aw, dad, it's not *that* bad – just needs some paint and a tune-up."

"Yeah, well you better not leave it out front very long – Old Man Packman'll complain. You know how he is!" I knew *exactly* how he was... "And don't expect me to rent a garage for you to put that piece of junk in!"

The next morning when I went out to look at my "dream car", I was like a man with a great behemoth of a hangover. The events of the previous day were acidly etched into my mind – a gruesome nightmare.

I quickly realized that this 65 dollar relic was simply beyond restoration and I needed to dispose of it and look for a more restorable Austin.

I called my friend Lark, bemoaning my situation.

"Look – you only paid sixty-five dollars for it, why don't we just pull it over here and you can let it sit on the lot next to my house – where the "grey ghost" is. Nobody is going to bother it there and you can use it for parts."

"Okay," I said, "let's do it!"

With the '33 Austin parts-car no longer a problem, I began my search again for a restorable Austin.

Immediately after I had disposed of my first American Austin, a *completely* worn out 1933 coupe, I began looking again, this time for a better version of the same car.

After school nearly every day, I would ride my 1940 Powell motor scooter over to Welston so that I could look in the used car lots and stop in at St. Louis Auto Salvage to see if an Austin might have made its way in there. For months I continued to do this as long as the weather wasn't too cold. During the middle of winter, I stopped.

One spring day, I began making my rounds again; I stopped in at St. Louis Auto Salvage and went to the counter to talk to Al Goldstein. He was used to my coming in asking about American Austins.

"Hi Al – did anyone bring in an Austin?"

He smiled: "Yeah – you should have come in here a month ago! There's one out there, but now it's buried in the middle of the yard!"

"Gee Al, why didn't you save it for me?"

"You know we can't tie up the space like that, Shamus why'd you stop coming around?"

"Aw.. it got too cold for me to ride the scooter."

Al shrugged and lifted his eyebrows. "That's life – right?"

I looked dejected, but walked out into the yard to try to find the Austin. After almost an hour of searching, I finally located the little car, half hidden behind a line of five larger, later model cars.

The Austin's body still had reasonably good green paint on it and the car appeared to be complete, with no large dents anywhere. I lifted the hood, which flopped off to one side. No engine! But *everything* else was there. I went back to talk to Al.

"I found the Austin, Al... but what happened to the engine?"

He looked at me sheepishly. "We sold it; got a hundred dollars for it."

I cringed "Aw gee... well, what d' you want for what's left?"

Al thought for a minute "Well, for you, Shamus... fifteen dollars."

"Okay," I said and got out the money and handed it to him. He handed me a receipt and the title.

"But now listen," Al said, "I can't tie up two men moving all those cars just so you can get to it. They'd have to cut up at least two of the cars – there's no room anywhere else to put 'em. So how you gonna get it out?"

I thought for a few seconds. "I'll get together a bunch of my high school buddies and we'll *carry* it out!"

Al gave a long laugh "*That* I'll have to see!"

The next day after school, Larkin and I drove to the junkyard in his '33 Chevy. The Austin's head lights were already off inside the car, removed when the engine was sold. The radiator had been loosened and pulled forward to remove the engine and we finished loosening the bolts and removed it, carrying it and the headlights to our car. We then inflated all the tires on the Austin with a hand pump. It was ready to be carried out.

On Saturday, I borrowed my dad's '47 Nash and went around picking up all my high school friends. Larkin McKibbin and Mal Clark drove to the junkyard in Lark's Chevy; Dan Leavitt and Al Schoenblat and Herb Faintich rode there with me. Everyone thought this would be a fun-funny experience carrying a car out of a junkyard.

We all walked down to where the tiny Austin sat hiding behind its larger junk mates.

"Okay, guys," I said, "Because the engine and radiator are both gone, the front end is pretty light; the main weight of the car's gonna be in the back. Let's get three on a side, but 4 closer to the rear. Okay?"

Herb Faintich went to the front trying to show off how strong he was. He tried unsuccessfully to lift the front of the car by its front bumper.

Dan gave a loud laugh and yelled "Herb can't lift the front – he's got a *faint itch*!" Everybody laughed.

We all began lifting on the car and managed to raise it a few inches, rolling it forward with its wheels starting to travel up the trunk of the car in front. Everyone got behind the Austin, pushing it up the back of the car in front and on up to the roof, along the roof and then down onto the hood and onto the next car ahead. This process was repeated two more times until we reached a four foot wide opening between the next cars. The Austin just barely squeezed in between the next two cars and we rolled it on out to the driveway for the junkyard. Someone had told Albert that we had gotten the Austin out. He opened the back door of the office and looked out.

"We got the Austin out Al" I yelled to him.

"Yeah, I see" he shook his head in amazement.

"We rolled it over the tops of the cars in front of it!"

"I'd never have believed it if I hadn't seen it," he laughed.

We then pushed the Austin on out to the street.

I chained the Austin's bumper to my dad's Nash got in and with one of the boys steering the Austin we pulled it the four miles to my home on Cornell. I removed the chain and we pushed the diminutive car into the garage, then we repositioned the Austin sideways in the very back. And there it stayed for another two years until I was finally able to get an engine for it.

To finish this thought, although my father still had enough room in the garage to put his car in, he did have to be a little more careful because there was only two feet of clearance between his Nash and the Austin. And it was an irritation to my Dad because he considered the Austin a "piece of junk". He had no appreciation for antique cars (or antiques of any kind); he could see no value in the older car's esthetic styling or in it's historic possibility. But he was no different from most other Americans in that respect.

Everything had to be up-to-date modern to have any value to him – regardless of how ugly or shoddy the item was constructed. Perhaps that is why there are so few antique cars or antique furniture pieces, or so few of the truly great, beautiful antique homes left. People want

212

everything new and modern – ugly looking and shoddily constructed with inferior materials – at least in this country.

But there are other cultures in this world where the traditional and beautiful *are* valued – perhaps not many, but there are at least a few. And *I* still have my Austin 75 years after I bought it out of the junkyard!

Now… does that tell you anything?… anything other than that I am quite old. Well… perhaps it does, but perhaps not…

William Piotrasche had a face like a jovial man-in-the-moon - round, with very close-cropped gray-blond hair and almost invisible eyebrows. He had, as his name implied, more the ethnic appearance of Polish or Slavic family ties; certainly not German, which he spoke fluently, and claimed was the result of his family's place of origin. But whatever he was or was not ethnically, more important by far, was the fact that he was the owner of an American Austin… a *running* American Austin… a *good* running American Austin!

My introduction to this unusual worthy came after many unsuccessful attempts to flag him down on the street. Always, it seemed, his little car was headed the opposite direction. One day, I succeeded in catching up with him at an intersection. At close range I could see the miserably sloppy welds that held fenders, doors, bumpers – everything – together, which had over the years broken from vibration on rough back roads. The car's hood was even covered with an old army raincoat tied down with leather belts. In sharp contracts to the drab gray car was its owner's effervescent smiling face.

"Want to sell this car? I asked"

"Oh my no!" – he was still smiling. "But you can come out and visit me if you want. I live by myself on the farm and I don't get much company." He may have been curious to know why any sane young man would ever want to buy his shabby, unimpressive little tinker-toy. All I knew was that I desperately needed that engine or his car. He gave me the directions to his farm, and I watched with avarice as he drove off silently – and smokelessly.

Several days later, after managing to borrow the family car, I drove to the Piotrasche farm in Creve Coeur, Missouri. From where I parked the car I couldn't see the Austin – nor could I discern any sign of life. It was early evening, and as I walked to the unpainted clapboard farmhouse, bats were already beginning to chase insects around the roof. The house appeared to be uninhabited, but I went to the front door and knocked anyway. There was no answer. Somewhere, I was sure, concealed in this sanctum sanctorum was my new acquaintance. Thoughts of insidiously arcane and esoteric activities that might be going on here fleetingly entered my mind. Suddenly all were dispelled by a friendly voice calling to me from the cellar doorway.

Bill, as I came to know him, welcomed me into the dirt-floor basement room where he lived. "Don't need all that space upstairs in the house.", he explained. "Besides, it's warmer in the winter and cooler in the summer down here." That made sense to me, though a lot of other things about him didn't. Bill was rather a strange fellow; basically a loner, he had never been married, but delighted in telling stories about his many exploits with women. And I have to admit that I was either intrigued or amused – but always delighted to know that he was accepting me as a friend (I *needed* that *engine!*)

Since my visits soon became a regular bi-weekly ritual, Bill eventually ran out of stories and our conversation began to center on some of his prominent eccentricities. For example, he drank "battery water" (distilled water) and he raised most of his own food. (Nobody else *I* had ever known did *that*.) He ate most of his food raw (my gawd – even raw *peanuts* – revolting!) And strangest of all, he ate no meat. No animal flesh of any kind. That, I thought was *truly weird*! I began bringing some of my friends with me on the visits, to see this incredible odd-ball.. so that we could have some good laughs about him when we got home.

Time passed – weeks, months and still I was getting nowhere with my attempts to buy Piotrasche's Austin. Every time I brought up the subject, he would counter with "What would I drive if I sold it? Besides, I've owned that car since it was new in 1934." (He had been an Austin dealer). I knew that the only way I was ever going to get the car was to offer to buy him another car that he liked better, and which would be easier to get parts for. That in itself was a stalemate – simply because there *was* no other car that he liked better. My only hope was that eventually I could somehow get him to a used car lot that had a Jeep – and give him a ride in it.

But until that time, I felt that I had to keep up the routine of my visits. Sometimes on those visits, instead of trying to explain why he lived in such a peculiar manner, Bill would simply just hand me a book to read. Wanting to be as agreeable as possible, but being just a dumb, very conventional kid, I would nod my head and spew an endless plethora of "um-hum, yeah… very interesting – how 'bout that!"

Then one day he stuck a small red book in my hands that would change my life forever. From almost the moment I opened the cover on Herbert M. Shelton's "Hygienic System" Volume II, I knew that what Bill Piotrasche had learned was the most profound discipline of healthful living ever discovered. Although *Bill* was unable to explain very well why he lived as he did, Shelton *was* able to. The extraordinary simplicity of the concept, when explained by Shelton, was overpowering – even for an 18 year old. I did not have to ponder long that concept of what was eminently natural for man as an animal.

At that point Bill began inviting me to go along with him to various health lectures and meetings. I always tried to drive him there in the family car – at first, as I told myself, to save wear and tear on "my" engine in his Austin. But the realization came to me that this was no longer my primary motive. I was beginning to understand that Bill was not a lone oddity in the world – that there were others like him – many others… and that healthful living was a growing concern of multitudes of people everywhere… and that all that was needed to change the world (back) into a better natural habitat was a few of the right people at that right place – at the right time. Perhaps they all awaited some Hygienic "messiah" – or perhaps were waiting patiently for the concepts to slowly diffuse. Whichever it may be, I suppose we're still going to have to wait a while yet.

But there was another extraordinary lesson that I learned from all of this. It was that one person *can* radically alter the life of another person – for that other's great benefit. Certainly, almost without realizing it, that is precisely what had happened to me.

Oh,… and Bill Piotrasche's Austin? *Never* did get it…

I finally lost contact with Bill Piotrasche; I had learned of a machinist who lived only a half mile from my home and also had a badly battered '33 Austin with an engine he had rebuilt. I became a friend of this fellow and he sold me the engine from his car when he decided to convert the drive train to a late model Crosley – a much more powerful and reliable system.

Years later, I learned that Bill Piotrasche had sold his Austin and bought a Ford Jeep from a used car lot, but I was never able to find out where the Austin had disappeared to.

A final note about Bill Piotrasche: Although Bill Piotrasche became a very important personal friend in my late teenage years, by the time I was 20 and attending Washington University School of Fine Arts regularly and avidly, I had little time for making long distance visits.

I did get Bill to allow me to store a '32 Packard convertible on his farm until I could attempt to get it running. Later, he allowed me to store a full ton truckload of small pieces of lumber from wrecked down obsolete store fixtures from Melman Fixture co. (I had no way to get the load to the family farm at Lone Dell Mo.). I finally gave the entire truckload to Bill who wanted to make a grape arbor with the smaller slats. That was probably my last contact with Bill Piotrasche.

Bill's parents had been Germen immigrants early in the 20th century and had purchased the farm in Creve Couer, Mo. (I can't recall whether it was 60 acres or 160 acres). After his parents grew too old to continue farming, they began selling off the tillable acreage to neighboring farmers. By the time his parents died, there was only 13 acres left of the original tract. Ten acres of that was on a fairly steep hillside which had eroded away to yellow clay subsoil; only three acres were flat ground around the house next to the county road (Marine Avenue). Bill had his small vegetable garden in what was the chicken yard next to the house.

Whether Bill inherited his Ford 8N Tractor or bought it with the money left to him when his parents died, I never learned. The tractor seemed to be fairly new and had a hydraulically operated blade which Bill used to do custom grading work for his neighbors and which provided him with a source for making his living (though his need for money was extremely minimal).

After about 1953, I saw nothing more of Bill Piotrasche (I was spending a great deal of my time traveling). Some time later, I heard from Sterling Ryan, owner of New Dawn Health Food store, where Bill Piotrasche occasionally bought items, that he had apparently been offered some outrageously high price for his remaining acreage by a subdivision developer and sold it. Bill then used the money to buy a farm near Petosi, Mo., sold his Austin and bought a Ford Jeep. That was the last I ever heard about him. Bill was about 25 years older than I was. That means he was born about 1910. I know that his natural hygiene diet kept him healthy, but if he were still alive, he'd be 115 years old – and he'd be some kind of national hero – he'd have been on the news media as the oldest living American! So, Bill Piotrasche – R.I.P.!

Jack Sophir, Jr. (Joaquin)

Feb. 1990

Addendum to "How I Found Natural Hygiene"

It's sad to realize that after over 40 years now since I was first introduced to natural hygiene, the membership of my local hygiene society is no larger than it was when I first joined it.

The population of this country has increased probably about 25% in that time – but junk food has proliferated with an unbounded ferocity. Even though there have been an almost endless number of clinical studies, experiments and research projects on the effects of and the need for natural health and even though these studies have received wide coverage in the news media, people in general are still as addicted as ever to their drugs (prescription drugs, coffee, cigarettes and liquor), devitalized foods and destructive lifestyles. The world is still under the pernicious influence of the refined (junk) food industry and its intended or unintended allies, the pharmaceutical industry and the powerful medical monopoly.

In my opinion, it is only through many more efforts like the Diamonds' "Fit For Life" – but aimed at the basically non-reading masses – that there will ever be a chance for a distinct difference in national health patterns.

The saddest part of all this is that sincere, devoted natural hygienists are severely limited in the choices they have for mates. It is often hard enough just to find someone who meets your standards for common interests, religious beliefs, physical appearance, etc., let alone find someone whose lifestyle (nutritionally) is compatible And what could possibly be more important in overall health than having a mate – one who is compatible in the most basic areas?

Jack Sophir, Jr. (Joaquin) Nov. 1992

Mose and the Carmaker

10/9/93

The kid had been wandering around the yard almost half a day., And that wasn't the first time. This seemingly aimless meandering had become an impassioned routine for him as he haunted even the most remote corners of Saint Louis Auto Salvage, the largest and oldest auto wrecking yard in the city. Populated with many stately, but forever silent remains of huge Packards, Cadillacs and Lincolns from the 1920's and '30's, that junk yard was a haven of delight for any imaginative autofile. In those less frenetic days of the early 1950's, a car could stay for years in its final resting place, the auto grave yard, before being cut up and sent "back to its maker".

Also well represented in the yard were the odd-ball makes – from tiny, to massive remnants of an age of automotive diversity and individuality. And since almost no one valued any of this as "collectable", the prices of the parts, or the cars themselves, ranged from reasonable to very cheap.

This was a warm, sunny, spring Friday with no school – the perfect day to tramp through acres of lifeless machines – sit behind the steering wheels of relics from a bygone era...dreaming in the automobile fantasies of boyhood.

At mid-day, after walking back up to the office, the kid approached the trio behind the counter. "What would you guys want for that '29 Packard opera-coupe with the stuck engine?" The Packard had been there for years. No one had ever bought a piece of it except for the headlights.

Billy was the first to answer. "Ah – you can have it for...what d'ya think, guys – 'bout a hundred dollars?"

"Nah, sell it to him for seventy-five." Albert chimed in. He was not only an agreeable chap, but glad to have the opportunity to move out some useless iron.

"You want the engine and radiator?" Bobby looked over at the kid. "They're no good anyway. Without 'em – take it for sixty." The big radiator would scrap out for twenty dollars and the engine an extra five – so by lowering the price fifteen, they made an extra ten. The kid didn't care how it worked out; the price sounded good.

It was a deal. Sixty bucks; the kid handed over three twenty dollar bills. None of them knew what he wanted to do with the Packard – or

218

cared. They had sold him a '41 Cadillac engine and a '42 Mercury frame earlier that year. As far as they were concerned, this kid was some kind of nutty car fanatic.

The kid caught Albert's attention. "Hay Al – remember that Mercury frame you sold me for twenty-five dollars?" Albert just smiled. "Well it's really too light for the Caddy engine. Can I sell it back to you and have you lift the engine off of it and put it down in the Packard?"

Albert was still smiling. "Yea, sure. Give you fifteen for the frame and we'll switch the engine around."

Al went to the back door and looked for a yard man. He yelled to the slim dark figure in the distance. "Mose; - can you hear me, Mose?" Then pointing over toward the kid – "He's going to show you which car he bought. Help him get it out."

There were five "yard men" – all of them men of color…and the blackest and tallest and thinnest was Mose. He had an almost painfully gaunt face with prominent cheekbones. But his lean looks belied the great power of that sparce frame. Fiery-eyed and scowling, he chewed incessantly on a plastic cigar holder with an unlit stub in it. A wide, thick moustache sprawled over his clenched teeth. He spat his words out as though they were tobacco juice. "Sheeit!" he grumbled loudly as he neared the office. The kid was reminded of a big, leggy, ugly, black spider every time he looked at Mose.

Threading their way through the maze of interlocking auto carcasses being picked over by parts vultures, Mose and the kid walked over to the '29 Packard.

"Sheeit! Wha'd a hell d'matta wit' Albert? He know ah gots ta move fo', fahve caws ta git to dis! Dat go' take me, Tate an' Levi ha'fa day to get dem caws out – we's go' hafta cut 'em all up, mos' likely. Ah still gots ta cut out a engine an' a reah en' an' git two brake drums…Simon go' kick my ass if ah don' git dat stuff t'day." Mose glowered at the kid.

"Listen, there's no big hurry on it. I don't have to get the car today."

Mose relaxed his perpetual scowl a bit. "Y'all come back t'marra' earleh an' we gits it out. Say, whut you go' do wit' all dis stuff? You buidlin' caws?"

Well…yeah. I'm going to make a "special"; lower it, chop the top. Put that big Caddy engine in it…"

"You is a caw makah..." Mose mused – then he half smiled, intrigued and a little bewildered. "You got a big shop wheh you go' do all dis?"

"Not really. But...I do have welding equipment and...I'm...I'm just going to have to work out all the rest."

Mose bit down hard on his cigar holder with a slight smile "See yuh t'marra' mawnin', Cawmakah."

The next morning was rank with anxiety. Carmaker found Mose positioning the tow truck in front of the first of the cannibalized hulks blocking access to the Packard. The later cars in the rows adjoining the Packard seemed amorphous and small next to its grand and distinctive old marquee. As Mose pulled a car out and flipped it over, Levi and Tate used their torches to cut it into sections small enough for the truck to drag to the cutter. All morning they worked, Carmaker busying himself with hand pumping the Packard's tires and unbolting the various lines, rods and wires that would still cause problems after the engine's mount bolts were cut. Finally, Mose was able to get close to the Packard and cut the engine loose.

The shrill blast from a local factory whistle signaled noon hour. Each of the yard men left his project, trudging up to the office to exchange his tool box for his lunch box. Lunch was a welcome half hour respite from heavy labor in the heat of midday. The heat was becoming as oppressive as the smoke from burning grease on the torched-off parts.

Carmaker sat inside his opera coupe and waited. Since Mose had left his tools at the Packard, he returned soon with his lunch.

"Ain'chu go' eat lunch?"

"Nah, I seldom eat lunch – especially on a day like today."

"Ah gots a extra b'lo'ny sangrich if you wants it."

"Thanks – no – no. That's really nice of you to offer it, Mose – but I'm – just kind of nervous about getting this car out of here."

Mose sat on the running board leaning against the back fender. He lit up the ancient cigar stub, puffed it a couple of times and let it go out.

"Ah wants ta ast you sump'n."

"Sure."

"You knows dehs hun'erts 'n hun'erts a guys comes in yeah buyin' pawts fo' deh caws – you's 'd' only one dat's *makin'* a caw. You *is* a caw makah, awright but Ah's cur'rus ta know whut you done wit dat Merc'ry frame Ah cut out fo' yuh...an' dem big ol' fendehs an' cowel offa dat henny daid-wagon. An' whut 'bout dat trunk an' back pawt a' duh body Ah cut off a Linc'n Cont'nent'l fo' yuh?"

"Oh…I…I still have all of it. I'll use most of it sometime. But the Mercury fame just won't work out because it was too light and the engine would also be set right over the front axel like it was in the Merc. If you look at this Packard, the radiator is over the front axel. That means the engine weight is a lot further back in the car where it ought to be. I'd have to extend the Mercury frame and front axel forward to get the engine weight far enough back. The Merc frame is too light as it is anyway and lengthening it would weaken it more. It's all just far more trouble than it's worth.

As the Carmaker explains his ideas, Mose sat in rapt silence. "See, this all started when they began pushing the engines further forward in the early '30's and that's what makes modern car's steering so unstable at very high speeds. The cars they're making today have the front of the engine eight or ten inches forward of the axel – that weight up front also causes excessive wear on all the front end parts. On top of that, it makes the cars look like hell – clumsy. And this was all done just so the driver could see over the hood easier!"

Mose was still contemplating. "You rilly does know 'bout caws. Someday you is go'n' build a *great* caw! Cawmakah!"

With that concluding prediction uttered in profound faith, Mose headed back to the office with his lunch box to clock in again.

Five months later Carmaker pushed open the grease splattered front door of the salvage yard again. He was looking down at the basement lights easily visible thought the cracks in the floor.

"How's the 'special' coming along?" Al queried.

"It's not."

"Wha'd 'yuh mean? Thought you'd have it pretty well finished by now."

"Well…there were problems…"

Al tried unsuccessfully to hide a wry smile. "Can't fit that Caddy engine in the Packard frame?"

"It's more than that – a *lot* more. There were so many things that I hadn't figured on when I bought that Packard. First of all the rear end ratio is so low that it would never work in a high performance car. There was no way to hook the Caddy drive shaft into the Packard rear end either. I'd have to go to a Cadillac rear end which would mean a lot smaller wheel size and that would never fill out the cut of those huge fenders properly. Then there's all that wood in the body. I didn't realize how much there was until I actually examined it closely. That would make a horrible job out of trying to chop the top and channel the body. And the frame is as heavy as on a ton truck – too much unnecessary added weight."

Albert looked over at his brother, Bobby and wrinkled his brow.

Carmaker continued. "Another problem – the wind blew the hood off in a bad storm and the engine got water in it and locked up. Worst thing though, was all the complaints. My family, the neighbors – and especially the city officials. Everybody was on my ass to get that 'thing', as they called it, off the street."

Al wrinkled his brow again and tried not to laugh. "So what d'ya want to do?"

"Sell it back to you. How much can you give me?"

Al looked at Bobby – Bobby looked at Billy – Billy looked over at Al. "Thirty bucks." They said in unison. "Where is it now?" Albert asked.

"Right outside on the street just at the edge of the drive."

Carmaker held out his hand and Al went to the cash register, pulled out a twenty and a ten and dropped them into the open palm.

Near the end of the day, Simon popped in, bossy and belligerent the way he thought a junk yard owner should be. He opened the back door and looked around – didn't see any of the yard men. "Hey, it's four-thirty," he bellowed, "one of you guys gotta take the tow truck and bring in those cars out on the street!" His harsh scream could be heard at the back edge of the yard.

Mose had no parts assignments. He was near the tow truck – climbed in and backed It up the drive. Turning and stopping it in front of the fist car, he got out, walked around and hooked up the chains and strap. Instantly he had recognized the Packard with the flat-head Caddy engine propped up by a pipe in the back. His scowl grew deeper; he clamped his teeth hard on the cigar holder.

Then with a shake of his head that seemed to vibrate his entire body, he thrust forward on the hoist lever. The hoist growled and groaned – stopped with the Packard dangling – still swinging slightly like a limp and lifeless corpse on a gallows. Mose watched it for only a moment. With eyes narrowed, he turned away and muttered in disgust, a final agonized "Cawmakah!"

Memories of St. Louis Auto Salvage

Rewritten 5/9/23

On Saturdays, I would often go with my Dad to his Morris Paint and Varnish Co. store on Easton Avenue, just below Union Avenue. Although I enjoyed wandering around the store, looking at everything, the main attraction for me as a young boy was to be able to go next door to Plegge's Pet Shop. I loved to look at the aquariums with all their tropical fish, the pretty painted turtles, and especially the puppies playing in their wire pens.

After spending most of the morning in the pet shop, I would go back to the paint store and wait for my father to take us home. We would usually go straight out Easton Avenue to Pennsylvania Avenue, then go left taking it all the way to Cornell, our home street.

On the way out Easton Avenue, we had to pass through Welston and at the far end of Welston on the south side we would pass the huge junk yard, "St. Louis Auto Salvage". I was fascinated by the hundreds of ancient cars visible through the wire fence bordering Easton.

Even as a four year old child, I had been cutting out pictures of the early 30's automobiles in the old magazines my mother gave me to cut up for my 'scrapbook'. I loved the esthetic lines of the early 30's cars and their occasional exotic styling. For years, I looked longingly at the cars in St. Louis Auto Salvage every time we passed by, not realizing that one day I would be old enough to be able to wander around in that wonderful yard of "corpus automobilia".

It may have been when I was about fifteen, when I first rode my bicycle to Welston. I have no memory as to why I rode it there, but I can recall riding past St. Louis Auto Salvage and stopping to view all the rusting hulks in the junkyard through the fence. I even rode along the side street that bordered the junk yard on the east, so as to be able to get a better view from its higher elevation.

About midway in the yard at the very east edge, I could see the remains of a 1935 Packard four door Phaeton – a huge, once princely car that looked as though it had been there for possibly twenty years. Nothing had been sold off of it and it was slowly rotting away into the ground. Its location was too inaccessible to get to it to cut it up, so there it stayed – perhaps forever?

At that same point, I remember there was a volunteer peach tree growing right in the fence line. Someone had dropped a peach seed there and it germinated and eventually grew into a large tree which had delicious nearly worm-free peaches on the overhanging branches in July. At first, I was able to get just a few peaches that fell outside the fence. In later years, I could get a lot more of the peaches by going inside the junk yard.

When I was sixteen, and I wanted to buy my first car, I had looked in the classified ads in the St. Louis Post Dispatch. I had managed to save up only $250 in the bank, so that strictly limited me as to what I could try to buy.

There was an older boy living on the street below ours, who had a 1934 Plymouth Coupe in beautiful original condition. He wanted $400 for it. I really liked the car and wanted to buy it, but just didn't have that much money.

The only car that I could find listed in the classified ads for $250 was a 1933 Chevrolet Coupe. I got my money out of the bank and went to the mid-town location to try to buy it.

The owner started up the engine and it seemed to run alright. But he didn't' let it run long enough for the haze of blue oil-smoke to be seen coming out of the exhaust pipe. Nor did he tell me that the clutch linkage was completely worn out and made it nearly impossible to get the transmission into gear!

In the garage, in its dim light, it was difficult to see that the car's fenders had been badly dented and poorly repaired and then repainted with a brush. I foolishly handed the man $250 and attempted to drive the car home.

My previous attempts to drive a car had been only two or three times in my dad's '47 Nash, and I had not been able to get the "feel" of smoothly coordinating the release of the clutch with the increase of pressing the gas pedal.

With a clutch that would barley release and my poor skill at releasing it, I was just barely able to start up from the many stop signs and get the coupe back home.

The following day, I looked more critically at my purchase and decided immediately to try to re-sell the car. I put an ad in the paper and the only guy who came to look at the car took one look at it sitting out on the street and said to me: "That car looks like it's hit everything including the freebridge! I wouldn't give you $125 for it!"

I was so disgusted I called my friend Larkin.

"Lark – hey Lark, you want to buy my Chevy coupe?"

"How much?"

"I paid $250 for it – I'll take $125."

"Well I don't have that much. But Ill trade yuh my '40 Powell scooter for it."

"Okay," I said, "It's a deal."

I had managed to adjust the clutch on the Chevy enough so that it could be driven slightly more easily, but still not well. The next morning after breakfast, I attempted to drive the car to Lark's to make the trade. Somehow, I started to fall asleep at the wheel before I had reached the end of my block. The car went over the curb and hit a tree, knocking the front bumper off. I got out and put the bumper in the trunk, then drove to Larkin's house.

Although I had to apologize for the bumper, Larkin thought nothing of it; he knew he was getting by far the better end of the trade (his scooter was worth only $75).

"I'll just get the bumper welded back on." he said. "Let's go look in the junk yard for a good clutch linkage."

We got in the '33 Chevy and drove to St. Louis Auto Salvage. After we had gotten permission to search the yard for '33 Chevrolets, we began looking for one with a usable clutch linkage. After searching for an hour we had to give it up. Of the few 33's we found, the clutch linkage was either gone – or worn out. We then went across the street to James Welding.

James agreed to build up the worn clutch linkage and weld the bumper back on for only four dollars – truly a bargain!

After James had welded the worn out hole in the clutch linkage and redrilled it, we put a new bolt in with plenty of grease on it, reassembled the linkage and never again had any clutch problem.

During my wandering in the junk yard, I had seen lots of interesting car parts which I then priced. Al Goldstein made such an attractive price on all of the parts (horns, headlamps, etc.) that I came back with my tools to begin disassembling some of the parts. Although I had to borrow a car in order to bring the parts back, this soon became a regular routine.

After several months of dissembling antique car parts, I began filling up shelving in our garage; placing apple boxes and orange crates all around the walls.

The area covered by St. Louis Auto Salvage probably amounted to something like four or five acres. That made it one of the two largest automobile junk yards in the city. There were literally hundreds of cars, trucks and busses in somewhat randomly placed rows – some of which had been jammed into corners and had been there perhaps decades.

I can remember seeing a section in the northwest corner having several double decker buses – which I know did not run on the streets since I had been a very small child. A year or two later, they were finally cut up and replaced by later cars.

I can remember sitting in a huge Diana four door sedan stuck in the middle of the yard. That one elegant automotive monster had been there almost forever. Nothing had been sold off of it; the car was such a rarity – but it had been standing out so long there was little left of parts of the body. Everyone (including myself) thought that it was unrestorable, though today, it would have been saved. I had liked sitting behind the steering wheel of that incredible car – just imagining what it must have been like to drive it!

The first year I roamed St. Louis Auto Salvage, there were still huge Packards from the 1930s, and massive Cadillacs and enormous "K" Lincolns – as well as a scattering of big Pierce Arrows and Marmons and Locomobiles, all long dead and by then largely forgotten.

After a few years of buying small parts, I got the idea of building an automotive "special". It was then that I began buying larger parts – the long, sweeping front fenders from a 1932 Henny hearse, the huge rear fenders from a '31 Pierce Arrow, the grill from a '40 Packaged, a trunk section from a 1940 Lincoln Continental, massive headlights from a 1930 Cadillac. Finally, I bought a 1929 Packard coupe on which to try to patch all of this together. It became an obviously impossible "morphydite" creation that never took place!

Still, as long as St. Louis Auto Salvage existed, I kept going back there. And you never knew what might be brought in.

I had always wanted to own a 1932 Hupmobile. That year was the epitome of Deco automotive designing. And the Hupmobile of that year was the most flamboyant of all the creations.

One day, I happened to be walking down into the yard at the auto salvage and there – right in the new line of cars was a 1932 Hupmobile! And it was a coupe! The car was shabby but complete and still in running condition! I ran back up the to the office to inquire how much they wanted for it. The price - $200! No less. They knew what it was worth! As a nineteen year old kid, I just didn't have that much.

Luckily, that day, an old car collector friend, W. Churchill Lowe, happened to come into the office as I was about to leave.

"Hey Church – there's a '32 Hupmobile that they just got in an' I'm tryin' to' buy it, but they want too much. Think you could get it for me for less?"

"Well, let's go look at it."

We went into the yard and Church lifted the hood on the Hup.

"It's only a six cylinder," he said with obvious disgust.

"Yeah, but it's a *coupe*!" I insisted.

"Now look," Churchill tried to explain to me, "You know that there are going to be some big expensive, really valuable cars that'll come in here. Cadillacs, Packards, Marmons. That's how I got my sixteen cylinder Caddy. I want to save my influence for buying those kinds of cars."

Churchill Lowe was a plumber b trade, and he had done plumbing work for the Goldstein family at a very reasonable price. They returned the favor by selling him cars at just slightly above their cost. I walked out of the St. Louis Auto Salvage dejected. But I figured I'd return in a few days and see if I could buy the Hup for less. When I returned a few days later, the Hup was gone.

When you walked in the door of the office of St. Louis Auto Salvage, if you looked down at the floor, the rough cut floor boards had small slits between some of them which allowed the lights from the basement to show through. I had always wondered what was in the basement and finally one day noticed the basement door open as I was going into the yard. When I took a look inside, I saw dozens of horns and headlights, mostly from 1930's cars, hanging on wires attached to nails driven into the upstairs floor joists. All the hanging items were badly corroded and covered with a thick layer of dust and dirt. The same was true of similar items hanging from the rafters in the office upstairs. It did not appear as though any of those items had bene sold for decades!

When I was about 23, I had found a 1932 Packard convertible coupe abandoned in a Washington University parking lot. I had it towed home. The car actually ran, but of course I had no title for it. I went to St. Louis Auto Salvage and spoke to Al.

"Hey Al – I've got a '32 Packard convertible I found, but don't have a title. You think there might be one in your file cabinet?"

"Well, Shamus, not with the current titles – but go look in the wooden file cabinet where all the older titles are. You might find something. Take anything you want out of there. Those cars were all cut up years ago."

I looked through hundreds of titles in the file. There was no title to match my '32 Packard. But there were lots of other interesting titles from odd makes long gone. I took several, including one from a 1926 Rolls Royce owned by the infamous safe cracker, Tobe Mundey, turned legitimate locksmith.

Over the next few years., I continued to roam the yard at St. Louis Auto Salvage. It wasn't very much later that they began "cleaning up" the yard. Suddenly all the double decker buses disappeared. And then the row of Model A mail trucks that was next to them.

Simon Goldstein, the owner, seldom came around any longer. Albert, his oldest sone took charge and began eliminating the "dead wood" – vehicles that had little or no sales potential for parts. Soon, all the ancient relics had been cut up and replaced by more modern cars and trucks.

The very last true large "classic" car that I ever saw come into St. Louis Auto Salvage was a 1930 Chrysler 8 roadster. Albert had the good sense by that time to put the huge classic right up against the fence facing Easton Avenue so that it could be easily seen from the street. The car had its original chalky paint and leather seat upholstery, but the top cloth was ragged and the top bows left folded down. Al priced the car at a thousand dollars – far more than I could manage to get together at the impecunious age of 20.

The Chrysler roadster sat there for only about a month until some California collector car buyer saw it and purchased it for some west coast collector.

I still made regular visits to the salvage yard, occasionally finding some misplaced oogah horn or a brass carburetor that had been overlooked.

And Albert was still very friendly to me – I even worked for him a couple of times driving one of his trucks. Simon Goldstein still came in usually at about 4:30. He would go to the back door of the office and yell as loud as he could to the yard men.

"Hey, Mose!" he would shout belligerently. "Mose! MOSE!! What the' hell ya doin'?" And long, slim, ugly Mose would answer just as belligerently: "Ahm here Simon! What th' hell ya want?"

"Gotta get all those five cars off the street!"

"Yeah – well Ah been wurkin' on dem caws de las' half hour – already got three moved in! Ah'll have 'em *all* moved in 'fo five!"

That would shut Simon up. I got to know Mose. He always called me "Cawmaker".

And I remember well, the big blond, Swedish – looking transmission rebuilder, Harvey. He too was very friendly and once spent a half hour explaining to me how to access certain of the transmission bearings in the more modern transmissions. I had no trouble taking apart a Model A transmission, but the later transmissions were much more highly sophisticated.

Sometime around 1970, Bobby Goldstein and his brother-in-law Billie Beckman left the St. Louis Auto Salvage, moving to Texas to establish a salvage yard there. They both stayed in Texas until their early deaths.

The vacant spot in the office had been filled by Earnie "Buddie" Goldstein, the youngest brother. Because the Goldstein family lived only a half block down from my own home, I got to know "Buddie" even though he was my younger sister's age and went to U. City High with her. But Buddie worked at the salvage yard only a short time. Some giant corporation bought all of the salvage yard acreage in order to erect an enormous new factory building (to manufacture what, I never learned). Suddenly ALL the hundreds of cars and trucks vanished into a "crusher" and were shipped out by rail for scrap.

Al Goldstein opened a small used car lot just across the street from the old salvage office. I would visit him occasionally to get him to notarize car titles. After a year or two, Buddie took over the car lot, Albert having developed an inoperable brain tumor.

A few months later, I got a phone call from Al. He just wanted to talk about old times. He knew he was dying. I tried to tell him that there were alternative cancer therapies that had a much higher success rate than the conventional medical cut, burn and poison methods of the M.D.'s. But Al insisted that the "doctors know what they're doing". In a couple of weeks, he was dead.

Buddie Goldstein stayed with the car lot until he got an offer to become the editor of the St. Louis Jewish Light. I kept in contact with him over the years calling him periodically. But the last time I spoke with him and he answered the phone, I said, "Hi Buddie – this is Jack Sophir!"

"Who?" he said.

"I'm Jack Sophir – don't you remember? I lived down the block from you!"

"Oh… yeah… raw turnips. I think I remember you. But that was a long time ago."

"Well, Buddie, it's been a couple of years since I talked to you. I just wanted to find out if you were still alright and how your family was doing."

"I'm okay; but my wife has developed Alzheimer's."

We spoke for a few more minutes about his brothers and brother-in-law, all of whom had passed away.

"Hey, Buddie - you remember that night before you were drafted into the army; when you walked down to my house and said "let's go to the Forest Park Highlands – I just want to do something fun before I spend 2 years in the army!" And I said, "But it's already so late, I don't see how we can get any girls to go with us."

"Oh, let's just go by ourselves – we'll have fun – just like we were little kids again!"

"So we got in my '38 Packard convertible and drove there and we went on *every* ride in the entire place! Just like a couple of kids! Remember that?"

"No... no, I don't. I don't remember it."

It seemed that Buddie's wife was not the only one with Alzheimer's. I never called Buddie Goldstein again.

After the demise of the St. Louis Auto Parts and Salvage, a few years later, there were other large auto wrecking yards that sprang up a little further west on what became "Martin Luther King Boulevard". But by then, there were no longer any of the great classic cars of the 1920's or 1930's to be found and sent to the wreckers. Now, when a truly great classic car does somehow manage to turn up under a pile of hay bales in some ancient barn, the owner will either place the car in an antique car auction or take it to an antique car swap meet putting a price tag on it of a hundred thousand dollars!

These great cars now, if they're found, seem to make their way into the collections of car museums or billionaire collectors.

The car collecting of 70 years ago is nothing but a memory. Everything has changed radically – and rapidly. Yes, there are still antique car shows – and "swap meets" – but fewer and less well attended each year. I never see antique cars being driven on the streets any longer. Modern traffic is too dangerous. Every year more vehicles using the same size and number of streets. How sad for those of us who loved the great styling and performance of the truly classic automobiles of the 20's and 30's!

The old St. Louis Auto Parts and Salvage yard is long gone. The Goldstein boys and their father Simon are all gone… and probably all the yard men I got to know as well.   It's all nothing but memories… and a few bits and pieces of automotive relics that I will intentionally keep until some 21st century thief manages to steal the rest of it.

But, at least there's one thing they can't steal – my memories of the great cars that came and went in the old St. Louis Auto Parts and Salvage yard!

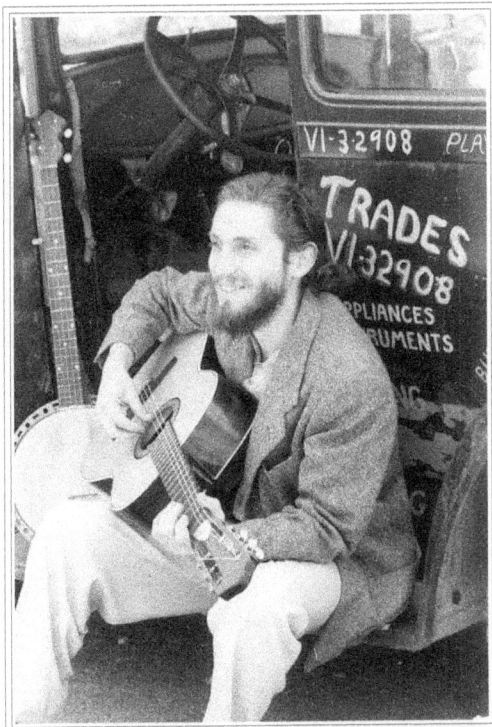

www.ingramcontent.com/pod-product-compliance
Lightning Source LLC
Chambersburg PA
CBHW021141090426
42740CB00008B/876